QUADROPHENIA – THE COMPLETE GUIDE.

By

LAYNE PATTERSON

50% of the Authors Royalties are being donated to The Teenage Cancer Trust. For more details of this unique charity visit: -
www.teenagecancertrust.org

DEDICATIONS AND THANKS: -

For: -

The Mad Ladies in my Life: - Liz, Ma, Kath, Laura, Kate, Kirsty and Amie
x

And the Hounds: - Bryan, Darren, Sam, and Terry x
Plus: -
My totally gorgeous Grandchildren, Laylah, Maisie, Summer and Bobby (one day when you are old enough we will watch Quadrophenia together!)
Dedicated to: -
THE WORLDWIDE WHO FAMILY
For the memory, of: -
The OX, Moonie, Michael Elphick, Roy Baird
And the (never) forgotten Mods, Barry Prior and James Smart.
Special Thanks and without whom: -
Graham Sharpe
Vince Deritis (rip)
Shawn Lee
Brighton and its people
West London and its people
The Brighton Argus
Simon Wells
and Kieran McAleer.
Pete, Roger, John and Keith for no other reason than being the top dogs of British Rock Music.
Thanks to: -
Phil Daniels, Leslie Ash, Toyah Wilcox, Gary Shail (Legend!) Mark Wingett, Phil Davis,
Garry Cooper, Trevor H. Laird, John Altman and Franc Roddam
for being all I hoped they would be in real life!

And finally, this book is further dedicated to all the Mods of the sixties who can still feel the sand beneath their fingernails.
(this line being unashamedly stolen from Alan Fletcher)

FOREWORD

This is an extraordinary achievement by Layne Patterson. He approaches the material like a fan but with the diligence of an academic.

It's an amazing piece of research that puts together the known and unknown facts about this iconic cultural event with insight, charm and affection.

It's a must-read for any Quadrophenia fan, any fan of The Who and all genuine Mods.

FRANC RODDAM,
Director, Quadrophenia.
April 2017.

INTRODUCTION

I was born in the summer of 1964, and lived in Harrow just a short walk from The Railway Tavern in Wealdstone (not Wealdstone and Harrow, as some people persist in calling it - there is no such place!) which at the time was a regular venue for a band called The High Numbers (*later The Who*). Little did I know at the time but that summer, and *The Who*, had just provided the material for an album and later a film called, QUADROPHENIA.

The Mod scene was something that I had very little knowledge of, with my favourite artist at the time being a certain Toyah Wilcox, and up until the late seventies I was, at best, only a casual listener to *The Who*. Around the same time a Mod band (also liked by lovers of the Punk scene) called The Jam had helped to re-ignite interest in all things Mod, and it was a time when everybody seemed to belong to some sort of youth culture group, everyone was either a Punk, Rude Boy or a Skinhead, etc., etc.

Anyway, in 1979 I remember a lot of talk about this new film made by *The Who* called *Quadrophenia*, it was on my list to see! Toyah had just released her first single and she was going to be in this film that everybody was now talking about! But wait, the film carried an X certificate, I was just 15 (that awkward age when getting refused entrance at the cinema in front of people would have been just too much to take!). Incidentally on its re-release in 1997 the film was awarded a 15 certificate!

Step forward my saviour Frazer Harris, who had a part time job at the ABC cinema in Harrow, and would gladly bunk me in to watch the film at my leisure. However, for some reason or another I never did get to see the film and slowly began to forget all about it. Approximately eighteen months later at still only 16, I was preparing to spend a boring Thursday night in watching something or other on the telly, when an old mate, Tim Parrot, phoned 'do you fancy going to the pictures to see *Quadrophenia* and *Scum* in a double bill?' The ABC cinema no longer held its previous fear of being proved to be underage, and before long I was settled down to see the film I should have seen in the same cinema some months previous! The ABC was absolutely packed to the rafters, and a very edgy atmosphere was present! Indeed, I well remember at least a couple of fights breaking out between a couple of local rivals!

As the film started and Phil Daniels walked towards camera, my main thought was of how long it would be before Toyah appeared on screen, when suddenly the scene changed! Phil Daniels, next appeared on his Lambretta riding through the streets of West London as the sound of *The Who* in the form of *The Real Me* crashed and banged on to the screen. The music made the hairs on the back of my neck stand-up, I was hooked!

The film made an immediate impact (how I wanted all my mates to suddenly go and buy a Parka and a Scooter realising that they had been Mods all along! suffice it to say this never happened) the music and film just seemed to compliment each other so well!

The next day (pay-day) I went to buy the soundtrack as well as the Alan Fletcher paperback novel, both of which are still in my possession, albeit showing their age a little! This film reinforced in my mind the brilliance of *The Who*, and if there is a better album than *Quadrophenia* out there, well I haven't heard it! This band from West London have been an important part of my life ever since, and they are still as relevant today as they were then – when your Granddaughter puts My Generation on the Juke Box you know your work is done!

Video rental shops started sprouting up everywhere, and *Quadrophenia* became a regular tape to hire, and many years on I have now lost count of the times that I have watched it! The avid collector of memorabilia connected with the film I found myself learning from various sources all types of information relating to the film, which gave me the ideal opportunity to re-watch the film and research them. Little did I know it but I had somehow subconsciously decided to put this all down on paper – possibly to exorcise this obsession with the film, possibly because I thought that such an important film needed a book entirely devoted to it! Subsequently Simon Wells wrote the excellent, *Quadrophenia – A Way of Life* in 2014, at last, this film had the book devoted to it that it so deserved. Simon became a friend during this period and I was delighted to assist him on one or two matters for his excellent publication, but thought at the time that this was, probably the end for my own project. Simon, however persuaded me that the type of book I was planning would still be a good idea, so the work restarted in earnest!

Simon has been mightily generous with his help since, and I thank him from the bottom of my heart for all his kindness. Also, I am extremely indebted to Kieran McAleer and Shawn Lee for help with locations, and Gary Shail for kind words. Franc Roddam who has been so encouraging and for agreeing to write the foreword – a true gent!
Lastly, but by no means last the legions of extras and scooter club members who have been more than generous reliving their time on the film, and allowing use of their various photographs – Franc Roddam has always said that the film wouldn't have got made without them, this book certainly wouldn't have!

With the renewed interest in the film caused by the 1997 re-release and subsequent video and DVD releases *Quadrophenia* is now firmly established as a cult British film! Today fans of the film can collect everything imaginable relating to *Quadrophenia,* with e-bay feeding the obsession to excess on its ever-busy pages. You may be a casual fan of the film you may be obsessed by it, you may just be curious about certain things relating to it, whatever, hopefully the following pages will prove to be of some interest.
Quadrophenia is and always will be my favourite album and as for the film, nothing has ever come close to shifting it from the very top of my Cinematic tree. Mr Townshend, and Mr Roddam – I thank, and salute you both!

LAYNE PATTERSON.
Norfolk, April 2017.

Every effort has been made to ensure that all information enclosed is correct, if you have any different or new recollections please feel free to contact me at layne.patterson64@gmail.com.

INDEX

CHAPTER 1.
A-Z
FULL PROFILE OF ALL PEOPLE CONNECTED WITH QUADROPHENIA

CHAPTER 2.
LOCATIONS
FULL LOCATION AND SCENE BREAKDOWN OF FILM LOCATIONS +
MUSIC LOCATIONS

CHAPTER 3.
THE MUSIC
ALL THE MUSIC FROM BOTH THE FILM AND THE ALBUM

CHAPTER 4.
STAGE SHOWS
THE VARIOUS QUADROPHENIA STAGE SHOWS

CHAPTER 5.
EXTRAS
REUNIONS, CONVENTIONS, DOCUMENTARIES ETC.

CHAPTER 6.
QUADS AND SODS
WEIRD AND WONDERFUL QUAD RELATED FACTS

CHAPTER 7.
THE SEQUEL
QUADROPHENIA 2?

CHAPTER 8.
MEMORIES AND QUOTES
VARIOUS MEMORIES AND QUOTES

CHAPTER 9.
APPENDIX

CHAPTER 1
QUADROPHENIA A-Z

A

THE ACTORS – Musical Connection.
Gary Shail and Gary Holton became great friends during Quadrophenia and with a common love of music founded the above band in which Joe McGann was also involved! An appearance on Channel 4's, The Tube followed which was coincidentally introduced by Leslie Ash who was hosting the show at the time.

PATRICK ALLEN – Voice-Over for UK Trailer.
Born 17th March, 1927 – Died 28th July 2006.

Patrick Allen was an unmistakable voice of TV commercials and Film Trailers, and was chosen for the one used in the UK following the abortive attempt to use Alan Lake. Allen was also an actor in his own-right and appeared in The Wild Geese alongside Sir Roger Moore.

JOHN ALTMAN – John Fagin the Mod.
Incredibly John Altman's performance is uncredited in the production, strange as his character is interwoven virtually throughout the whole film! Altman is, undoubtedly, best known for his role of 'Nasty' Nick Cotton in EastEnders, a part that he first played at the show's inception in 1985, and went on to play on an infrequent basis until he was finally killed off in 2015. In 2001 he had returned once again to play the baddie and was voted that year's rear of the year!

Altman was up for the part of the Ace Face in the film (having been put up for the role by Patsy Pollock who he was dating at the time) but, of course lost out to Sting. However, he was pleased to be part of the film anyway, and is always a popular figure with fans of the film when he attends any re-unions or conventions.

Altman's other work has included parts in An American Werewolf in London and playing George Harrison in The Birth of the Beatles. Altman was originally born in Reading, Berkshire, but moved at a young age to Kent. Married in 1986 he divorced eleven years later, and is currently busy on various projects including a short film and an album of his own music. Altman continues his acting career, which of late has been extensively in the Theatre, and is always a much-sought after 'baddie' when pantomime time comes around. A little-known fact is that his Grandfather was Johnnie Schofield who was a constant in British films during the thirties and forties, including The Arsenal Stadium Mystery in 1940.

MISCLEANOUS INFORMATION

Books: In the Nick of Time – Autobiography – John Blake Publishing 2016.

Websites: http://www.johnaltman.info

JOHNATHAN AMBERSTON – Misc. role in Production.
Amberston had a brief role within the production, mainly dealing with the extras that were used and later went on to work on Aliens in 1979.

DALLAS AMOS – Hairstyling (1973 album booklet).
Dallas Amos provided the Hairstyling on the iconic booklet that accompanies the original 1973 album.

DAVID ANDERSON – Unit Manager.
Anderson is now working as a Director in the advertising industry and work includes commercials for Dettol, Eurostar and Heineken.

ADAM ANT – Potential Actor in film.
Born; 3rd November 1954

Adam Ant (real name Stuart Goddard) was considered for the role of Ace Face after just completing the role of Kid in the Derek Jarman film, Jubilee. The film also starred Toyah, with the two appearing in a fictional band called The Maneaters! Following this film Ant went on to pursue a musical career, and formed Adam and the Ants who had major success in the early eighties. After the group were disbanded Ant combined both music and acting, whilst all the while battling a serious mental illness. Now thankfully in better health Adam Ant is back again both recording and touring

LEON APSEY – Construction Manager.

Many projects in the British Film Industry include the 1999 Star Wars film The Phantom Menace and The Mummy in the same year. Other work included A Fish Called Wanda 1988 and the 1977 production of Jabberwocky on which he worked as a carpenter.

LESLIE ASH – Steph.

Born; 19th February 1960

Leslie Ash was born at her family home in Mitcham, Surrey, but whilst still a baby her family moved the short distance to Streatham. Her parents later opened a decorating shop, which was later purchased by Leslie and her husband, Lee Chapman and turned into a bar, SOUK which they still own.

Leslie made her television debut at the tender age of four in a commercial for Fairy Liquid; this was being made by a family friend, and led to her catching the acting bug.

At the age of eleven Leslie joined her sister Debbie on a five-year course in singing, dancing and drama at the Italia Conti School, where she enjoyed a few minor roles such as her appearance in the TV series, The Boy with Two Heads. She then stumbled into modelling whilst still trying to get her acting career off the ground, these were primarily with the many girls' teen magazines that were prevalent in the seventies, such as the likes of Jackie and Mirabelle.

At the age of seventeen she was being offered more and more TV commercials, including ones for Levis and Clearasil, these lucrative assignments gave her the opportunity to buy her first flat as her parents had by this time emigrated to Spain. At the time her sister, Debbie (who later went on to marry stuntman, Eddie Kidd) was starting to make her name as a dancer with Hot Gossip. Leslie, herself had auditioned for them but was rejected, a move that was to ultimately do her a massive favour as it focused her to concentrate fully on acting, which was to prove extremely profitable in the following years.

At eighteen years of age she auditioned for the role of Steph in Quadrophenia, having just completed a film, Rosie Dixon – Night Nurse, and was now ready to grab another slice of the limelight! Ash claims to have earned just £500 for her portrayal of Steph. Whilst the cast were being given lessons on scooters at the Hendon Police College the female cast members and Leslie, (in particular) became firm favourites of the Policemen training them with no shortage of others to have them as their passengers!

Following her success in Quadrophenia she was still doing a fair bit of modelling as the film had not yet given her the expected flood of offers for her acting skills.

One of her first post-Quadrophenia jobs was in some sketches that were used in The Two Ronnies, and then followed a period of various one-off appearances in comedy shows such as, Shelley and Outside Edge; she then went onto co-present The Tube with Jools Holland, covering for Paula Yates, who was on maternity leave. In her autobiography, Leslie freely admits that these were not her most polished set of performances in a show that was famous for her many gaffes. She famously interviewed Paul McCartney in a car on his way to a job as he was too busy to come into the studios! The Tube was filmed live in Newcastle on a Friday, and the crew were famous for their drinking exploits, something that Leslie got sucked into, and was possibly the start of a problem that was to blight her for many years to come. Around this time, she was dating the comedian, Rowan Atkinson, with the newspapers even hinting at a wedding! In 1983 Leslie was back on the big screen with a role in The Curse of the Pink Panther.

In 1984 she returned to mainstream TV with a bang in the ITV show, Cats Eyes in which she played the part of Fred. Cats Eyes was a spin off from The Gentle Touch which starred Jill Gascoigne. The show aired in April of the following year and was a huge success; leading to her being sought after for many more roles.

In December 1986, she met footballer, Lee Chapman who was, at the time playing for Sheffield Wednesday. A romance blossomed and the pair were married in July 1988. Thereon in they led a somewhat nomadic life as Chapman moved from club to club, enjoying a reputation as a journeyman leading goal-scorer.

A brief spell playing in France was followed by a return to England to play for Nottingham Forest, but within eighteen months they were on the move yet again to Leeds United. It was here that Chapman enjoyed his most successful period in the game, as his goals went a long way to winning the 1991/92 Football League Division One Championship, this was the last year before the top tier of English Football became the F.A. Premier League.

During his time at Leeds United one of Chapman's team-mates was the mercurial Frenchman, Eric Cantona. When Cantona left somewhat unexpectedly for bitter rivals, Manchester United it was rumoured that he had been involved in affair with Ash, and was the reason that he had been sold. There was never any real substance to these rumours that were strenuously denied by both parties, but for many months when appearing at away grounds Cantona would be greeted with the unflattering chant of 'He's French, He's Flash He's shagging Leslie Ash!'

Leslie was an actress very much in the public eye at the time as she had been appearing in Men Behaving Badly, the show having been the brainchild of, Beryl Vertue. The first incarnation of the show was at the time on the ITV network, and included Harry Enfield before being replaced in the second series by Neil Morrissey, however it was dropped in 1992 as its makers, Thames Television lost their franchise. The BBC later took on the show where it went on to enjoy massive success!

Men Behaving Badly in which Leslie played the part of Deborah was to go on for six seasons and was hugely popular, catapulting all the stars of the show to stardom, including a top thirty song that Ash and Quentin released off the back of the show's popularity. Martin Clunes, Neil Morrissey and Caroline Quentin are very much sought after actors as was Leslie Ash prior to her well documented health problems. Her big roles following Men Behaving Badly were, Where the Heart is and Merseybeat.

In January 2003, she hit the headlines after a cosmetic procedure to enhance the size of her lips went dreadfully wrong. The injections that she had gave her an allergic reaction that saw them swell to well above their normal size. The red-top newspapers had a field day cruelly showing unflattering photographs and dubbing it her 'trout pout'.

In April 2004 Leslie suffered two broken ribs following an accident at home, and was admitted to hospital. Speculation was rife that her injury had been caused by the hands of Chapman; there had already been various other accusations of domestic violence in the past, most notably from her estranged sister, Debbie. The later has repeated these accusations on various occasions, usually for financial recompense, as her own career seems to have all but disappeared! Another allegation of domestic violence came from an ex-employee of their bar, TEATRO'S. There was also a very public fall out with her co-star, Caroline Quentin following an incident where Chapman kicked her door in looking for Ash who had fled there following an argument!

When Leslie was admitted to hospital she caught an infection in her back which she was told not to worry about it, however, this turned out to be a form of MSSA which ultimately led to severe spinal damage. She was told that she may never walk again and would be confined to a wheelchair. Whilst a full recovery is out of the question, and she has accepted the fact that she is now permanently disabled she has made massive strides and is able to walk albeit with the aid of a stick. Bravely in 2015 she announced that most of her health problems are behind her and that she was looking to resume her career!

Ash went on to successfully sue the hospital where she caught the infection, and has campaigned long and hard for cleaner hospitals to reduce the risk of further problems. In September 2007, she published her long-awaited autobiography which was very well received, and praised by many reviewers for its frank honesty.

MISCLEANOUS INFORMATION

Books: My Life Behaving Badly – Autobiography – Orion Books 2007.

Websites: www.menbehavingbadly.com

LESLIE ASH and CAROLINE QUENTIN – Musical Connection.
Following the success of Men Behaving Badly the two female stars of the show released a record that went on to reach number 25 in the charts. The song in question was Tell Him, a cover of the sixties tune by The Exciters in 1962. The picture below shows the record cover of their one and only release!

JOHN ASTLEY – Sound Engineer – 1973 Album.
John Astley has worked producing, mixing and arranging extensively within the music industry. Astley has worked on projects with the likes of Level 42 and Abba and is the younger brother of Pete Townshend's ex-wife Karen Astley.

B

PHIL.B - *(Mod extra at Brighton).*
Phil was a member of The Barnsley Vikings Scooter Club who earned himself an uncredited role as an extra in the film.

ALBERT BAILEY – Boom Op.
Bailey went on to work as sound recordist on the following British films, My Beautiful Launderette 1985, My Son the Fanatic 1988 and the 2002 production starring James Nesbitt, Bloody Sunday. He was nominated for a BAFTA for the former and won the Irish equivalent an IFTA for his work on this project.

ROY BAIRD – Producer.
Born; 1933

Died; May 2010

Baird worked on several films as Assistant Producer including, Casino Royale the James Bond spoof starring, David Niven in 1967. Also, credited with Producer or Executive Producer on the likes of That'll Be The Day 1973, The Devils 1971, he also worked with Roger Daltrey on Lisztomania 1975, McVicar 1980 and Buddy's Song in 1990.

CARL BARAT – Musical Connection.
The frontman from both The Libertines and The Dirty Pretty Things was talked about by Roger Daltrey as a possible lead in a proposed West End production of Quadrophenia.

RICHARD BARNES – Special Mention on 1973 Album.
A long-term friend of Pete Townshend since their Art School days he was given a special mention on the original album for Directing and advising on the photo shoot for the concept book which accompanies it. Barnes has gone on to write various books such as, MODS and THE WHO-Maximum R&B.

AMANDA BARRIE – Original choice for Mrs. Cooper.

Amanda Barrie was the original actress cast to play the part of Jimmy's mother, but was sacked after just one days filming. Her interpretation of the part was not what Franc Roddam was looking for, something that Barrie is quick to acknowledge as she was going through a lot of personal traumas at the time. She is on record at regretting not being part of the finished film, but accepts full responsibility for it. Barrie of course went on to become a household name after playing the part of Alma Baldwin in Coronation Street for twenty years up until 2001. Barrie was also in a couple of Carry On films including the lead in Cleo, acclaimed as one of the finest in the series! The following picture shows her in a continuity photograph that was never actually needed!

MICHAEL BARRY - (youth on bicycle).

A bit of an obscure one this, look out for a young lad on his cycle. He frantically tries to keep up with Jimmy's scooter as he gives Steph a lift home from work through the streets of Shepherds Bush. This chap was on his bike in the area when he noticed the film being made, earning himself an unplanned part in the finished production.

SEAN BARTON – Film Editor.
Sean Barton came on board after Franc Roddam had dispensed with the services of Mike Taylor. Barton worked with John Altman who took the role of George Harrison in the 1979 film Birth of the Beatles, and then went on to work on the Star Wars film, Return of the Jedi 1983 followed by three Franc Roddam projects K2 1991, War Party 1989 and the television version of Moby Dick 1998. Other work has included Guest House Paradiso, This Year's Love both 1999 and Photographing Fairies 1997, he also Directed the 1991 film Witchcraft (Curse 3: Blood Sacrifice) which starred Hammer Horror veteran, Christopher Lee. More recent projects include the 2000 TV movie, Jason and the Argonauts.

THE BEATLES – Musical Connection.
Although no music of the Fab Four is heard during the film their poster is briefly glimpsed in Jimmy's sister Yvonne's bedroom. Ringo Starr is of course the father of Zak Starkey the current drummer with The Who.

PERRY BENSON (Eric the post room assistant).
Although Perry only had a small role alongside Phil Daniels and Hugh Lloyd in a scene at the advertising agency's post room he enjoyed a slightly larger part as Formby in Scum. He has continued to work on a mixture of roles on television including the part of Carly alongside Gillian Taylforth in the BBC play, Stars of the Roller State Disco as well as an appearance in Black Adder. More recent work has included a part in the 2000 BBC film, Last Resort and the part of Bones in the Ray Burdis police comedy, Operation Good Guys, and alongside James Nesbit in the BBC drama, Murphy's Law. He worked with Burdis again on the improvisational drama, Final Cut. The later also staring fellow Quadrophenia co-star Ray Winstone. Benson also appeared in both the TV and film versions of; This is England and latterly, the ITV show, Benidorm. Benson is still a close friend of Phil Daniels to this day.

JOHN BINDON – Harry North.
Born: 4th October 1943,

Died: 10th October 1993

John Bindon played the part of local gangster, Harry North, in what was a case of art imitating real life. Bindon had a somewhat colourful private life, which led to him being typecast as either a heavy or an underworld figure. It is a shame he was never really allowed to show the full extent of his skills, but with Bindon there was always so many other things going on!

Bindon was born in Fulham, West London, where he excelled as a very talented Rugby player, but he inevitably slipped in to a life of crime, something that tarnished his name for the rest of his life! In 1967 he played the part of the aggressive husband in Ken Loach's critically acclaimed, Poor Cow for which he received rave reviews. However, he continued to act on a sporadic basis and indeed Quadrophenia was to be his last film!

He was said to have had an affair with Princess Margaret as well as a string of various models! and in 1968 was awarded a Police bravery award for saving a man from drowning in the River Thames near Putney Bridge.

In 1977 Bindon was hired as a bodyguard for Led Zeppelin as they toured America which it is said where he developed a taste for hard drugs an addiction that was eventually contribute to his death. The tour was dogged by violent outbursts from Bindon, where he was to even receive a suspended prison sentence.

In 1978 Bindon was involved in a fight with a local man, John Darke, in which Darke was killed, Bindon fled the country with serious knife wounds, but returned to face trial at the Old Bailey. In November 1979, he was found not guilty, thanks in no small part to a glowing character reference from none other than Bob Hoskins.

Following this incident Bindon hardly ever worked again and plummeted into a life of severe drug addiction and died of an AIDS related illness just a few days after his fiftieth birthday.

BINGO? (Mod extra at Brighton).

A scooter club member (possibly Barnsley) Bingo was a Scooter riding extra in Brighton, and is featured in the picture with Martyn Scully later in chapter.

PHIL BIRCH (Mod extra at Brighton).
Phil was a member of the Modrapheniacs scooter club who was involved for about a week's filming in Brighton.

JESSE BIRDSALL – Aggressive Rocker.
Born   13th February 1963

Birdsall appeared alongside Gary Holton as one of the aggressive Rockers and is perhaps best known for his portrayal of Marcus Tandy in the ill-fated BBC show, Elderado. However, he has continued to work on a regular basis with film credits such as, Wish You Were Here in 1987, and television appearances in the likes of Bugs and Footballers Wives.

He has been married to Gwyneth Strong (Cassandra in Only Fools and Horses) since 2000 and was involved in a well-publicised attack on a fellow drinker in a London pub the year before! Birdsall was less than popular with his co-star, Gary Shail during filming as he chatted up and stole his girlfriend, Tammy Jacobs, who had played the role for real in the film!

JOHN BLUNDELL (Rocker on road to and in Brighton).
Blundell is an instantly recognisable actor from around this period and is seen at the front of the pack of Rockers that ride Chalky off the road, and later in the fight at the café. Blundell appeared in both the TV and film versions of Scum as Banks, and later re-united with Ray Winstone in, Nil-by Mouth in 1997. TV work has included parts in Juliet Bravo and Shoestring; however, Blundell has concentrated predominantly on a career in the Theatre. Blundell was involved in some of the early improvisation during casting alongside Johnny Rotten, he was also considered for the part of The Ace Face before Sting.

BLUR – Musical Connection.

A track from their celebrated album, Parklife, entitled 'Clover over Dover' was said to be homage to the closing scenes from Quadrophenia. Phil Daniels also appears on the 1994 single, Parklife. Daniels was at the time playing for the NME football team when it was mentioned by one of the editorial staff that Blur were interested in him performing on the song, his original contribution was set to be a lot less prominent, but in the end all parties were delighted with the finished product!

ALFIE BOE – Vocals for Jimmy in Pete Townshend's Classic Quadrophenia.
Born; - 29th September 1973.

Alfred Giovanni Roncalli Boe, was born in Blackpool, Lancashire with both Norwegian and Irish heritage and was in fact named after Pope John XXIII. Having started his working life as a trainee mechanic it soon became evident to his workmates that his talents lie elsewhere, and after being urged to audition for an Opera Company he very quickly went on to study at the Royal College of Music and Royal Opera House.

Boe's big break came when he took the lead for La Boheme on Broadway before going on to play the role of Jean Valjean in Les Miserables on both sides of the Atlantic. TV work has included a role as a music hall performer in Mr Selfridge.

ELLY BONGO – (Mod at Brighton).
Elly was a member of the Barnsley scooter club who was enlisted as an extra during the Brighton scenes.

MICK BONNER (TWIZZEL) (Rocker on road to and in Brighton).
Bonner plays the part of the Rocker to the right-hand side of Chalky when he is ridden off the road on route to Brighton.

BONNIE – (Rocker girl on road to Brighton).
Bonnie was the other–half of Tigger and both were associates of fellow Rocker, Tom Ingram.

BOOKER T & THE M.G.'s – Musical Contribution.

This well-known group was originally formed by Booker T. Jones along with Al Wilson (drummer/guitarist), Lewis Steinberg (drummer), and Steve Cropper (lead guitarist). It was Steve Cropper who composed the classic; 'Green Onion's' earning him a gold disc at the tender age of just sixteen.

Further hits for the group included, Hip Hug Her, Groovin, Soul Limbo, Hang Em High, Time is Tight and Mrs Robinson. Cropper was also to enjoy writing credits on many other songs including the classic Dock of the Bay sung by Otis Redding and Midnight Hour performed by Wilson Picket.

The group split up in 1972 but reformed in 1974, however tragedy struck the group in 1975 when Al Jackson, who had joined the group after its original inception, was murdered, this threatened the group's future for a while, but they resolved to carry on and still tour and release the very occasional album.

TIM BRINTON - (Newscaster in cut scene).

Tim Brinton was engaged to record a scene as a Newscaster on 19th October 1978; however, this never made it to the finished print. Having worked for both the BBC and ITN in this role for real, he went on to enjoy various cameos in the likes of Carry On-Emmannuelle, Budgie and Dixon of Dock Green. Less than a year on from his work on Quadrophenia he went on to sweep to power in Margaret Thatcher's Conservative Government as an MP for Gravesend in the 1979 General Election. Brinton lost his seat at the next election before joining UKIP in 2003. Tim Brinton passed away in 2009 having suffered badly from dementia in his final years. The following picture shows Tim Brinton around the time of filming.

RAY BROOKS - (Voice-Over for Cigarette Advertisement).
The unmistakable voice of Ray Brooks is heard during the cigarette advert at Jimmy's workplace. Brooks has worked extensively in this area over the years as well as appearing in a string of TV and film productions. Brooks first became prominent in the gritty 1966 BBC play, Cathy Come Home, which led on to countless roles including a part in Carry On Abroad in 1974. Brooks ended a two-year stint in EastEnders in 2007 where he played the hapless husband of Pauline Fowler. Brooks was married in 1961 having borrowed his suit from a BBC wardrobe, and has three grown up children.

RICHARD BRYAN – Producer of Cigarette Advertisement.
Well versed maker of advertisement films and features who was known to Franc Roddam during his days in the Advertising industry. Bryan was enlisted to produce a realistic advertisement, referred to in the movie as 'the people like you film'. It was voiced by Ray Brooks and starred an unnamed Czechoslovakian actress. Bryan went on to work on the BBC show, Masterchef, and is also credited as the Assembly Editor of, A Funny Thing Happened on the Way to the Forum.

PETER BRAYHAM – Stunt Arranger.

Vastly experienced in both Television and Film, Brayham's' work on the former has included Space 1999, The Prisoner, The Professionals, Blake's 7 and Boon alongside Michael Elphick. Film work includes the second James Bond adventure From Russia With Love, Listzomania (which starred Roger Daltrey) 1975, Tank Malling in 1988 starring Ray Winstone, Life is Sweet 1990 which includes a brief appearance from Timothy Spall and the 1997 Spice Girls offering Spiceworld. Brayham's last project was the BBC TV series, Life on Mars, before succumbing to cancer in December 2006.

BRENDAN? – (Mod Extra at Brighton).
Brendan was a member of Modern Coasters scooter club who was involved in the Brighton scenes.

JAMES BROWN – Musical Contribution.
James Brown was born in South Carolina in May 1933 and forced himself out of abject poverty to become one of the biggest ever stars of Popular and Soul music. The Godfather of Soul, has enjoyed a remarkable career that has seen countless hits both sides of The Atlantic, apart from Night Train other notable hits have included, Papa's Got a Brand-New Bag and I Got You (I Feel Good) both from 1965.

Brown's personal life has never been without incident and has included spells in prison and as recent as the age of sixty-nine was charged with domestic violence. The Godfather of Soul became ill and developed pneumonia and passed away on Christmas Day 2006 at the age of 73.

RAY BURDIS – Potential Actor.
Ray Burdis was another product of the Anna Scher stage school, and had appeared in the BBC version of Scum before going on to work on the Film version. It is more than conceivable that Burdis was considered for a role in Quadrophenia, what is known is that he took part in an improvised audition with both Sting and John Blundell. Ray has gone on to work the other side of the camera and was involved in the likes of The Krays in 1990, and is also working on the proposed film, To Be Someone, which is an alternative take on what happened to Jimmy next.

ROGER K BURTON – *Clothing Supplier.*
Roger Burton had a market stall selling clothing when he was approached by one of the film's makers to see if he could supply some Mod clothing. Burton had been a Mod himself and was therefore a perfect choice. After Quadrophenia he went on to set up a business that hired these out for other films. Burton's collection is believed to be the UK's biggest of 20th century youth clothing. Burton is now based at the Horse Hospital in Bloomsbury, London, having since worked on many films including, Absolute Beginners. Burton has also worked on other projects such as TV commercials and Music videos, working with the likes of Bob Dylan and Depeche Mode.

C

JENNY CAMPBELL (*Rocker on road to Brighton*).
Jenny Campbell is the Rocker girl that rides on the back of one of the Rockers motorbikes on the way to Brighton. She went on to work with Michael Elphick on a couple of episodes of Boon, but it appears that she sadly died sometime around the year 2000.

JACK CARTER – *Construction Manager.*
A distinguished career within the British Film Industry has included working on the following productions; Here We Go Round the Mulberry Bush 1967, If 1968, Women in Love 1969, Spring and Port Wine 1970, Gumshoe 1971, Steptoe and Son 1972, O Lucky Man and Steptoe and Son Ride Again, both 1973. An initial acquaintance with The Who was made in the 1975 film, Tommy.

Further work has included, Equus and Sinbad and the Eye of the Tiger both 1977, Superman 1978, A Nightingale in Berkeley Square and Agatha, both 1979. Into the eighties, Carter has worked on the following; Reds 1981, Privates on Parade and The Return of the Soldier both 1982, A Private Function, Another Country, Eureka and Greystoke: - The Legend of Tarzan, all 1984, followed by The Mission in 1986. More recent work has included Nuns on the Run 1990, Sense and Sensibility 1995, All the Little

Animals 1998 and Captain Jack the following year completes the impressive list.

THE CASCADES – Musical Contribution.
The all-male group from San Diego enjoyed global success with, Rhythm of the Rain. They were, however, unable to repeat this fate with any of their subsequent offerings! The core of the group namely, John Gummoe, Lenny Green and Dave Wilson all met whilst serving in the US Navy.

The band was to endure many personnel changes over the years and worked under various names including, The Thundertones, until their only hit came along. Gummoe left the band to pursue a solo career and was subsequently replaced on lead vocals by Gabe Lapano, they went on to record Maybe the Rain Will Fall which enjoyed limited success. Recently, two of the original group's members have again teamed up with Gummoe.

DAVE CASH (Radio London Announcer).
Dave Cash's unmistakable voice is heard over the Radio London airwaves, as Jimmy prepares himself for Brighton. Cash was bought up in London but having spent some time in Canada he acquired the North American accent that was to become his trademark. At the time of filming Cash had moved on to Capital Radio, where he stayed for twenty-one years before leaving to pursue a writing career, he is currently back on the airwaves with Radio Kent.

ESTA CHARKHAM – Casting Assistant.
Esta was friends with the actress, Frances Tomelty, who was, at the time married to Sting, and was rumoured to have recommended him for the role of the Ace-Face. Esta went on to work on Scum and Breaking Glass in 1980 before moving on to various TV projects such as Producer of Boon from 1987 to 1989 and also worked on, One Foot in the Grave. Esta now runs a theatrical agency in London and is sister of Beth Charkham, also an agent!

JEANETTE CHARLES – Jimmy's Mother 1973 Album Booklet.
Jeanette Charles took the part of Jimmy's mother for the booklet that accompanied the 1973 album. Charles made her living from acting as a

lookalike for the Queen, and appeared in countless TV shows and Films such as, National Lampoon's European vacation.

Charles was born in 1927 and retired on 2014. When I questioned Ethan A. Russell about it he told me 'We cast the model that got all her work as the Queen Lookalike as Jimmy's mum. A fun idea I thought'. The following picture shows Jeanette as The Queen! Her agent at Lookalikes, Susan Scott further told me that 'she still often speaks about it'.

CHRIS CHARLESWORTH – Executive Producer (re-issued album).
The Executive Producer on the re-issued album has also contributed to projects by John Lennon and Deep Purple.

THE CHIFFONS – Musical Contribution.
An all-girl band that hailed from the Bronx area of New York and comprised of Judy Craig, Patricia Bennett, Sylvia Peterson and Barbara Lee Jones, who died in 1992. The group went on to enjoy much success throughout the sixties with hits such as; He's So Fine, One Fine Day and Sweet Talkin' Guy.

It was the first of these three hits that was to put the group back in the news in the early seventies, when George Harrison was successfully sued for plagiarism. Harrison later admitting that his hit, My Sweet Lord bore more than a passing resemblance to it.

On the back of the renewed interest in the song the group re-released it in 1972 when it reached number four in the British charts.

JEREMY CHILD – Michael in Advertising Agency.
Born: 20th September 1944

Without doubt Child is the only Baron to appear in Quadrophenia! His full title is Sir (Coles John) Jeremy Child, 3rd Baronet, and was rather predictably educated at Eton, before moving onto the Bristol Old Vic Theatre School. His film roles include A Fish Called Wanda and Wimbledon. Child has been married three times, once being to the well-known actress, Deborah Grant.

THE CHORDS – Musical Connection.
After reading about the search for a band for Quadrophenia in the NME, The Chords were auditioned, but rejected. It was said that they were considered as too similar to The Who. The Chords of course went on to be at the forefront of the 1979 mod revival.

ALAN CLARKE – Potential Director.
Born: 28th October 1935   Died: 24th July 1990

The much-missed Alan Clarke was famous for his realistic approach to Film and TV making. Clarke had just finished the BBC version of Scum, that was subsequently banned and remade in 1979 for the big screen; this of course featured many Quadrophenia actors including Phil Daniels and Ray Winstone. The excellent, Rita, Sue and Bob Too! followed in 1987, which was three years before he sadly succumbed to Lung Cancer, in what was a major loss to the British TV and Film industry. Alan Clarke's is survived by his son Gabriel, the well-known ITV sports reporter!

LOLLY CLARKE (Rocker girl at Brighton).
Lolly was a local girl living in Brighton who saw an advert in the Brighton Argus for extras. A visit to the Job Centre followed where she was photographed and later offered a part. Lolly was used for a day, and paid £10 for her services, even getting to appear in The Melody Maker in a special feature about the filming. Lolly was provided with a dark wig to hide her highlighted hair, and remembers fighting on the beach against

Toyah in a scene that never made the final print, but said she was delightful and very nice. 'Toyah was very apologetic and frightened she might hurt me, she was lovely' Lolly recalls. Sting did not leave such a lasting memory on her though and she recalls him swanning around in his big grey coat like the big 'I am' also that his favourite quote was 'hey be careful with the clothes'. Lolly befriended another extra Chrissie Hancock, with the two becoming good friends before eventually losing contact in the mid-eighties (If you know of Chrissie's whereabouts please contact the author and I will reunite them). Lolly Clarke is happily married and is now known as Lolly Dobrijevic, living and working as a teaching assistant in Leicestershire. Lolly has two teenagers who no doubt think it's pretty cool that mum was in Quadrophenia.

PAUL B. CLAY – Music Editor.
Paul Clay had an uncredited role in editing music on the film, and has worked extensively on both the big and small screen on the likes of Columbo and Murder She Wrote.

DAVE CLAYTON - (Mod at Brighton).
Dave was a Mod extra in the Brighton scenes and was a member of a Nottinghamshire based scooter club.

BRYAN COATES – Location Manager.
Coates was the man responsible for sourcing some of the terrific locations that were used in the film giving it that unmistakable air of authenticity. Other work has included Raiders of the Lost Ark in 1981 and Clash of the Titans in 1996. Coates also acted as Assistant Director in the 1996 British sci-fi production of Fahrenheit 451, which starred Julie Christie. In 1985 Coates was tragically killed in an aircraft crash on his way back from Morocco. He had been to view potential locations for his new project, The Jewel in the Nile, which went onto star Michael Douglas. Bryan Coates leaves a legacy of outstanding work in his chosen field within the British Film Industry.

ADEY COBB (Mod extra at Brighton).

Adey was a Mod extra in the Brighton scenes and was a member of a Nottinghamshire based scooter club.

NEIL COLLINS – (Rocker on road to Brighton).

Neil was a friend of fellow Rocker, Tom Ingram, who asked him if he wished to be in a film. Collins big moment comes at 59minutes and 59 seconds into the film when he veers on to wrong side of the road in Beachey Head.

FRANK CONNOR – Unit Photographer.

Frank Connor's impressive collections of Photographs are seen extensively on the special unseen pictorial footage section of the DVD, and later video offerings of the film. Connor's work also features on the pull-out album sleeves from the original 1979 gatefold format album. Film work has included The Elephant Man 1980, Gandhi 1982, Octupussy 1983, Cry Freedom 1987, Red Planet 2000 and What a Girl Wants 2003. Connor also has many minor acting roles to his credit including Battle Stations 1956 and the 1973 version of Superman.

NORMAN COOK aka FATBOY SLIM – Musical Connection.

Norman Cook a long-time resident of Brighton was the DJ at the 1997 re-release after party of Quadrophenia in Brighton. A former member of The Housemartins he topped the charts the following year with Praise You, and in 2002 played to a packed audience live on Brighton Beach.

GARRY COOPER – Peter Fenton.

Born; 2nd June 1955

Garry Cooper was born in Hull, East Yorkshire in 1955 and reputedly shared the name of the famous Hollywood star due to his mother's love of the film industry, although she afforded him an extra 'r' in her son's case!

Cooper left school in 1973 at the age of 15 and joined the Humberside Theatre Company as an assistant stage manager, with his first professional appearance being at the Norwich Theatre Royal as Benjamin in Joseph & His Amazing Technicolour Dreamcoat. Cooper then continued to tour the country as part of a repertory company, slowly but surely building up a name as a fine young theatre actor. After three years, he went on to formal training at stage school, and then went onto work with the Glasgow Theatre Company, from which he was allowed to take a three-month sabbatical to make Quadrophenia.

Cooper has always combined his film and television work with that of the theatre, which is where he has probably enjoyed his greater success. As he was a few years older than the rest of the cast he was originally up for the part of Ace Face, but ended up getting the one of Pete Fenton. Having been highly recommended to Franc Roddam by casting director, Patsy Pollock an impressive improvised screen test with Jimmy Pursey was to follow. Only a small amount of screen work had been done prior to this role, in which he is perfect, with an air of slight aloofness from the rest of the Mod group, and portrays a figure somewhat above his younger co-Mods! It is a tribute to the acting skills of Cooper that he delivers one of the finest performances in the whole film. He later went on to play Tommy in the excellent P'tang, Yang, Kipperbang in 1982.

Cooper's theatre work is extensive, to say the least! with notable roles such as Pavlik and Lawrence in Britannicus which was directed by Simon Callow, and also as Peter in Salonica at the Royal Court, which was directed by a then unknown, Danny Boyle who would later go on to work notably on Trainspotting.

In 1997 Cooper took the Paines Plough and Drum Theatre production of Long Time dead to the Edinburgh Festival in which he played the part of a veteran mountain climber, Grizzly. It was a critically acclaimed production written by, Rona Monro and centred on the adventures of a small group of mountaineers, indeed Cooper was awarded the Actor of the Year award from the trade newspaper, The Stage. Cooper was between jobs when he heard the news, and was doing some plumbing work. He tells the story about having one hand stuck down a u-bend clearing some human debris and the other hand on his mobile receiving the news!

Although a very accomplished stage actor Cooper is very affable when asked about his time making Quadrophenia, and says that he was proud to have been in the film, quoting the famous chemist scene, as his favourite part. His worst being the scooters, as he was known to have come off his on several occasions, and had to be strongly coaxed back on to them after one particularly nasty fall! He is still a keen follower of his home town football team, Hull City.

RAY CORBETT – Assistant Director.
Vastly experienced within the British Film Industry as well as the occasional project in America his credits include the following: - Baby Love and The Adding Machine both 1969, The Cat and the Canary and Midnight Express both 1978. S.O.S. Titanic followed in 1979, and then in 1980 Corbett was involved in three films all as Production Manager Inseminoid, McVicar which starred Roger Daltrey, and Babylon which was written by Martin Stellman and starred Trevor Laird. Further work in several roles includes the following impressive list, Pink Floyd: - The Wall, The Trail of the Pink Panther both 1982, The Keep, The Curse of the Pink Panther, Monty Python's: - The Meaning of Life all 1983, Greystoke: - The Legend of Tarzan, The Razors Edge both 1984. Mona Lisa starring Bob Hoskins followed in 1986 then came Nature of the Beast 1988, a straight to video sci-fi film starring Iggy Pop entitled Hardware came along the following year and in 1991 he renewed his acquaintance with Roger Daltrey in Buddy's Song.

CROSS SECTION – Mod Band in Goldhawk Club.
Cross Section was a young five-piece outfit from Kent that had been formed in 1978. The band comprised of, Dene O'Neill the seventeen-year-old drummer and Josh Phillips just a year his junior who played keyboards, both hailing from Rochester. Eighteen-year-old Lawrence Merton played bass, whilst his younger brother (by a year), Vince was the lead singer, and both came from nearby Rainham. Phil Kitto from Gillingham completed the band on rhythm guitar and vocals, and at just fourteen was the youngest member of Cross Section.

The band were managed by Vince and Lawrence's father, Bob, who had been entering them enthusiastically in talent shows in which they had played pop and rock classics as well as some self-penned efforts. Bob's eagle eye spotted an advert in The Melody Maker asking for new bands that were interested in appearing in Quadrophenia to send in a demo tape. Cross Section were amongst nine groups that attended an audition at The Electric Ballroom in Camden, after performing two songs, including, Bonie Maronie they left unsure of their fate, however as they were leaving Roger Daltrey who had been sitting in on the audition asked if they would mind getting their hair cut short for the film. Daltrey had seen something in them that he had liked, although their appearance was that of a seventies rock group, they were sent three songs to learn, High Heal Sneakers, Dimples and Boom, Boom The latter two saw Phil Kitto take the vocals, although only the first two were used in the film. Cross Section recorded their songs at Ramport Studios in Battersea during which they were given period style haircuts and costumes before moving onto filming which lasted two days at Lee Studios in Wembley, and Covent Garden.

As part of their deal they were offered a demo recording with Polydor, and eight weeks later they returned to the studios to record a further three tracks, by their own admission they were dire, and no contract was to be offered, these songs had a more rock feel to them. The band initially experienced trouble getting paid for some unexplained reason; a problem that was resolved by The Musicians Union, later on Josh Phillips was to work with Pete Townshend who said he thought that they were still owed some money, which was actually sorted out by Townshend himself.

After the film the band were kept busy, but was unable to turn the Mod scene to their advantage and continued to play rock covers and self-penned efforts. A band that had promised so much soon began to suffer internal problems with various factions forming within it, and less than a year after Quadrophenia they had split-up.

So, what are the group's members up to today? Josh Phillips is still a professional musician and has worked as a session singer with Pete Townshend also keeping busy with jingles. Phil Kitto still plays and lives in Tenerife. Vince Merton is also still playing (mainly Mod-type music), his brother Lawrence is also now back playing and performing. Dene O'Neill lives in Norway where he appears with a band called, Steam and writes scripts for Norwegian T.V.

The later was asked about Quadrophenia and said that he had been proud to have appeared in the film and as they had only appeared briefly at the start he felt that he could watch it impartially and thinks that it's still a great little film. There is also a Kansas based Gospel group by the same name, however they have no connection with the original group. In 2014 they reformed to appear at a charity event in Sussex organised by Kenney Jones, and were galvanized into returning to the studio with a new CD in the pipeline!

THE CRYSTALS – *Musical Contribution.*
The Crystals were an all-girl group from Brooklyn, New York comprising of, Dee Dee Kershaw, La La Brooks, Pat Wright, Mary Thomas and Barbara Alston and were yet another discovery of Phil Spector.

The group enjoyed their first commercial success with There's No Other (Like My Baby) in 1961, with their Quadrophenia contribution of Da Doo Ron Ron becoming a hit for them two years later. Further hits included, It's My Party and Chapel of Love, their unforgettable sound makes them a favourite for the countless sixties themed albums that are available, and they are still performing live some forty years on from their big success.

BILL CURBISHLEY – *Producer.*
Curbishley has been involved in various aspects of The Who for over 40 years; he acted as Producer or Executive Producer on most of their projects including McVicar and The Kids are Alright. He has also worked on most of The Who's direct to DVD projects including, Amazing Journey: The Story of The Who in 2007. Curbishley was originally part of Track Records and also managed amongst others, Marc Bolan. Curbishley set up Trinifold Management and went onto to manage the legendary Robert Plant. Trinifold was subsequently sold in 2002, but Curbishley remained as manager of The Who. Curbishley was born in East London and is the older brother of Alan, the former West Ham United manager and also of Paul who had a small uncredited part in Quadrophenia.

PAUL CURBISHLEY *(Spiders Friend).*
When Bill Curbishley the manager of The Who got involved in the production of Quadrophenia it was perhaps excusable that he found a

minor role in the film for his younger brother, Paul. His big moment in the film is when the mods leave the Ballroom and he persuades Spider to go for a scooter ride whilst Chalky and Dave go in search of somewhere to sleep. Paul also features on the cover of Meaty Beatty Big and Bouncy as a scruffy child. Phil Daniels says that he was very talented footballer like his brother, Alan. Indeed, he actually had a short spell at West Ham United, and the following picture is during this period.

JOHN CURL – Newsreader on 1973 Album.
Newsreader in a small segment of the track from the original album, Cut My Hair. John Curl was also engaged as an Audio Consultant on the 1972 musical documentary, Fillmore, which included amongst others, The Grateful Dead.

D

PHIL DANIELS – Jimmy.
Born;   25th October 1958

Paolo Sedazzari – 'It's impossible to imagine anyone else but Phil playing Jimmy. He was born for the role, just as DeNiro was for Travis Bickle or Richard E. Grant for Withnail'.

Phil Daniels was born at the Royal Free Hospital in Islington, North London right in the heart of Arsenal F.C. territory; however, he has always favoured the Blues from the west of the capital, Chelsea F.C. This led to a few run-ins with none other than Johnny (Rotten) Lydon, another local, who followed Arsenal and was himself later to be considered for the role of Jimmy!

Daniels spent his formative years in nearby, Kings Cross where his Father was a caretaker (one of his more famous tenants being the Carry-On star, Kenneth Williams!), the younger brother to two older sisters, he also had a brother who sadly died of a rare bone disease at just 3 years of age! At the age of twelve Daniels got well and truly bitten by the acting bug, and joined the Anna Scher Theatre Workshop, which is where he met and forged a lifetime friendship with Trevor Laird (the two are still regular visitors to Stamford Bridge!). It was ironically the same year that he was on a train journey back from a day out in Margate that crashed, and claimed the life of 6 of his fellow passengers, one of whom was the Driver and was subsequently later discovered to have been drunk.

Daniels' career really got off the ground in 1976 when at the age of eighteen; he had an uncredited role in Bugsy Malone and a couple of TV roles in Four Idle Hands, and The Molly Wopsies.

His first prominent role came the following year when he appeared in the TV drama, Raven, for which he was critically acclaimed, and was a role that set him on the path to bigger and better things. After his role in The Class of Miss MacMichael he landed a part in Zulu Dawn. This was the perfect vehicle for the young Daniels to display his talents to a far wider audience in the role of Pullen, the Quartermasters assistance. Although, only a relatively small role in which he ultimately meets his death, it was a superb performance that had an early day Jimmy Cooper written all over it! Zulu Dawn does not crop up very often on TV these days, but is an absolute must see if you get the chance!

During the filming of Zulu Dawn, Daniels was known to disappear during periods of filming inactivity and camp out in the wilds, which led to him contracting an illness that made him look less than perfect for his upcoming audition for the part of Jimmy Cooper in Quadrophenia. Daniels mother had answered an advert in The Sun newspaper in July 1978 on his behalf. The advert said that they were looking for somebody to play the lead in the upcoming new movie by The Who, fortunately for all concerned Mrs Daniels instinct that this would be good for her son proved to be correct! Indeed, unbeknown to Mrs Daniels his agent had already put him up for the role!

Daniels had two auditions for the role of Jimmy, with the first by his own omission being not very good due to his illness. However, by the time he was screen-tested he was in a much better state, and although eight other actors were seriously considered, Daniels performance that day convinced Franc Roddam that they had found their Jimmy. Roddam also liked the fact that he looked slightly similar to a younger Pete Townshend.

The story of Quadrophenia was not unknown to Daniels as he was a big fan of The Who, and knew the original album very well. He particularly likes the scene when he is seen on his Scooter at the canal tow path in pouring rain when the track 'I'm One' cuts in. Filming the ending first was important to Daniels as he felt he knew where his character was going; also, he was delighted that he was able to improvise largely during the film. He had been taught the craft at Anna Scher's, and the film is littered with many of these performances, think the 'Mr Fucking Postman' scene and the interplay between him and Kate Williams on his return from Brighton to realise how good at his art he is.

Daniels also says that at the time he was living a similar lifestyle at home which all helped in his development of the character.

Of course, Daniels went on to deliver an incredible performance in the film that was to make him so well known, but as is inevitable in such a high-profile role there were also negatives connected with it!

Indeed, Daniels will of course, be forever Jimmy, but following Quadrophenia it would sometimes see him overlooked for other roles, a victim of his own success? At times in the past Daniels had appeared to be a little waspy when being interviewed about his latest project, and was constantly asked about Quadrophenia. However, these days with the film being re-evaluated constantly, he is happy to talk and celebrate a glorious moment in his past!

Franc Roddam has gone on record as saying that Phil Daniels was his true partner in the film. Daniels was twenty at the time of filming and showed unbelievable maturity beyond his years to deliver the role, his co-star, Kate Williams was equally impressed with him, and on only her first day on the film they filmed Jimmy's less than triumphant return from Brighton. A truly memorable scene, that is a testament to their expertise in their craft! It is hard to imagine the scene being quite so poignant between Daniels and his original on-screen mother, Amanda Barrie.

Following Quadrophenia, Daniels and many of his co-stars quickly moved on to make Scum. The film version was virtually a carbon copy of a version that had been made for BBC2 the previous year, and was subsequently banned.

In Scum, it is Ray Winstone that is the central figure, with Daniels part of the supporting cast. Indeed, Winstone gets to exact his revenge on Daniels for his treatment of him in Quadrophenia. Winstone is seen coshing Daniels in the infamous scene that sees him whack him with a sock full of snooker balls. Out of shot somebody switches the prop with one full of a rolled-up sock, Daniels joked 'I was shitting myself that they didn't mess up on the swap'! Although not really a major role for Daniels, Scum was and is a important part of his repertoire in which he delivers a frighteningly realistic performance in a film, made by Alan Clarke that was to actually change the way British Borstals were run!

Following Scum, Daniels went on to work on Breaking Glass, alongside Mark Wingett and Hazel O'Connor who had beaten off Toyah Wilcox for the lead role of Kate. It is a film that rarely gets aired on TV these days and very much of the eighties, in which Daniels plays the part of Danny who was Kate's manager, and eventually her lover. It has certain similarities to The Commitments and worth searching out on DVD. In 1984 Daniels played the older brother to Tim Roth in the BBC play, Meantime, which also featured Gary Oldman. It portrays a depressed Britain of the mid-eighties and life on the dole in a gritty Mike Leigh production that was very well received at the time. The following year Daniels played the part of Billy Kidd in Billy the Kid and the Green Baize Vampire. The role was that of a London snooker player, reputedly based on Jimmy White, the film saw Daniels re-united again with both Alan Clarke and Trevor H. Laird.

The rest of the eighties were littered with various TV and Theatre roles including a superb performance as the lead in The Clockwork Orange at The Barbican. The eighties also saw periods of unemployment for Daniels when he was even forced to sign on the dole. Daniels joked about the time at a convention saying 'I used to get some strange looks, there's nothing worse than being famous and skint'.

Phil Daniels had always been something of a musician having fronted Phil Daniels and the Cross in the late seventies as well as being part of a band with Trevor Laird named Renoir, and through this and his love of Football he ended up playing for the NME staff team. In 1994 Blur were working on a song called Parklife that required a narrative and it was suggested by one of the NME team that Phil Daniels would be ideal, and indeed he was! And a seminal part of the Brit-Pop phenomenon was subsequently created.

Parklife is still a very popular record and who can say they haven't listened to it and not chipped in with the obligatory "It's got nothing to do with your 'Vorsprung Durch Technik' ya Know"?

The year after the success of this song Daniels was working again with The Who, as the narrator of the 1996 performance of Quadrophenia in Hyde Park and the subsequent tour.

Regular work has continued to follow including the SKY TV comedy, Time Gentleman Please, in which he played the permanently inebriated Terry for two years. In 2004 a very watchable part in The Long Firm was followed by Outlaws before the move to EastEnders. EastEnders was a part of Daniels life for two years before refusing to renew his contract to pursue other work. One of Daniels latest film roles was as Grouch in Freebird, where he played the part of an aged Rocker.

In 2008 Daniels run the London marathon in a very respectable 4 hours 49 minutes, and was the first to be voted out in Strictly Come Dancing. In his autobiography, he speaks about his dislike as being called 'common' by one of the judges, referring to him as 'that Australian twat with the double-barrelled name'.

He lives in North London not far from where he grew up and lived with his long-term partner, Jan Stevens until her sad and sudden death in October 2012. The pair met and had been together since the early eighties, they met when Jan was working in the music industry. The couple have a daughter, Ella, Bella, Mandela Daniels who was given the slightly elongated name to commemorate the fact that Nelson Mandela had been released from prison the day before her birth. One of Phil Daniels prized possessions is the stripy boating jacket that he wore in Quadrophenia, which he says still fits him, although sadly his trademark Parka from the film was stolen years ago, from a car, after taking it to show some fans at a reunion. In the following photograph Phil Daniels receives a birthday kiss from his co-star, Leslie Ash whilst on location in Acton.

PHIL DANIELS AND THE CROSS – *Musical Connection.*
The short lived musical project of Daniels' which went on to have an album released in 1979.

DENNIS DAVIDSON ASSOCIATES – *Public Relations.*
Dennis Davidson Associates (DDA) is an extremely well established Independent PR company for both the film industry and the corporate media, boasting offices in both London and Los Angeles. Amongst the many films that they have been involved in are McVicar in 1980 and The Kings Speech in 2010. Dennis Davidson set the company up in 1970 having previously worked as a management trainee at his local ABC cinema in Chester before moving to London to work in PR for ABPC.

Former employees include Tom Parker-Bowles the son of Camilla, who was involved in a drug scandal that hit the national press in the late nineties.

PHIL DAVIS – Chalky.
Born; 30th July 1953

Phil Davis never attended Drama School, but it is something that has certainly not hampered his career. Davis has enjoyed a busy and full career having become one of the most well-known faces on TV over recent years, in a career that has also seen him branch off into writing and directing.

Born in Grays, Essex, he went on to join the National Youth Theatre in Stratford which (with the help of none other than Joan Littlewood) helped to shape and hone his craft. Davis moved on to various TV roles prior to Quadrophenia, which included the lead in the 1977 BBC play, Gotcha which was written by Barrie Keeffe. A stunning performance was very well received and saw him receive the Time Out – Best Performance of the year award.

The following year he was asked to audition for the part of Jimmy Cooper. However, at 25 he was a few years older than his rivals for the role. Davis was known to be a little disappointed at the refusal but in the end said he was delighted to be offered the role of Chalky. Chalky is blessed with some of the films funniest moments, including the hilarious Chemist scene. Davis commented that he felt that the original script was a bit stiff, but that the improvisational methods used bought it to life, and that at times he felt as if he didn't have a clue what was going on. "Somebody would shout action – and chaos would ensue". Davies was felt to have had a somewhat similar look to Roger Daltrey at the time, and like Franc Roddam, was less than happy with the stunt scene in which he is ridden off of his scooter on-route to Brighton, "look out for his dodgy wig" he jokes!

Following Quadrophenia a host of TV appearances followed as well as a role in Pink Floyd's, The Wall in 1982 along with various other members of the Quadrophenia ensemble. In 1989 Davis wrote and directed his first TV play, Skulduggery, for the BBC, which he followed up with a couple of directorial roles on TV dramas. In 1995 he transferred his craft to the big screen when he directed I.D., a gritty British drama about football hooliganism in the eighties; he also had a small part in the film as a policeman. The following year it was back to the acting with amongst others a role in the Mike Leigh film, Secrets and Lies, which starred

Timothy Spall and Trevor H. Laird in a superb comedy drama that was nominated for no less than five Oscars.

From then on Davis started to become a main-stay of most TV dramas, cropping up in all sorts of roles, large and small!

In 2004, and released the following year was the highly-acclaimed Vera Drake, in which, Imelda Staunton played the lead role of a female abortionist in the 1950's. Davis played the husband in what was one of his finest hours. The film received countless awards and was even nominated for three Oscars. Davis himself was nominated for a BAFTA and won the best actor award from the British Independent Filmmakers Guild. A superb film from the cannon of Mike Leigh that is must see for any fan of British Cinema at its best!

Recent work has included Dr. Who, and The Curse of Steptoe, in which he superbly played the part of Wilfrid Brambell. When asked by mistake at the 2008 convention by somebody how he had enjoyed being a certain TV show, he answered that he had not actually been in it. Phil Daniels cut in with a rather accurate "It was the only bloody thing you haven't been in lately". A very busy and much sought after actor Davis continues to crop up regularly on both small and large screen, with many projects already in the pipeline!

Davis is married to actress, Eve Matheson who starred in the BBC comedy show, May to December ,and the couple have a Daughter Amy. When he can Davis likes to play the occasional round of Golf, and has played many times with Phil Daniels, he also keen on watching Football and supports West Ham United.

LOREN DAY (Steph's friend Shirl).
Loren Day appears in what would seem to be her only film as Steph's friend, who we learn as they head off to their accommodation is called Shirl (presumably short for Shirley).

JEFF DEXTER – Assistant Choreographer.
Dexter was working as a Mod DJ when he stumbled upon the cast having dancing lessons in a Soho studio. Dexter was enlisted to assist Gillian Gregory with some of the dance scenes after offering advice on certain dance moves, and was particularly heavily involved in teaching Sting.

Dexter was a close friend of the late glam-rock star, Marc Bolan, and was on set for all the Dance scenes, also carrying out some rehearsal work at the London Dance Centre in Covent Garden. Dexter is pictured below during rehearsals for the Brighton Dance Hall scenes!

MICHAEL DICKINS (Mod at Brighton).
Dickins originally hailed from South London but moved to Worthing whilst still at school and very soon joined a local theatre group. Following this he landed an uncredited role in Quadrophenia and has since gone on to work on films such as, Gladiator and Skyfall.

LESLEY DODD (Mod girl at Brighton).
This instantly recognisable girl appears in various scenes during the Brighton sequences. A prominent blond bouffant hairstyle somewhat akin to the infamous Myra Hindley, is seen bouncing around quite a bit; surely this elegant head of hair was the work of a wigmaker! Lesley Dodd does not appear to have continued acting after this minor role. The following picture shows Lesley (right) with Claire Toeman and Stuart Turton in a continuity photograph.

BILL DRAKE – Scooter Advisor.
Drake was a Scooter enthusiast whose Vespa 150 GS (registration no: - 809 ARW) was used by Gary Cooper during the film, although it wasn't actually authentic to the era! Drake subsequently left his advisory role in the project as he was constantly overruled by Terry Wells, (the Property Master) over what scooters were being used.

E

ADRIAN EDMONSON – Ace Face (1996 Hyde Park Concert).
The British comedy star, probably best known for his role in The Young Ones took the part of the Ace Face, in the 1996 show at Hyde Park. Edmonson is married to Jennifer Saunders.

ROYSTON EDWARDS (Mod in London and Brighton).
Royston Edwards was a member of a small bunch of Scooterist's known as the 5.15 club. Edwards and co used to meet at a pub in Sevenoaks Kent, and very soon fell in love with the scene, and eventually ended up at a rally in Southend, which is where he, like many who attended, were invited to take part in the film.

Having seen an advert in a newspaper entitled 'Who wants to be a star?' which was looking for people to play lead roles in the film, Royston sent away the required photograph, and was quickly invited to an audition. Although, missing out on a lead role, Royston was to become a widely used extra throughout the film.

Royston immediately left his job and committed himself to the full 3 ½ months of filming.

Although there are, of course, many scooters that feature in Quadrophenia, Royston's Lambretta adorned in a union jack paint design is right up there with any of them. In particular, a certain Roger Daltrey was very impressed with it! Edwards was to go on and work extensively on the Brighton scenes, where he constantly crops up. It was somewhat of a labour of love for Edwards, although he was of course paid, as well as receiving a fee of £300 for the hire of his bike.

Royston told his story in serialised form in Classic Scooterist Scene over a couple of years in what was a real insight into the filming, and well worth checking out. Royston has attended the cast reunions and the 2008 convention where he was more than happy to talk about his time working on Quadrophenia. Truly one of the unsung heroes of the film, and one without whom the film would not have got made as Franc Roddam was to say.

MARK ELLIS (Mod at Brighton).
Mark Ellis is briefly seen sitting on a yellow scooter when the Mods are converging on Madeira Drive, Brighton.

MICHAEL ELPHICK – Mr Cooper (Jimmy's Father).
Born; 19th November 1946

Died; 9th September 2002

Michael Elphick was born in 1947 in Chichester, West Sussex, and although was said to have had acting ambitions at an early age, he left school at 15, and became an apprentice electrician. It was during his apprenticeship that he was sent to carry out some work at his local theatre, a job that was to change his life! For it was whilst carrying out his electrical duties that the acting bug well and truly bit him. He was encouraged by Laurence Olivier who was performing there at the time to audition for the Central School for Speech and Drama in Swiss Cottage.

Elphick very soon changed his career path when at the age of 18 he won a scholarship that was to launch his career. Although regular television appearances were made throughout the late sixties and early seventies it wasn't until the end of that decade that he really began to get noticed. Elphick had made his acting debut in an Italian production, Fraulein Doctor which starred, Suzy Kendall as a secret-agent during the First World War.

1979 saw him star in not only Quadrophenia, but also in the classic Dennis Potter play for BBC, Blue Remembered Hills. Elphick went on to appear in many classic British films such as The Krays, Withnail and I, as well as the night porter in the 1980 David Lynch production of The Elephant Man.

In 1981 his first major television role came in the mini-series Private Schultz. This lead to a constant flow of television parts including the part of McGowan, in Auf Weidershen Pet, alongside fellow Quadrophenia actors, Timothy Spall and Gary Holton, this classic show being the creation of none other than Franc Roddam! A particularly memorable role was as Pasha in the 1984 film, Gorky Park for which he was nominated for a BAFTA.

Other notable roles included playing alongside Pauline Quirke as Barkis, in David Copperfield, as well as the lead role in the BBC comedy, Three Up, Two Down. It was, however, the part of Ken Boon in the hit ITV series, Boon, that made him a star playing alongside David Daker and Neil Morrissey in a show that went on to run for seven series.

In 1993 BBC lured him from ITV, and he went on to star as Harry Salter in Harry, in which he played the part of a freelance journalist who was a recovering alcoholic. It was to prove an ironic part for Elphick as he had a constant drink problem that was never really cured. He said that he had got his drinking under control by the mid-nineties after finally admitting his problem, and joining Alcoholics Anonymous, but it was to prove only a temporary cure.

From Harry Salter, he went on to play the part of Harry Slater in EastEnders in what proved to be his final role on television, Elphick appeared overweight and looking somewhat ravaged by the effects of alcohol, but nevertheless, delivered a quality performance in an extremely challenging role. In the controversial role, he played the part of Kat Slater's uncle who we later learned had raped her and made her pregnant when she was still a child.

EastEnders should have been the vehicle to revamp this extremely talented actor's career, but he was fighting a losing battle with the bottle and admitted to being drunk 'virtually every night', indeed his drinking was said to have nearly cost him his job. He had begun drinking heavily again in 1996 when he was devastated by the death from cancer of his partner of thirty-three years, Julia Alexander. Two years later he entered the Priory Clinic in Roehampton in an unsuccessful attempt to beat his alcoholism, but drink was something that would be with him for the rest of his life.

Elphick completed one last film shortly before he died, Out of Bounds, which was released in 2003 and starred Sophie Ward in a story centring on a girls Boarding School.

Michael Elphick became the first actor with a leading role in Quadrophenia to pass away, when on 9th September 2002, having complained about chest pains to his daughter he was rushed from his home in Willesden Green, North West London, to Hospital but died later that day. Elphick was cremated back in his birth place in Chichester.

His ex-co-star from EastEnders, Barbara Windsor leading the tributes: - 'I liked him very much. He was a terrific actor and has left a great legacy of great shows'. Neil Morrissey another ex-co-star from Boon said 'Michael has been a great friend and mentor for many years. He was one of the best actors this country has ever produced and will be sadly missed'.

The actor who was famous for his for his croaky voice and craggy features was in fact just 55 years old when he died, just 11 years older than his screen son, Phil Daniels.

MISCLEANOUS INFORMATION

Books: - Michael Elphick: The Great Pretender Biography by Kate Elphick and Nigel Denison – The History Press 2013.

BEN ELTON   (youth at party).
In a blink and you'll miss it appearance the popular entertainer and author (allegedly) appears at the beginning of the house party scene. Elton is said to be seen sipping a beer as Jimmy enters the front room. I'm not sure if this is an urban myth or not! Franc Roddam could not confirm the fact, but said he would be thrilled to think he was is in it!

CAROLINE EMBLING (schoolgirl on train).

Caroline Embling is the blond-haired schoolgirl that takes an interest in Jimmy during his trip back to Brighton on the train, however he does not reciprocate, asking in aggressive manor 'what you looking at?'. Embling went on to work on a couple TV mini-series Edward and Mrs Simpson, and Claire. The year after Quadrophenia was made she played the part of Susan in Bloody Kids, alongside Gary Holton, Jesse Birdsall, P.H. Moriarty and Tammy Jacobs, she was also part of the scriptwriting team. Embling does not appear to have acted on screen for over twenty years.

JULIE EMSON – (Mod girl in 1973 album booklet).
Julie was a girl local to Ramport Studios in Battersea and spotted as an ideal Mod for the album booklet, she is seen sitting down against a wall as Jimmy looks on astride his scooter.

MARTIN EVANS – Electrical Supervisor for Polytel Films.
A varied role in film work as best-boy, gaffer and rigging electrician has included work on the following; Steptoe and Son 1972, Jesus Christ Superstar and The National Health both 1973, Stardust and Swallows and Amazons both 1974 The Man Who Fell to Earth and The Eagle Has Landed both 1976.

A very busy decade of work in the eighties includes contributions to the following; The Bitch 1980, Raiders of the Lost Ark and Reds both 1981, Pink Floyd: - The Wall 1982, The Jigsaw Man, Never Say Never Again and The Hunger all 1983. Later work in that decade numbers amongst it Indiana Jones and the Temple of Doom 1984, Water 1985 and Hamburger Hill in 1987.

More recent offerings have included the following, Carrington 1995, The Mummy 1999 and Pitch Black in 2000.

RICHARD EVANS – Contribution to Album (re-issued version).
Evans worked on the re-issued album and went on to work on the 1989 film, K9.

_F_

RUPERT FARLEY (uncredited Mod in London and Brighton).
Farley makes regular cameos throughout the film as a sharp dressed Mod. Early action sees him confront Ferdy for pills after seeing that Jimmy had just scored. Farley is also seen sitting next to Jimmy in the courtroom scene. A regular Theatre performer as well as appearing in TV and film roles which include, The Comic Strip Presents and Heartbeat, as well as a part in the 1997 film Mrs Brown alongside Billy Connelly. Farley was also used as a voice over artist on the TV series, The Animals of Farthing Wood. Picture below shows a camera run-through of the courtroom scene, with Farley wearing black-collared T-shirt sitting next to Phil Daniels.

RON FAWCUS – Production Assistant on 1973 Album.
Having worked on the original album in 1973 Fawcus went on to work with the likes of Ronnie Lane.

HARRY 'AITCH' FIELDER (uncredited Policeman in Brighton).
Fielder is one of those unsung heroes of British TV and Film having appeared in countless uncredited roles in both mediums. Fielder was

bussed down to Brighton from London to take part in the riot scenes and has also appeared in the likes of Fawlty Towers and Star Wars.

Eagle-eyed viewers will notice a timber yard opposite Alfredos in Islington when Jimmy and co depart, this was coincidentally the very same yard that Fielder worked in before turning to acting!

JULIAN FIRTH (Michael).
This well-established actor has an all too brief, but constant role throughout the film as the part of Michael, a Mod on the fringes of the main group. He is seen drugged up in the pub toilet prior to the house party, at which he eventually arrives, only to be pushed out of the way by Pete as he leaves with Steph. Julian also appears throughout the Brighton scenes, notably as he and his fellow Mods march along the promenade singing 'we are the mods'. An excellent actor, who sadly appears very much on the outside of the film, his character although un-credited, did have a name, Michael.

Julian's big break came just after Quadrophenia, when he landed the part of Davis in Scum, in which he has a pivotal role. His character suffers the infamous horrific rape in the greenhouse before going on to commit suicide. Julian's other notable roles have been Absolute Beginners in 1986 and the 2006 production of The Queen. Julian also crops up regularly on television including ten appearances during the nineties in Cadfael.

FLEAGAL? (Mod extra at Brighton).
A scooter club member (possibly Barnsley) Fleagal was a scooter riding extra in Brighton and is featured in the picture below Martyn Scully later in this chapter.

ALAN FLETCHER – Story Consultant.
Fletcher was the man chosen by Pete Townshend to write the novel that accompanies the film, which is well worth a read as it gives further character information not explored in the actual film. Along with Pete Townshend and Chris Stamp he was credited as story consultant. Fletchers' other novels include Learning Curve, Brummell's Last Riff and Blue Millionaire. Brummell's Last Riff was submitted as a script, but later rejected by Granada Television, unperturbed he sent the script to Pete Townshend which led to him being used for Quadrophenia, he was given a

copy of a rough script to develop the novel from, which went on to sell 90,000 copies on the back of the film's success. The subject was one that Fletcher knew very well as he had been a Mod during the sixties. Fletcher lives in Nottinghamshire, and although his main job is an Insurance Broker, he still writes about the Mod scene, and is angered when 'sloppy journalists' sometimes portray the scene as all about fights on Beaches!

FLOWERED UP – Musical Connection.
A Camden based band in the Madchester mould they were active from 1989 till 1994 and fronted by two brothers Liam and Joe Maher. In 1992 they released the song Weekender which samples Jimmy's resignation speech from the film and went on to reach number 20 in the UK. The full video which lasts in excess of seventeen minutes is well worth a watch and is to say the least very heavily influenced by Quadrophenia. Sadly, Liam Maher died of a Heroin overdose in October 2009!

MIKE FLYNN – Second Assistant Director.
Flynn worked alongside Kieron Phipps as Second Assistant Director. Flynn has also worked on the following films, Gumshoe 1971, The Hit 1984, The Grifters 1990 and High Fidelity 2000.

BARBARA FRANKLAND – Mod Girl in Brighton Club Scene.
Barbara Frankland was used as an uncredited extra in the Brighton Club scenes that were actually filmed in London. A product of the Barbara Speake Stage School she has appeared in things as diverse as The Benny Hill Show and Star Wars-A New Hope in 2015. Barbara is now known as Barbie Denham.

GEOFF FREEMAN – Unit Publicist.
Freeman has worked on such productions as the classic 1963 production of Cleopatra with Elizabeth Taylor and Richard Burton, Under Milk Wood 1972, The Tamarind Seed 1974, which starred Julie Andrews and Omar Sharif. Further projects include The Rocky Horror Picture Show 1975, The Eagle Has Landed 1976, Zulu Dawn and Scum 1979. Work in the eighties lists the 1985 Terry Gilliam film, Brazil, The Living Daylights 1987 and Shirley Valentine in 1989. Recent work includes The Mummy 1999, The

Mummy Returns 2001 and Die Another Day in 2002. Freeman sadly died of Pulmonary Fibrosis in 2006.

STEPHEN FRY – Actor in 1996 Hyde Park Show.
The star of many TV and stage shows including, Blackadder Goes Forth and QI had a small role as the Hotel Manager in the 1996 show at Hyde Park.

RACHEL FULLER – Orchestration on Pete Townshend's Classic Quadrophenia.
Born; 24th July 1973.

Rachel Fuller was born in Ipswich, and like Alfie Boe was born the year of Quadrophenia's original release. Primarily Rachel is an orchestrator, which is how she came to meet Pete Townshend in 1996 having worked with him on The Lifehouse Chronicles. Rachel soon became Pete's other-half, and has worked on various other projects of her own highlighting what an accomplished singer and musician she is! Along with Mickey Cuthbert she was responsible for the now legendary, In the Attic shows that used to be streamed on line during The Who's tours. The likes of Townshend would sometimes just pop-in and bash out an improvised or rare Who related song, as well as other material in what are much missed shows! Rachel and Pete Townshend finally married in December 2016.

G

MARVIN GAYE – Musical Contribution.
Marvin Gaye was born in April 1939 as Marvin Pentz Gay Jnr, named after his father, who was a minister in the Apostolic Church. Gaye's contribution to music (black music, particularly) is almost impossible to comprehend having countless hits whilst with the Tamla Motown label in his own right, as well as many as part of a duet.

A famous partnership was forged with Tammi Terrell, with the duo enjoying several hits together, however, tragedy was to strike when she collapsed and died of a brain tumour in Gaye's arms whilst on stage in

1968. The tragedy had a profound impact on Gaye, but he soldiered on and had a world-wide number one in 1971 with, What's Going On? The early eighties saw Gaye descend into a deep cocaine addiction but he carried on producing quality songs such as Sexual Healing in 1982, however two years later whilst living back with his father he ended up having a violent row. The ensuing chaos saw his father shoot him dead just one day before his 45th birthday, and the world was robbed of one its finest soul singers of all time.

JOHN GAY – Lou (Mod friend of Danny).
John Gay enjoys some very minor moments on the screen as one of the many Mods at Brighton, also as Danny Peacocks mate at the Tailors 'Fucking rent-a-tent init'. Gay also appeared alongside another Quadrophenia actor in the form of Patrick Murray, when the two of them appeared in the 1980 production of Moon over the Alley.

DAVID GIDEON THOMPSON – Executive Producer (Polytel).
Thompson also worked in a similar role in the 1988 production, Eye of the Dictator, which was the story of Josef Goebbels.

DAVID GILMOUR – Musician in 1996 Hyde Park Show.
The legendary member of Pink Floyd played the part of the bus driver in the 1996 show at Hyde Park, he was made a CBE in 2003 for his services to music.

SIMON GIPPS-KENT (Sandra's boyfriend at Party).
Born: -25th October 1958. Died: -16th September 1987

Simon Gipps-Kent was born on the same day as Phil Daniels; he is the disgruntled boyfriend of Sandra the host of the house party – 'bleeding Prince Phillip' as Spider addresses him! Gipps-Kent was a instantly recognisable face from Children's TV and Film during the seventies, including, The Tomorrow People, as well as various productions for The Children's Film Foundation. His last recorded roles on TV were in 1982 in Blackadder and alongside Gary Shail in an episode of Metal Mickey. Tragically Gipps-Kent died in 1987; with an official coroner's report stating that it was 'misadventure due to Morphine poisoning. The internet, however, is awash with many other theories, suggesting many sinister alternatives. For more info see: - www.simongipps-kent.info.

ROBERT GLENISTER (Mod at Brighton and London).
Sharp eyed viewers can spot Robert Glenister in the Kitchener Road party scene, as well as in the mayhem in Brighton. Glenister is the son of Director, John Glenister and brother of Philip. He has appeared in countless TV roles such as, Spooks and Doctor Who, and has a daughter, Emily with actress Amanda Redman. The following photograph shows Robert Glenister during a break from filming with Roger Daltrey and other cast members.

GARY GLITTER – Musician in 1996 Hyde Park Show.
The disgraced former glam-rock star from the seventies played the part of a Rocker in the 1996 Hyde Park show, and then made appearances as the Godfather on the ensuing tour.

ROBERT GLOVER (Mod extra at Brighton).
Robert Glover was a member of the Barnsley scooter club who was used as an extra in the Brighton scenes.

WILLOUGHBY GODDARD – TV SHOW APPEARANCE.
Born; 4th July 1926. Died; 11th April 2004.

Willoughby Goddard's dulcet tones can be briefly heard when he is viewed on an episode of The Avengers that is being watched by Mr and Mrs Cooper. Goddard was a large proportioned English actor who crops up on many shows such as, The Invisible Man and Danger Man, predominately paying similar roles. In the episode of The Avengers viewed he plays the part of the Deacon.

GREEN DAY – Musical Connection.
Green Day's 2004 hit album entitled, American Idiot was their successful foray into the world of rock-opera. The album's main protagonist is also a sufferer of a personality disorder, with one of his alter egos named Saint Jimmy, which has led to much speculation that one of its main inspirations came from Quadrophenia! Whether this is true or not is the subject to a lot of conjecture as Green Day very rarely discuss their work in public, although it is patently clear that definite parallels exist.

GILLIAN GREGORY – Choreographer.
Very experienced choreographer who has countless films and stage shows to her credit. Stage work has included many West End productions and projects at the Regents Park open-air theatre as we'll as the 2001 Broadway production Seven Brides for Seven Brothers. Film credits include Mahler 1974, Privates on Parade 1982 which starred Michael Elphick, Return of the Jedi 1983 a film in which John Altman had a minor role. Gregory also worked on the 1975 film made by The Who, Tommy. In 1987 Gregory won the prestigious Tony Award as choreographer for Me and My Girl on Broadway.

DAVID GRIGGLESTONE (Mod extra at Brighton).
David Grigglestone was a member of a scooter club and used in Brighton, ridding his own bike called Dave. Grigglestone is also seen wearing a parka in some of the riot scenes in Brighton; this same parka is now on display at the Littledean Jail exhibition.

H

FREDDIE HAAYEN – Without Whom.

Although not technically a member of the crew Haayen (sometimes credited as Haaven) is given special thanks in the credits. He was the president of Polydor Records and was responsible for signing The Who to the label.

CAROLINE HAGEN – Production Assistant.
Hagen went onto work on the 1980 film Breaking Glass with the late Dodi Fayed, where she renewed her Quadrophenia affiliation with Phil Daniels and Mark Wingett.

STEVE HAMILTON – Special Effects Technician.
Hamilton went on to carve out a successful career in special effects on films such as Tomb Raider in 2001, and Die Another Day the following year. In 2007 Hamilton won a VES award for outstanding special effects in Harry Potter and the Order of the Phoenix. A little-known fact is that he is the son-in-law of Julie Andrews.

CHRISSIE HANCOCK (Rocker girl at Brighton).
Chrissie Hancock was a local girl who landed a role as an extra during the Beach scenes.

DON HANN (associate of Harry North).
Hann was one of the heavies that were in Harry North's company at the Boxing Gym at the back of the Pub. Hann had a few minor roles on TV including one alongside Martin Sheen in the 1975 production of Sweet Hostage.

HAPPY? – (Mod extra at Brighton).
Happy was another of the Modrapheniacs Scooter Club who was present in the Brighton scenes.

SLIM HARPER (musical connection).
Harper's 'Got Love if you want it!' provides the basis for 'I'm the Face', in what today would be called sampling.

CAROL HARRISON (record shop assistant).
Carol has a minor role in the film, playing the part of the assistant in the record shop who tells Jimmy which booth to go into in order to listen to his

selected song. Carol has had a varied career on stage and television, including roles in A Touch of Frost, The Bill and more notably for her role in the BBC comedy, Brush Strokes. She also starred alongside fellow Quadrophenia actor, Ray Winstone in the 1992 production of Get Back for the BBC, this show also saw her playing alongside a young, Kate Winslet.

Her other film work has included parts in the 1999 film, Human Traffic and a small part alongside Michael Elphick in the 1980 production of The Elephant Man.

However, she is probably best known for her part in EastEnders as Lisa Raymond (Grant Mitchell's mother-in-law). In the soap, she played the part of Tiffany Mitchell's mum, who went on to have an affair with her husband. Carol's partner for many years was the actor, Jamie Foreman, who played alongside Ray Winstone in the hit film, Nil by Mouth. Foreman is the son of the infamous gangster, Freddie Foreman who had many dealings with another actor from the film, John Bindon. Carol continues to juggle her career as a busy actress, and mother of her son, Alfie, with a future return to EastEnders never ruled out. Carol is currently working on her production, 'All or Nothing' an excellent musical about The Small Faces.

PAUL HARRISON (Rocker in Brighton).

One of the many colourful characters in Brighton, Paul Harrison is an artist and musician who has made the place his home. Paul moved to Brighton at the age of thirteen, from Berkshire. Harrison was in his mid-twenties at the time of the film and described himself as a 'bit of a beach bum', when his mum noticed the advertisement for extras. Although, Harrison had been a teenage Mod at the time of the original riot in 1964, they were looking for Rockers, so he borrowed a leather jacket and got hold of an old bus conductor's hat and duly went along to Brighton Job Centre. Three days of filming followed for which he was paid £20 per day. Local TV showed interested in the story of somebody acting in a film about an event that he had actually been at so he was duly featured on South Today.

Following his work on the film he had various jobs including one that took him to Spain for five years, and now has an artist's studio back in Brighton, check out http://www.harrisonsbrighton.co.uk for more information. Quadrophenia was not the first experience he had with The Who, as when he was away with the Merchant Navy in New Zealand he bumped in to Pete Townshend, who later turned up on their boat with the rest of the band and members of The Small Faces. A surreal afternoon followed when the ship's captain agreed to open the bar for his esteemed visitors. Harrison said that working on Quadrophenia was a most pleasant experience and was even complimented by Sting for his acting after seeing the previous day's rushes. The following picture shows the back of Paul Harrison (right) in a scene that didn't make the finished print!

WILF HARVEY (Rocker in Brighton).
Wilf Harvey is seen briefly throughout the Rockers scenes in Brighton. He is most recognisable when he is at the centre of three motorbikes that roar up to confront the Mods on the beach opposite shouting 'kill the bastards'. Wilf hailed from Hangleton, just along the coast in Hove, and was a motorbike enthusiast. He was sadly killed some years later when he tried to stop an attack on a woman.

MARK HAZEGROVE (Mod extra at Brighton).
Mark Hazelgrove was enlisted from an unknown scooter club and used in the Brighton scenes.

COLIN HAWKER (Mod extra at Brighton).

Colin was a member of Modrapheniacs scooter club who was involved in the Brighton filming and is seen pictured with John Wardzinski in his section further on in this chapter. The smart suit sported by Colin was ruined by leaning on to the sign behind him which was covered in wet paint!

TED HIGH – Production Buyer.
High worked on the 1994 film, Stanley's Dragon and the 1983 TV series The Outsider, and was also credited as Set Decorator Buyer on the 2001 TV version of Murder on the Orient Express.

THE HIGH NUMBERS – Musical Contribution,
The High Numbers was the name albeit briefly for The Who between July and October 1964. The one and only release under this name was, Zoot Suit with, I'm The Face on its reverse, both songs feature on the film and its subsequent soundtrack.

MALCOLM HIRST – Second Boom Operator / Sound Maintenance.
Uncredited in the film Hirst went on to work on, Prostitute 1980, Puccini 1984, Hidden City 1988, Life is Sweet 1990 and the 2002 production of All or Nothing.

SIMON HOGUE – Script and Story for Quadrophenia 2.

BARRIE HOLLAND – American Tobacco Buyer at Jimmy's work.
Barrie Holland is a veteran of more than 200 films and countless TV roles on both sides of the Atlantic. Barrie has shared scenes with the likes of Robert DeNiro and Harrison Ford appearing in such films as Return of the Jedi and Indiana Jones. Following pictures show Holland in Quadrophenia (in middle) and a recent publicity shot.

SIMON HOLLAND – *Production Designer.*
Television work has included The Magical Legend of the Leprechauns in 1999, a project that was also worked on by Roger Daltrey. Film work has included The Emerald Forest 1985, Scandal 1989 and Nuns on the Run in 1990.

GARY HOLTON – *Aggressive Rocker (Wesley'Wez'Brooks).*
Born: 22nd September 1952,   Died: 25th October 1985.

Holton was only used for one days filming when he and Jesse Birdsall are seen attacking Gary Shail. The two Gary's were to become good pals as they talked about music in the Bramley Arms pub whilst awaiting their call. Holton is perhaps best known for his role of Cockney carpenter, Wayne Norris in Auf Wiedersehen Pet, in which he delivered a superb performance in what has become a classic series. Holton had previously been part of the Old Vic Theatre Company before joining the Royal Shakespeare Company. His first love seemed to be that of music and was a member of the glam rock outfit, Heavy Metal Kids who were to enjoy a fair amount of success, mostly abroad.

Holton had many other minor television roles, as well as a series of well-known adverts for Tennants Pilsner Lager. However, he struggled for many years with a drink and drug addiction which was to eventually cost him his life!

During a break in filming for the second series of Auf Wiedersehen Pet he was to take a fatal mixture of Alcohol and Morphine and was found dead at a friend's flat in Wembley, Middlesex, in a now demolished estate very near to the famous stadium. It subsequently transpired that Holton had recently been offered, but turned down the role of Nick Cotton in EastEnders, A role which of course went to his co-star, John Altman.

Holton had struggled with his addiction as well as acute financial problems and sadly at just thirty-three years of age his life was over. Holton was cremated in Golders Green almost a month after his death, with the service being attended by all of his co-stars from Auf Wiedersehen Pet. Later Gary's ashes were laid to rest alongside his Grandparents in Wales. A much-missed star who surely had so much more to offer!

MISCLEANOUS INFORMATION

Books: Fast Living: Remembering the Real Gary Holton – Biography by Teddie Dahlin – New Haven Publishing 2013.

JOHN LEE HOOKER – Musical Connection.
The legendary blues singer was the original artist to record Dimples in 1956, which he also wrote. The number was, of course, covered by Cross Section in the early part of the film. Hooker died in 2001 at the age of 83 and had a phenomenal career recording over one hundred albums. He is cited by countless artists including Pete Townshend and Eric Clapton as a major influence.

GRAHAM HUGHES – Photographer 1973 Album.
Hughes was responsible for the superb iconic photograph on the front cover of the 1973 album, which cleverly features the four members of The Who in the reflection of the scooters wing mirrors. He is the cousin of Roger Daltrey, and the decision to use his photograph on the cover is known to have upset Ethan A. Russell.

RON HUISON – Special Effects 1973 Album.
Huison worked on the special effects used on the original album and went on to work as a musical producer. Huison has worked with the likes of

Echo and the Bunnymen, Judge Dread and Cliff Richard, and now lives in Florida.

DAVE HUMPHRIES – *Screenplay.*
Further script work has included The Haunting of Julia 1976, Full Circle 1977, and The Stud in 1978. Humphries has subsequently moved into the sound department working on amongst others, A Casual Affair 1994, and Beautiful People in 1999. TV work has included Target, Shoestring, Dempsey and Makepeace, The Professionals and Minder. Dave Humphries was sacked by Franc Roddam as he was unhappy with the draft script, however due to contractual obligations he retained his credit on the finished film.

DEWI HUMPHRIES – *Camera Operator.*
Humphries' is now a successful TV Director working on projects such as Harry Enfield and Chums and The Vicar of Dibley. Previous film work includes the 1978 production, The Boys from Brazil which starred Gregory Peck and Sir Laurence Olivier.

I

BILLY IDOL – *Ace Face in Quadrophenia American Tour/Classic Quadrophenia.*
Idol took the part of the Ace Face when Quadrophenia toured America, and reprised this role in the Classic Quadrophenia version in 2015. A former member of Generation X, before going on to have a very successful solo career. Songs that done very well for Idol included Rebel Yell, and White Wedding, he still tours and is now based in America. In 2015 Billy Idol once again revisited Quadrophenia when he contributed vocals on five tracks on Pete Townshend's Classic Quadrophenia, also doing likewise at the World Premiere at the Royal Albert Hall in July of that year.

MISCLEANOUS INFORMATION

Books: - Dancing with Myself– Autobiography – Simon and Schuster 2015.

CATHY INGRAM (Rocker girl in Brighton).
Cathy is the sister of Tom Ingram and was used as an extra in scenes at Brighton and can also be seen in the courtroom scene.

TOM INGRAM (Rocker in Police Van in Brighton).
Ingram has gone on to work in TV, Stage and Cinema, with his last role of note playing the part of a London Gangster in the 2006 production of Him and Us. Ingram is the easily recognisable Rocker in the police van who has a bit of a push and shove with Jimmy, and then has his fingers shut in Ace Face's cigarette case, cutting his fingers in the process!

Ingram is also part of the main posse of Rockers with John Blundell who ride Chalky off the road on the way to Brighton. The scene which was filmed in Denham, Bucks, meant that he and a few pals had to ride up to the location from his home in Beckenham, Kent.

Ingram is more than willing to relive his memories of the film which he is asked to do on a regular basis, even where he now lives in Long Beach, California. He is still acting and producing, and runs Vegas Weekenders and has an ever-growing property portfolio. For more details of Tom's weekends check out www.vivalasvegas.net.

GEORGE INNES – Alfredo's Café Owner.
Born: 8th March 1938

George Innes is one of those unmistakable British actors who crops up extremely frequently on both the small and large screen. A busy stage career has also seen appearances in both the West End and Broadway.

London born Innes' notable film credits include, Billy Liar, The Italian Job, A Bridge Too Far and Stardust. A very full television career both sides of the Atlantic have seen appearances in things such as M*A*S*H and The Sweeney. A small, but notable, part in Quadrophenia saw Innes deliver an extremely memorable cameo.

JOHN IRELAND – Sound Engineer.
Working extensively within the British film industry, Ireland's film work includes the following, Where's Jack 1969, Hitler: The Last Ten Days 1973, The Medusa Touch 1978, Lost and Found 1979. Working with Roger Daltrey on McVicar 1980 and Buddy's Song 1990 followed by

Blame it on the Bellboy 1992, G.I. Jane and Tomorrow Never Dies both 1997. Recent work has included, The World is Not Enough 1999, Enigma and To End All Wars both 2001.

MAXINE ISENMAN – (Mod girl in 1973 album booklet).
Maxine was a friend of Julie Emson who lived near the Ramport Studios in Battersea and was used a Mod girl in the album booklet. Maxine is viewed leaning against a wall next to Julie as Jimmy looks on astride his scooter.

J

TAMMY JACOBS (Spiders Girlfriend).
Tammy Jacobs had a small, but memorable part in the film as Spiders girlfriend. Tammy was also the real-life girlfriend of Gary Shail, who had turned up with him for his audition, Franc Roddam looked at her and said 'bring her along' and so she was duly written into the film. During filming, she split up with Shail and went off with Jesse Birdsall, whose character had beaten him up in the film. Jacobs went on to work on Bloody Kids in 1979 alongside Birdsall, in a film probably best remembered as the one that Richard Beckinsale was filming at the time of his death. Jacobs had a part as a policewoman, and liked it so much she went on to be one in real-life!

THE JAM – Musical Connection.
The seminal Mod group with Punk attitude coincidentally enjoyed much of their early success when Quadrophenia was released. Modfather, Paul Weller has gone on record as saying he is not the films biggest fan; however, one of the extras was definitely a fan of his as he can be seen sporting one of their patches on his Parka. The Jam were formed in 1974, ten years after the events in the film took place!

TONY JAMES – Potential Actor.
Tony James was at the time a band mate of Billy Idol in Generation X, and was considered for a role within the film. A few years older than the core cast it may have been the role of Peter Fenton that he was being linked with. Following the end of Generation X, James went on to play with Sigue Sigue Sputnik, and is now both a Producer and Musician.

LAVERNE JANES (Mod girl at Brighton).
Laverne was a member of the Modrapheniacs scooter club who was involved in many of the Brighton scenes.

RICHARD JOBSON – Potential Director of Quadrophenia 2.
Richard Jobson made his name as the front man for the seventies Punk outfit, The Skids, who enjoyed chart success with the likes of Into the Valley in 1979. Jobson went onto have a career in TV presenting before moving into film-making predominately in Scotland. In 2012 when an official sequel was being mooted his name was linked with the role of Director.

GLYN JOHNS – Associate Producer, Love Reign O'er Me and Is it in my Head.
Johns has worked on various projects with The Who, including Amazing Journey – The Story of The Who, also worked on the Rolling Stones Rock and Roll Circus in 1966.

LlOYD JOHNSON – Clothing Supplier.
Lloyd Johnson was the proprietor of Johnson's Modern Outfitters who were based in the Kings Road during the 70's 80's and 90's, and his company were responsible for supplying many of the shirts and suits used.

MICHAEL JORDAN – Sound Recording (Dolby Digital 5.1 and DVD).
Jordan has worked on dozens of films which list the following, East Side Story 1988, Small Kill 1992, Full Cycle 1994, Captain Jack 1995, The Mouse 1997, and the 2002 production of Anne B. Real.

_K_

DAVID KAY – (Mod extra at Brighton).
David Kay was a member of the Barnsley scooter club who was used for many of the Brighton scenes.

BARRY KEEFE – Potential Screenwriter.

Allegedly, Barry Keefe was sounded out to write the screenplay for the film but was busy on other projects, more than likely to be Hanging Around which went on to feature both Phil Daniels and Michael Elphick. Keefe actually began as a Journalist before changing his writing skills, which saw him go on to write (amongst other things) the superb, Long Good Friday in 1981.

TERRY 'CHAD' KENNETT – *Jimmy in 1973 Album booklet.*
Kennett is the original Jimmy as pictured in the iconic booklet that accompanies the 1973 album. Kennett was enjoying a pint in The Butchers Arms near the recording studios in Battersea when he was spotted by Pete Townshend. During the photo shoot, he had to attend Court after 'borrowing' a bus, however Ethan Russell pleaded with the Magistrate to let him go as he was needed for remainder of the project, and obviously done a good job as he was allowed to leave with no charge! Kennett was 23 at the time, and a paint sprayer. He sadly passed away in 2011 aged 61.

ERIC KENT - *Dave's boss at work.*
Eric Kent was a mainstay of many London based dramas from the seventies, including roles in Dempsey and Makepeace and, The Sweeney. Kent also had a small role in The Sweeney2 film, continuing to work up until 1990 when he appeared in Comic Strip Presents. A well-known face if not name from his many roles, he sadly died in December 2012.

LYDON KIRBY - *Advisor for 1973 Album booklet.*
Kirby was a Mod who was well known to The Who and was used as an advisor to Ethan A. Russell when he shot the photographs for the 1973 album.

THE KINGSMEN – *Musical Contribution.*
The Kingsmen were formed in Portland, USA, in 1960, releasing their big hit, Louie-Louie in 1963 which was actually a cover of a song by Richard Berry some eight years previous. The band were dogged by internal turmoil following their early success, which resulted in various changes in personnel, notably with Joe Easton the lead singer being replaced by the drummer Lynn Easton.

Further hits included Money, and Jolly Green Giant, before they called it a day in 1969. The band has reformed on various occasions since then. Their coupe de grace – Louie-Louie will not go away and has become somewhat a darling of the advertising men, appearing alongside such products as California Wine and the Quadrophenia inspired advert for the energy drink, Lucozade.

THE KINKS – Musical Contribution.

The seminal Mod group who were great rivals of The Who scored a number of hits in the sixties including, You Really Got Me, which is sung during the film by Jimmy. The song was, of course sung on two occasions by Jimmy during the film whilst at work and at the public baths. The Kinks were predominantly Dave and Sir Ray Davies, and scored countless hits such as the classic, Waterloo Sunset.

L

TREVOR H. LAIRD – Ferdy.

Trevor Laird was born in the Angel Islington, on 30th August, 1957, and left school at sixteen to take up an apprenticeship in electronics. Laird had been attending the Anna Scher Theatre workshops where he was advised to follow his dream and move into acting as a profession. It was at Anna Scher's where Laird first met Phil Daniels.

The two started a band together, Renoir, and were even given tips on playing their instruments by the Kemp brothers who went on to form Spandau Ballet, and lived nearby.

Laird had appeared in a couple of minor TV roles, but Quadrophenia was to be his first film. Franc Roddam and Pete Townshend had watched him doing some improvisation work with Phil Daniels at his audition, and Laird had reminded Townshend of a guy he used to buy pills from in the sixties. So, they offered Laird a part in the film and wrote in the part of Ferdy.

Laird delivers a cool performance who seems to retain an air of aloofness from the rest of the group. Impeccably dressed throughout, he does not have a great deal of actual dialogue in the film, but the impression that he makes speaks volumes of his acting skills. Indeed, his little shrug of the shoulders after the fighting in East Street is a small but golden moment! Laird was the only one aware that the cameras were still rolling, so decided to 'throw one in', indeed this moment is often mentioned, and is a particular favourite part of the film for Franc Roddam.

Following on from Quadrophenia, Laird soon went on to work on two critically acclaimed films, Babylon as well as a small part in The Long Good Friday in which he is nearly killed by fellow Quadrophenia actor, P.H. Moriarty. He also had a very brief time in between jobs as a porter at Smithfield Meat Market.

Laird has continued to flit between the small and large screen in various roles, and has worked extensively in the Theatre. As a member of the National Theatre, Laird has worked on the likes of; Twilight Zone, Moon on a Rainbow Shawl, Foxes, Sunsets and Glories, An Enchanted Land, Strange Fruit, A Midsummer Night's Dream, Twelfth Night, Mama Dragon and Othello. As well as being a Director of the Black Theatre Company in Liverpool.

Laird is a big fan of music, especially classical jazz and the likes of Miles Davis; he is happily married with young children and still best mates with Phil Daniels. Indeed, the pair are still regular spectators at Stamford Bridge to watch their beloved Chelsea F.C.

Trevor Laird turning up with Phil Daniels for his audition that day must have been fate, as you simply can't imagine Quadrophenia without the fine performance that is delivered!

ALAN LAKE – Voice Over Artist.
Born 24th October 1940 – Died 10th October 1984.

Alan Lake was the original choice for the official UK trailer of the film, but was replaced as it was felt his voice wasn't right for it. Lake was married to Diana Dors until her death, and had many minor roles in TV shows in the seventies such as Dr Who and The Sweeney. When Diana Dors died, Lake found it hard to deal with the grief and sadly took his own life just five months later.

KIT LAMBERT – Pre-Production and Executive Producer of 1973 Album.

Kit (real name Chris) Lambert was a young film-maker who had met Chris Stamp whilst working for the BBC. Lambert was looking for a band to promote, and to make a short film about, and ended up one day at The Railway Pub in Wealdstone where The Who were playing. The rest, as they say, is history! Lambert was to be a major influence on Pete Townshend, and encouraged him to write his own material and to be more experimental. Lambert went onto produce a lot of the band's music in the sixties, with the help of his young protégé, Townshend! Lambert and Stamp also set up Track Records a label which went onto showcase some of the bands finest work. Lambert is actually credited in a production role on the 1973 album, but it is unclear how much actual impact he had on it, as he was heavily into drink and drugs at the time. Although it was the idea of his Father, Constant (a founder of The Saddlers Wells Theatre) who first sewed the idea of a rock opera in Townshend's head 'don't let the bloody upper-class have all the operas' he was reputed as saying.

By the end of 1973 Lambert was to have little to do with The Who, he was no longer their manager and, was too unreliable to use as a Producer. Lambert died at the age of 46 in a bizarre accident which saw him fall down the stairs in his mother's house.

MISCLEANOUS INFORMATION

DVD: - Lambert & Stamp – Documentary – 2105.

ALEX LANGDON – Jimmy 1996/7 Quadrophenia Tour.
Alex Langdon was the young actor who was used to narrate and play the part of Jimmy in the backscreen film that accompanied the Hyde Park performance of Quadrophenia, and the subsequent tour. Langdon went on to a few minor TV roles, but looks to have disappeared from acting now.

CY LANGTON – Remixing Engineer.
A former roadie with The Who, Langton also worked on The Kids Are Alright 1978 and McVicar 1980. Musical work has also included the Roger Daltrey solo project Martyrs and Madmen in 1997 having worked the previous year on the John Entwistle Anthology album.

KEVIN LAWN (Mod extra at Brighton).
A scooter club member (possibly Barnsley) Kevin was a scooter riding extra in Brighton and is featured in the picture below Martyn Scully later on in this chapter.

KEVIN LAWTON aka GINGER (Mod and Rocker extra at Brighton).
Ginger was a member of Preston scooter club that landed a role of an extra at Brighton. He is most prevalent in the scene when Jimmy and The Ace Face are shoved into a police van, and he is seen dressed as a Rocker. The filmmakers were short of a Rocker for this scene so made him dress as one much to his obvious disdain which is clearly visible in the film. Ginger is still a well-known face on the Scooter scene, organising his own annual charity ride-out! The following picture shows Ginger next to Sting on right, with Steve Orridge on left, and Robin 'Yob' Williams to his left.

LEE LIGHTING LTD (UK) – Lighting Services.
Lee Lighting have worked on countless films which include, Alien 1979, Absolute Beginners 1986, 101 Dalmatians 1996, Angela's Ashes 1999, Billy Elliott 2000, Bridget Jones Diary 2001, as well as About a Boy and Bend it Like Beckham both 2002. The TV work is also extensive and numbers amongst it the following, The Bill, Red Dwarf, The League of Gentleman, Brookside and Casualty.

LEVIS JEANS –Clothing Supplier.
The world-famous Levi Jeans Company get a special mention in the credits as they also do in the 2000 production Nurse Betty, which starred Morgan Freeman and Renee Zellweger.

LUCITA LIJERTWOOD (Ferdy's Mum).

'Him not in, him gone out', a brief but unforgettable line delivered by an actress who crops up in various film and TV roles. Lijertwood was born in Trinidad in 1920, and died at the age of 72 in London. Although she never shared a scene with her screen son, Trevor Laird, they went on to work together a few times in the future. Lijertwood was apparently very protective of Laird and even used to bring him food so he didn't have to suffer the mobile catering! Trevor remembers her as a 'lovely woman' who appeared in various TV shows such as Only Fools and Horses and The Bill. Lijertwood also appeared in a few films such as Pink Floyd The Wall in 1982. An actress who delivered a small but memorable scene!

LINDA? (girl with Ferdy at party).
Linda was an actress known to both Trevor Laird and Phil Daniels, possibly from the same drama school. Linda is seen briefly with Ferdy and was originally meant to be seen pairing off with him until it was decided to drop that part of the scene.

HUGH LLOYD – Mr Cale.
Born: 22nd APRIL 1923   Died: 14th July 2008.

Hugh Lloyd is an extremely well-known figure in every field of British entertainment, particularly in that of comedy.

Born in Chester, and an ardent fan of his home town football club he left school and spent two years as a reporter with the Chester Chronicle, but it was acting and entertainment that was his first love.

During the Second World War, he joined ENSA, before going on to work in repertory theatre until 1957.

Following on from this he joined the cast of Hancock's Half Hour, which saw his career really take-off, and also saw him become a constant presence on both stage and screen, appearing in a string of hits on both mediums.

Lloyd also appeared in many serious roles including work with the Royal National Theatre, he lived in Worthing and although his work in Quadrophenia was filmed in London, he was known to have visited the set when they were in Brighton.

In the 2005 new-years honours list he was awarded an MBE for his services to drama and charity, and continued to work, albeit on an infrequent basis write up to his death at his home in Worthing in 2008.

PHILIP LOCKE – TV SHOW APPEARANCE.
Born; 29th March 1928. Died; 19th April 2004.

Philip Locke plays the part of Moxon in an episode of The Avengers called, The Frighteners, which is watched by Jimmy's parents in the film. Locke's other work includes appearances on TV in Dr. Who, and The Champions.

JAMES LOMBARD aka 'FUZZ' (Nicky the Mod).
James Lombard also had a small role in Scum as Jameson, and has acted infrequently ever since. However, it is as 'Fuzz' that he is better known in the music industry, where he has been a vocalist and musician with the likes of Inferno, as well as enjoying a solo career which earned him an OBE. Lombard's last big acting job was in 2006 film, The History Boys.

LONDON ORIANA CHOIR – Choir for Pete Townshend's Classic Quadrophenia.
The London Oriana Choir is an amateur choral group with over 100 singers and based in London. First formed in 1973 by Leon Lovett, who was their first conductor and musical director, the choir has gone on to tour all over Europe.

JOHN LOVING (Mod extra at Brighton).
Loving was a member of the Modrapheniacs scooter club who was recruited as an extra when he attended a scooter rally in Southend.

BOB LUDWIG – Re-mastering of original album.
Ludwig was responsible for re-mastering the re-released album, and has worked regularly with the likes of Eric Clapton, Bruce Springsteen and Neil Young.

JOHN LYDON – Screen-tested for the role of Jimmy.
Born 31st January 1956.

Lydon was at the time still known as Johnny Rotten, and was screen-tested for the lead role. Franc Roddam had asked Toyah to coach him for the role, and he was said to have delivered a superb audition, her honest opinion was that he was 'fucking brilliant'. However, the idea was dropped when the films insurers got cold feet, Roddam has gone on record as saying that he could have easily played the role, and is sad that no footage of the screen-test survived! Rotten was the front man of The Sex Pistols from 1975-78 before embarking on a distinguished career with Pubic Image Limited. Lydon has also gone on to make many diverse TV appearances including the infamous Country Life Butter Advertisements.

DEREK LYONS (uncredited Mod).
Lyons had a small uncredited role in the original Star Wars movie in 1977, and went on to work on Gandhi in 1982. Recent work has included the ITV series, Secret Diary of a Call Girl.

'IRISH' JACK LYONS – Story Consultant.
Irish Jack is something of a legend amongst fans of The Who. Jack who originally hailed from Cork in Southern Ireland was living in West London in the sixties, and a massive follower of the band. He became friends with Pete Townshend and the rest of the band and who officially nicknamed 'Irish Jack'. It is thought that Jack was a major inspiration for Jimmy Cooper, and even had a song Happy Jack recorded in his honour!

Jack was employed for a short while advising on the film, and writing scenarios for possible inclusion in the script. Jack now lives back in his native Ireland and infrequently reads from his 'Mod memoirs' at select gatherings. Jack has also contributed to various books about his beloved group, members of which he is proud to call his friends.

M

DOUGIE MACDONALD (Mod extra at Brighton).
Macdonald was an extra who lived in Brighton, and almost certainly saw the vacancy at the local job centre for extras in the film. Macdonald was paid £15 per day for filming, but also received compensation of a further

£14 after being bitten by an Alsatian dog in the scene where Sting pulls a policeman from his horse.

ANDY MACPHERSON – Mixer for Re-issued Album.

FRANK MAIDMENT (Mod at Brighton).
Frank Maidment was a member of Modrapheniacs Scooter Club who acted as an extra in Brighton.

MANFRED MANN – Musical Contribution.
Manfred Mann was born in 1940 in the South African town of Johannesburg where he harboured dreams to move to England and play Jazz, and at the age of 21 that is exactly what he did. Mann supplemented his earnings by doing musical reviews for the press, but it was in 1962 that a meeting in Butlin's, Clacton (of all places!) was to change his life, for this is where he met Mike Hugg.

Mann and Hugg very quickly formed The Mann-Hugg Blues Brothers, and were subsequently joined by Paul Jones as they moved into a more R&B direction. Late in 1962 they were spotted by Kenneth Pitt who directed them towards the Producer, John Burgess, the later persuading them to change their name to Manfred Mann. Their first single was an instrumental offering entitled, Why Should We Not, although it didn't do well it created interest in the group and the follow up of, Cock-A-Hoop fared much better. This led to them being invited to record a theme tune for the new Mod inspired music show, Ready Steady Go, that song being 5-4-3-2-1.

From then on, they went onto enjoy constant success with such hits as Do Wah Diddy-Diddy. In 1967 Mann and Hugg moved into commercials before forming Emanon, then Manfred Mann Chapter Three, which was to evolve in Manfred Mann's Earth Band in 1971. They continued to enjoy success with hits such as Blinded by the Light in 1976, and still perform well over forty years from their first hit.

ANGELA MARSHALL (voice-over for riot at Brighton Beach).
Marshall was amongst a group of people who supplied voice over material for the riot on the beach. Marshall is now the librarian of Cine-Sound who supply sound effects to various films, adverts and television programmes.

PETE McCARTHY (rioting Mod on Brighton Beach).
This well-known travel writer and presenter has a small part as an extra in the Beach scenes, instantly recognisable in a blue suit with orange tie, he goads the police during the ensuing melee. McCarthy has presented travel programmes on both television and radio, and was author of the million selling book, McCarthy's Bar. He died at the tragically young age of 51 in October 2004 of cancer. A much-missed author who also had a spell as a stand-up comedian and went on to write for the likes of Mel Smith and Griff Rhys Jones.

SIR TREVOR McDONALD – 1996 Hyde Park Show.
The legendary ITN newscaster was somewhat typecast in his cameo role as a newsreader during the 1996 show at Hyde Park. Sir Trevor has won more awards than any other newsreader in the history of British Television.

MIKE McGARRY – (Mod extra at Brighton).
Mike McGarry was a member of the Modern Coasters Scooter Club and was enticed at the Southend Scooter Rally to join the production in Brighton for a week. Mike appears in various bits of the action in Brighton, and was part of the Ace Face's posse when they are viewed on their scooters after the scenes in the Night Club. The following picture shows Mike showing off an injury sustained during filming!

<u>ANDY McKAIE</u> – *Special Thanks – 1973 Album.*

<u>GEORGE McMANUS</u> – *Special Thanks – 1973 Album.*

<u>JOE McMICHAEL</u> – *Special Thanks – 1973 Album.*

<u>PETER McNAMARA</u> *(Mod at house party).*
McNamara is viewed very briefly at the house party when the revellers are doing their stuff to My Generation, and is seen in an annoyed state after somebody ruffles his tie. McNamara is one of those instantly recognisable faces that constantly crops up in many TV roles in which he tends to play somebody with an aggressive misdemeanour. McNamara's countless TV roles include, Grange Hill, Holby City and The Bill.

<u>THE MERSEYBEATS</u> – **Musical Contribution.**
The Merseybeats started life in 1961 as The Mavericks, but changed their name a year later. They first enjoyed commercial success in 1963 with, It's Love That Really Counts. The following year their success was further cemented with amongst other, Don't Turn Around, I Stand Accused and Wishin' and Hopin'.

Veterans of the famous Cavern Club where they appeared countless times alongside The Beatles, it was in 1966 that (under the name of The Mersey's) they recorded the classic Sorrow which was amply covered by David Bowie.

Although the band have gone through countless line-up changes over the years they are still actively touring today with founder member Tony Crane very much still at the helm.

<u>MICK?</u> *(Mod extra at Brighton).*
Mick was the No.1 from the Barnsley Vikings Scooter Club who had answered the advert for the lead role, but ended up as an extra.

<u>MIDGE</u> *(Mod extra at Brighton).*

Midge was a member of the Barnsley Vikings Scooter Club who earned himself an uncredited role as an extra in the film.

RANDY MILLER – Special Thanks – 1973 Album.
Miller has worked on various musical projects including The Flintstones film.

GARETH MILNE (Stuntman).
Gareth Milne is viewed as a Rocker on the bike next to John Blundell, as well as a stuntman. He was seriously injured during this section of filming in Denham, Bucks. Local Gypsies had dumped a burnt-out car that Milne crashed in to, and was forced to miss a few days filming after having several stitches following a severed artery in his thigh. Milne has gone on to appear in hundreds of other productions ranging from Dr Who, and The Bill on TV, and India Jones and the Temple of Doom, and The Bourne Ultimatum on the large screen. Indeed, for the later he was part of a stunt ensemble that won an Outstanding Performance award from the Screen Actors Guild in 2007.

DERRICK MORGAN – Musical Contribution.
A major star of the ska music scene who hails from Jamaica, Morgan began having hits as early as 1960. Inevitably he was to become one of the flagship artists of Trojan Records, and went on to inspire a legion of fans that still ensures he is a much sought after entertainer.

P.H. MORIARTY – Barman.
P.H. (Paul) Moriarty was born in London and did not begin his acting career until he was in his late thirties, soon becoming an instantly recognisable face that crops up time and time again in British productions. He was working on the Docks (after various other careers including that of a boxer) when he was discovered by a film crew and offered a part, he was never to look back and went onto appear in amongst other films, Scum, The Long Good Friday and Lock Stock and Two Smoking Barrels, as well as countless TV appearances. Somewhat typecast in the role of a 'heavy' he now lives in Sussex and told the author that he was extremely proud to have appeared in such a film as Quadrophenia, and is still making regular film and TV appearances.

ALAN MORRIS aka DJ KING JERRY – Advisor.

Alan Morris was a DJ in the very early days of Mod in the Brighton area. He played alongside some of the biggest names at the time including The High Numbers later known as The Who. In 1964 he was known as the figurehead of the Mod movement locally and was called 'the King of the Mods', which led to him being used as the inspiration for the Ace Face in Brighton. Morris has been a DJ since he was sixteen and is still going strong as he nears retirement age. In fact, he is the co-founder of soul survivors a regular disco in the area playing Mod and Soul music. Morris still lives in the area and just prior to Christmas 2007 was mistakenly believed to be dead, in fact a number of his fans turned up to pay their respects at what they believed to be his funeral. Thankfully DJ King Jerry is still very much spinning his wheels of steel in this life!

REDMOND MORRIS – Location Manager.

Morris went on to work on, Yanks 1979 and the 1981 James Bond offering, For Your Eyes Only which starred Roger Moore. Later work included Reds in 1981 and Privates on Parade in 1982 and the 1983 Dennis Potter screenplay, Gorky Park. In 1992 he worked as the First Assistant Director on The Crying Game, and as co-producer on Interview with a Vampire in 1994. Morris has since moved on to the role of co-producer on various projects in conjunction with Neil Jordan the Irish writer and Director.

RICHARD MORRISON – Title Designer.

Morrison was responsible for the 'sickly yellow' titles (as Franc Roddam described them) at the films start. Morrison went on to work with Roddam again on K2 in 1991, with recent work including, The Golden Compass in 2007 and Vantage Point in 2008.

MOTORHEAD – Musical Connection.

Although the band was not formed until 1975 a Rocker is seen in the film with one of their T-Shirts! The Heavy Rock group were fronted by the infamous Ian 'Lemmy' Kimister who sadly died of Cancer on 28th December 2015.

JOHNNY MOYCE – Driver and Stand-in for Phil Daniels.

Moyce was a friend of Phil Daniels who acted as his driver, and also stood in for him whilst lighting was being set up, it was a role he was to continue during the 1980 film, Breaking Glass.

JIMMY MUIR (associate of Harry North).
Muir was one of the heavies that were in Harry North's company at the Boxing Gym at the back of the Pub. Muir went on to have a few minor roles on TV, including an appearance in Russ Abbott's Madhouse in the eighties.

GEOFF MULLIGAN – Camera Operator (2nd Unit).
Although sometimes uncredited Mulligan has an impressive list of productions to his name which include, Superman and International Velvet both 1978, The First Great Train Robbery 1979, Octupussy 1983, King Ralph 1991 and Blame it on the Bellboy 1992.

ANGIE MULVEY – (Mod girl at Brighton).
Angie was a member of the Modrapheniacs Scooter Club and joined the action in Brighton for a week. Angie was one of several females who were required to wear a period style wig! The following picture shows a recent photo of Angie still very much wearing a Parka!

GLEN MURPHY (Rocker in Brighton).
Glen Murphy, perhaps best known as George Green in London's |Burning had a small role as a Rocker in the Brighton scenes.

NICOLE MURPHY (Mod girl at Brighton).

Brighton born Nicole Murphy (her married name) was sixteen at the time of the filming when she landed the part of an extra during the scenes in her home town. Murphy is a nurse at nearby Worthing Hospital, and lives in Hove with her husband and five children. In 2007 Murphy made an unsuccessful attempt to succeed the current Labour MP for the Brighton Pavilion ward.

PATRICK MURRAY – Des.

A small cameo from an actor who went on to be known universally as the hapless, Mickey Pearce, in Only Fools and Horses. Murray played the role of Mickey Pearce for over twenty years after being spotted in a Pizza Hut advert by Producer, Ray Butt. Murray had previously appeared in both versions of Scum with Phil Daniels, as well as The Class of Miss MacMichael. Other early work includes the film, Last Summer, alongside Ray Winstone.

Murray's father was an Irish immigrant, with his mother coming from Spain. Born in Greenwich he still lives in the area, and used to run a local pub, and supports the local team, Millwall F.C.

N

KIM NEVE – Yvonne Cooper.

Somewhat of a mystery woman, little is known of the actress that played the part of Yvonne Cooper, and Quadrophenia appears to be the end of her brief acting career! In the DVD commentary Franc Roddam is highly complementary of her brief role, and it is likely that it was originally planned for her to have a larger part in the film, indeed her character features more prominently in Alan Fletcher's novel.

Prior to Quadrophenia, Kim Neve had a small part in, Born and Bred a television series in 1978, and appeared in a couple of early episodes of Grange Hill playing the part of Lucy.

RON NEVISON - Engineer and Special Effects (1973 album).

Engineering and special effects work on the 1973 album was followed by work on Tommy in 1975, and more recently appeared in a 2004 TV show about Eric Clapton.

BERTIE NICHOLAS – Coordinator of Promotional Material.
Bertie Nicholas was an Advertising Agent who was tasked with coordinating some of the promotional material that accompanied the film.

JOHN NICHOLSON - Supplied Police Vans for the film.
John Nicholson's Car Sales and Hire Company supplied the infamous Black Mariah's used in the Brighton riot scenes.

O

OCEAN COLOUR SCENE – Musical Contribution.
Not strictly a contribution, more of homage to the film. The group who help to keep the Mod-scene alive include the following line 'write another song that Jimmy heard the day he caught the train' in their classic song The Day we Caught the Train. The group have also acknowledged the part of another Jimmy, Jimmy Miller who they worked with on their preceding album.

JOHN HENRY ODDY (Mod extra at Brighton).
John Henry was a member of the Barnsley Scooter Club who was involved in the scenes in Brighton.

KEVIN O'DRISCOLL - Production Manager and Accountant.
O'Driscoll was chiefly responsible for the production accounts and has enjoyed similar roles on the following; Return of the Pink Panther 1975, The Pink Panther Strikes Again 1976, Noble House (TV mini-series) 1988, Small Faces 1996, Her Own Rules (TV film) 1998 and also the 2000 TV mini-series, In the Beginning.

STEVE ORRIDGE – (Mod extra at Brighton).

Steve Orridge was a member of Barnsley scooter club who earned a role as an extra in Brighton, and is seen in Ace Face's posse. Steve is pictured (see Kevin 'Ginger' Lawton) with Sting.

THE ORLONS – Musical Contribution.
This group which hailed from Philadelphia were at the very forefront of fun-filled dance numbers, originally formed at the start of the fifties, they were originally known as Audrey and the Teenettes.

The group were formed at junior school and comprised of Audrey, Jean and Shirley Brickley, Rosetta Hightower and Marlene Davis. However, as Audrey was just thirteen her mother refused to let her sing in clubs, which meant that her and her sister, Jean left the group.

The remnants of the group were very soon joined by Stephen Caldwell, following various other changes in the line-up they achieved a couple of minor hits in 1962. The same year saw them act as back-up singers on Dee-Dee Sharp's, Mashed Potato which went on to reach number two, and was followed by the group's big break-through on their own, The Wah Watusi. The song went on to reach number two in the USA charts and was followed up with, Don't Hang Up, this preceded a down period in the bands history, and various personal changes ensued before Audrey Brickley re-joined them. In 1977 tragedy struck when Shirley Brickley was killed in her own home by a burglar, but the band continued, and enjoyed success right up to the eighties, and can still occasionally be seen on tour, albeit with a very different line-up!

OVERBOX – Musical Contribution.
Overbox are a six piece Milan based rock-combo who are heavily influenced by The Who in the seventies. They are as yet unsigned, and show-case their music via the internet on sites such as Myspace. In 2006 they produced an album, Who's Jimmy, which included many of the songs from Quadrophenia, and are linked together with a narrative. An interesting take on the project, for more details view their website on www.serialsinger.net.

P

CHARLIE PARKER – *Musical Inspiration.*
Born: 29th August 1920 – Died: 12th March 1955

The legendary Jazz saxophonist who died at just 34 years of age in 1955 was well known for fusing Jazz music with other genres such as The Blues. His personal life followed a troubled path with a well-known Drug and, Alcohol problem contributing to his early demise! Townshend has said he drew inspiration from him when writing Anyway, Anyhow, Anywhere, which is glimpsed when Jimmy watches Ready Steady Go on his TV.

CHRIS PARSONS – *Bouncer at Nightclub.*
Parsons still a teenager at the time of filming was glimpsed in the Brighton Nightclub scenes, and has gone on to work on things such as Breaking Glass in 1980 and Raiders of the Lost Ark the following year.

GUIDO PASTORELLI *(Mod extra at Brighton).*
Guido is the younger brother of Guilio and was 16 at the time of filming being paid £15 per day. Guido was used as a passenger on the scooter scenes.

GUILIO PASTORELLI *(Mod extra at Brighton).*
Guilio is one of the proprietors of the legendary Armando's Scooter shop in Sheffield, which was started by his father in the sixties. Guilio was paid £25 per day, and is viewed as one of Sting's posse.

JEFF PAYNTER – *Camera Focus.*
Paynter has worked on many British films which include, Superman II 1980, An American Werewolf in London 1981 and the 1985 production of Santa Claus which starred Dudley Moore, as well as the 1990 film, Strike it Rich. Paynter also worked on the 1984 TV mini-series, Lace.

DANIEL PEACOCK – *Dan the Mod.*

It is hardly surprising that Peacock ended up in the entertainment industry as he is the son of well-known actor, Trevor Peacock, who is perhaps best known for his role in The Vicar of Dibley.

Peacock was bought up in Barnet, and attended the local Ashmole School before going on to have a busy career as an actor, writer and director. Quadrophenia was his second film, following on from the big screen version of Porridge in the same year.

Peacock continued to work extensively in the comedy field notably in The Comic Strip series for channel four, and in 1983 he wrote and starred in the British film, Party - Party. Peacock has continued to work in all three fields and combines them all where at all possible. Peacock has one of those faces that seem to be forever cropping up on our screen, and was part of a double act that starred in some very successful adverts for the Do It All chain in the eighties.

CHRIS PEARCEY - *(Mod extra at Brighton).*
Chris Pearcey is an extra who was used for scenes on the Beach, and in East Street in Brighton.

TOM PETCH - *(Scooter riding Mod at Brighton).*
Tom Petch was a member of the York Scooter Club, he heard about the film and managed to get himself a part as an extra in the Brighton scenes. Petch also appears in the court room scenes and was paid £75 for his time.

JOHN PEVERALL – *Associate Producer.*
Peverall went on to work as Associate Producer on another Who project that of McVicar, in 1980. Peverall's work has also included Producing and Directing in his own right, but the highlight for him came in 1979, when alongside, Barry Spikings and Michael Deeley he won an Oscar for Special Achievements in Visual Effects for their work on the 1978 production of Superman. A little-known fact is that he is the uncle of well-known TV astrologer, Russell Grant.

JOHN PHILLIPS – *Magistrate*.
Born: 16th July 1914, Died: 11th May 1995

John Phillips delivers a totally believable role as the Magistrate, in which he apes the famous 'Sawdust Caesar' speech that was originally delivered by Dr George Simpson during the original sixties troubles.

A long career on screen and stage Phillips would play a host of authoritarian figures such as Policeman and Army personnel, and even a magistrate in the sixties TV show, Dixon of Dock Green. Phillips has made countless TV appearances in such shows as The Avengers and The Persuaders; he passed away in Oswestry in 1995 aged 81. The following picture shows a production still of John Phillips, and his fellow Magistrates.

KIERON PHIPPS – Second Assistant Director.
Phipps many projects have included, Midnight Express and Superman both 1978, Hopscotch 1980, Pink Floyd: The Wall 1982, Monty Python's The Meaning of Life 1983, Greystoke: The Legend of Tarzan 1984 Return to Oz and Billy the Kid and the Green Baize Vampire both 1985. Further work lists, Absolute Beginners 1986, Empire of the Sun 1987, Shirley Valentine 1989 and Four Weddings and a Funeral 1994, Braveheart 1995 as well as Martha, Meet Frank, Daniel and Laurence 1998, which starred amongst others, Ray Winstone.

OLIVER PIERRE – Tailor.
Born: 19th October 1953, Died March 2005

Pierre was a French born actor who had a career that flitted between France and the UK. His first role was in a French production of Dracula, before going onto play the part of the Tailor in Quadrophenia in 1978 when he was in fact only twenty-five years of age, although his appearance on screen would suggest somebody of more advanced years!

A small role as a Chef followed in the 1980 production of The Long Good Friday, after which a number of minor roles followed in such TV shows as Lovejoy. Pierre's last recorded role was a Journalist in the 2002 French TV show, Miroir d'Alice Le, however, he sadly passed away at just fifty-two in 2005 back home in France.

PATSY POLLOCK – Casting Director.
Pollock worked on the critically acclaimed 1995 production of Braveheart with Mel Gibson with other work including Restoration 1995, In the Name of the Father 1993 and Last Orders 1997 which starred Ray Winstone. Pollock was also credited as co-producer of the 1986 Alan Clarke film Rita, Sue and Bob Too. Pollock was re-united with Timothy Spall and Phil Daniels in the 2000 production of Chicken Run, the former playing the part of a Rat!

POLYDOR – Film Soundtrack.
Polydor can trace its history back to 1913 when they formed in Germany, now operating as part of the Universal Music Group. The Who, following their departure from Track Records, have released many albums and singles on this label, as have fellow mods, The Jam. The Company was first established in the UK in 1958 as a subsidiary of Deutsche Grammaphon, this company incidentally were responsible for the release of Pete Townshend's Classic Quadrophenia in 2015.

POLYGRAM VIDEO – Video Distributors.
This now disbanded video distribution company was owned by Phillips until 1998, and then the Seagram Corporation for a further year until 1999 when it closed.

POLYTEL (UK) – Production Company.
Worked in conjunction with The Who Films and were also responsible for producing the 1977 TV mini- series for TV, Marie Curie.

CHARLES PREECE – Script and Story for Quadrophenia 2.
Charles Preece worked with Roy Baird and Sam Hogue on the draft script of Wont Get Fooled Again/Quadrophenia 2. Preece has since worked on TV documentaries such as, The Other Loch Ness Monster.

BOB PRIDDEN – Sound Engineering on 1973 album.
A stalwart from The Who camp since 1966, Pridden worked on the original album and has been a sound recording engineer both in the studio and on the road until he retired in 2016. Pridden has also appeared on the bands many DVD's, and is a well-known and popular member of The Who team to its legions of fans.

BARRY PRIOR – 1964 Mod.
Barry Prior was a seventeen-year-old Mod and trainee accountant who fell to his death on 18th May 1964 following the infamous bank-holiday riots in Brighton. He and some pals had camped a few miles up the coast in Saltdean, and sadly fell from the cliff-edge and died, when he is believed to have become disorientated in the early hours of the morning! Pete Townshend has always denied that Quadrophenia was based on him in anyway, but his uncle later went on to work for The Who, so his existence and tragic end would have surely been known to members of The Who. Either way, he retains a kind of cult-status by those who knew of, or have subsequently heard about him. In his book, Mod – A Very British Style (2013) its author Richard Weight muses the following 'Quadrophenia *was a film about mods for the punk generation, based on the true story of Barry Prior, a teenager who committed suicide by riding his Lambretta over the cliff in 1964, after a Mod gathering in Brighton'*. It is perhaps unfair to say that he committed suicide as there is no evidence to support this, and indeed his scooter was still intact on the top of the cliff! More information on this tragic story can be found at the following site, which was created by Simon Wells.

quadropheniaslostmod.blogspot.co.uk

P.J. PROBY – Musical Contribution – Hyde Park and subsequent tour.
Born: 6th November 1938

The noted singer, songwriter and actor took the part of The Godfather during The Who's UK tour of Quadrophenia.

SERGEI PROKOFIEV – Musical Contribution.
The famous Russian born composer who died in 1953 was known to be an influence for some of the arrangements used by Pete Townshend on the original album. Some of his work being sampled on I've Had Enough. Prokofiev died some twenty years before the album was released in 1973.

THE PURPLE HEARTS – Musical Connection.
An Essex based punk band that started life as The Sockets in 1978 but changed direction upon Mod's re-birth later that year. The group were signed by Fiction which was part of the Polydor group, with their final release for them being, Jimmy, which was inspired by Quadrophenia and reached number sixty in the charts. They are also believed to have sent in a demo asking to be considered for the part of the band at The Goldhawk in the film.

The group still perform today, but their last commercial release entitled Friends Again was back in 1986.

JIMMY PURSEY - Screen-tested for the role of Jimmy.
The front man from Sham69 was another who was considered for the lead role. Apparently, in his audition he really went for it, and put so much into his performance that he cried! One can see why he was indeed considered, and it's perhaps a shame that we have never seen him in any acting role at all!

Q

CAROLINE QUENTIN – Musical Connection.
Following the success of Men Behaving Badly, Leslie Ash and Caroline Quentin went on to release a record that was to reach number 25 in the

charts. The song in question was Tell Him, a cover of the sixties tune by The Exciters in 1962.

R

RANK FILM LABORATORIES (Denham) – Technical Services.
Countless films that this company have been involved in include, The Omen 1970, Carry On Matron 1972, The Boys From Brazil 1978, Alien and The Life of Brian both 1979, Who Framed Roger Rabbit 1988 and Braveheart 1995.

RONNIE RAMPTON – Best Boy.
Rampton who acted as the Best Boy (aka Chief Lighting Technician) has also worked (sometimes as Gaffer) on a number of British films, which include the following; To Catch a Spy 1971, The Bitch 1979, Pink Floyd: The Wall 1982, Local Hero 1983, and The Madness of King George 1994. TV work has included The Canterville Ghost.

BOBBY RAMSEY (ringside trainer and Security co-ordinator).
Ramsey made many minor appearances on TV and film normally as a Heavy, including a role alongside Stacey Keach in the 1977 film, The Squeeze. Ramsey was an associate of The Krays in the sixties (namechecked in the 2015 film, Rise of The Krays) and also served as a security co-ordinator on the film. Ramsey passed away at the age of 84 in 2004.

RAY (Colindale)? – Uncredited Rocker.
Ray a member of a North London Motorbike club can be glimpsed a few times during the fight scenes in Brighton.

READY STEADY GO! – Musical Connection.
Ready Steady Go was the staple viewing every Friday evening for any self-respecting Mod, and was first broadcast in December 1966. Initially RSG was broadcast exclusively in the London area, but was soon networked to the whole country. The opening line of 'the weekend starts here!' saw a show presented by Keith Fordyce and Queen of the Mods, Cathy McGowan that headlined acts such as The Who, Georgie Fame, and The Kinks. In the film, Jimmy watches The Who perform Anyway, Anyhow,

Anywhere, which was filmed at Redifusion Studios in Wembley – the very same studios that Quadrophenia used for some interior scenes!

MELINDA REES – *Continuity*.
A much-understated role within Film and Television who are sometimes not even credited for their work at all! Television work has included the ITV wartime drama Danger UXB.

LINDA REGAN (*Rocker girl on road to and in Brighton*).
Linda Regan is the blond girl sitting on the back of John Blundell's bike on the road to Brighton. Linda was initially supposed to have a fight with Leslie Ash; however, this idea was subsequently scrapped as Ash did not want to do it! Although Linda and John Blundell were on the 'other side' they were both part of the gang when filming stopped and spent three happy weeks on location in Brighton. Regan appeared for a few years as a yellow coat in Hi-De-Hi, as well as various other roles on both the big and small screen, such as in the 1971 film version of On the Buses. Recently she has turned to a new and successful career as a crime novelist. Linda is married to the actor Brian Murphy, best known for his role as George Roper in George and Mildred. The following picture shows Linda Regan (right) in a publicity shot with Roger Daltrey.

RENOIR – Musical Connection.
Renoir was the name of the band that Phil Daniels and Trevor Laird played together in the late seventies. Phil Daniels played lead guitar, Gary Kemp later of Spandau Ballet was also a brief member of the band.

RHINO VIDEO (US) – Distributors (video).
This company have been responsible for distributing such diverse projects as the 1936 film, Sweeney Todd: The Demon Barber of Fleet Street and the 1966 TV series, The Monkees.

GARY ROBERTSON - (Mod extra at Brighton).
Gary Robertson was a member of the Modrapheniacs scooter club who was used in the Brighton scenes.

FRANC RODDAM – Director.
Franc Roddam was born on 29th April 1946 in Stockton-On-Tees in the North East of England.

In 1964, Roddam was aged eighteen, and very aware of the Mod movement, and what was going on down in places like Brighton, although not a Mod himself he says that many of his friends were.

Roddam ultimately travelled south where he studied at, and graduated from the London Film School. A personal nod was given to his old haunt in Quadrophenia, when it was used as a location in the scene where Jimmy scores some pills from Ferdy. The London Film School is something that is still dear to Roddam's heart, and he has continued to help raise funds for them as and when he can.

After graduating Roddam began his career with the BBC as a Director, and was to go on to make a fly on the wall documentary in 1974 called, The Family. It was highly acclaimed, and about an everyday family called the Wilkins, setting the bench mark for many such programmes that have since followed. It was basically the start of reality TV and the success of it opened the door for Roddam to move on to his first drama.

On 9th November 1977 Pete Townshend was at home watching a docudrama called, Dummy which was a story about a deaf girl named Sandra X who had been forced into prostitution. It caused an absolute storm at the time, with its content even being debated in Parliament. Townshend was extremely impressed in the way that thirty-two-year-old Roddam had handled the subject, and although he didn't know it yet, he had just subconsciously found his Director for Quadrophenia!

Dummy was later to be awarded the prestigious 'Prix Italia' drama award, and was the launch-pad for the actress who played the lead, Geraldine James to going on to much bigger things!

Dummy was what undoubtedly lead to Roddam being offered Quadrophenia, Nick Roeg and Alan Parker were also said to have been in the frame, but rookie Roddam was to be the one who ultimately won the role!

There were many obstacles for Roddam to overcome when he took on the role of Director, not least that there was no completed script! Roddam helped to lick this into shape, although he later admits this was used more as a reference point than an actual definitive script, with the actors being heavily encouraged to improvise. Roddam's first day of work was in the middle of June, three months later he found himself on set for the first day of filming!

Pete Townshend had a slightly different idea of what direction the film should go in, and turned up at a pre-production meeting with tapes of stringed music to add to it. Roddam, however, said that he was very much against making another 'Tommy' and wanted Quadrophenia to be much more realistic, and not surprisingly given Roddam's documentary background many of these techniques were employed.

Keith Moon also paid Roddam a visit, saying that he had a great idea 'why don't they direct the film together', Roddam politely laughed it off by saying only if he could drum on the next album by The Who.

Roddam always talks about Phil Daniels as being his partner in the film, but it is quite clear that the way Roddam decided to go about making the film in a very much 'hands on' way made it the success it was to ultimately become.

Roddam's highlight as a Director during the film must surely be the beach fight scenes, shot with frightening accuracy that gave it an air of supreme realism. Indeed, whilst preparing for a re-take he approached the extras and told them to really go for the policeman as they were mucking about and 'fucking up the scene', job done!

Looking back at the film now it is impossible to think of anybody else directing it, and it was indeed a masterstroke by the Producers employing somebody like Roddam who was firmly rooted in the real-life documentary genre.

In 1983 Central TV aired a new series called "Auf Wiedersehen Pet" with Roddam being credited as Executive Producer. It was based on an idea following a visit to his native north-east where he had chatted with some pals that had just returned from working in Germany as bricklayers. They had been unable to get such work in their own country, and their story was ideal for an eighties audience! Auf Wiedersehen Pet, went on to become a massive hit, launching the careers of amongst others, Jimmy Nail and Timothy Spall. It was also a vehicle for many ex-Quadrophenia actors such as the late Gary Holton and Michael Elphick, as well as Ray Winstone. Following the success of the first series, a second was scheduled that saw the group encamped in Spain. It was during the filming of this series that Gary Holton died, and led to the end of the programme until a triumphant return in 2001.

Roddam met with Jimmy Nail and a decision was made to bring the lads back, this time on the BBC. It was with some trepidation that the old gang reassembled to try and recapture the magic of the eighties. Although, somewhat different from the old-days, it was still a very, very good series which was followed by another and a Christmas special.

After the first series of Auf Wiedersehen Pet, Roddam went on to direct a few films including War Party in 1988 and K2 in 1991, and worked on a few TV projects. However, Roddam now tends to work in executive producer roles with his major successes being the devising of new TV shows. Such a show was Master Chef, which first hit the screens in 1990 and has spawned various spin-offs such as Celebrity Master Chef, and is still one of the most popular shows on BBC. Roddam is also a founder and chairman of ZIJI Publishing, which includes in its roster the multi-million selling novel, The Last Templar.

Roddam was also heavily involved in the re-mastered DVD releases of Quadrophenia, and has been a welcome guest at many reunions and special screenings in recent years, where he enjoys something of a cult-status!

NIC ROEG – *Potential Director.*
It is easy to see why Nic Roeg's name was thrown into the ring; his unique style is one that could have quite easily had suited Quadrophenia! He had recently finished directing David Bowie in The Man Who Fell to Earth and had previously worked on Walkabout (one of Phil Daniels favourite films) in 1971. Later work was to include Roald Dahl's, The Witches in 1990.

THE RONETTES – *Musical Contribution.*
Sisters' Veronica (Ronnie) and Estelle Bennett teamed up with their cousin Nedra Talley to perform as a dance group at the Peppermint Lounge in New York. They then changed direction and became a singing group known initially as, Ronnie and the Relatives. Later they changed their name to The Ronettes, and were spotted by a certain Phil Specter who signed them launching them on the road to fame. Spectre and Ronnie later married, however this ended in a very messy divorce, which saw the pair involved in litigation relating to the rights of their back catalogue.

ROBERT ROSENBERG - *Re-issue Executive Producer (1973 album).*
Rosenberg worked on the re-issued album and has gone on to work with The Who on many occasions, including Amazing Journey: The Story of The Who as Executive Producer, and has also many other credits within the music industry.

BILL ROWE – *Sound Re-Recording.*
Rowe received two major honours for his work in the eighties and nineties, when a BAFTA was awarded for his work on The Killing Fields 1984 and then an Oscar for the 1997 production of The Last Emperor. Further work has included Dr Jekyll and Sister Hyde, Dulcima both 1971, Dracula AD

1972, Tommy, Listzomania both 1975 both starring Roger Daltrey. Other work includes, Give My Regards to Broad Street and Cal both 1984, The Mission 1986 as well as Unbreakable 2000.

MICKEY ROYCE – Ken 'Jonesy' Jones the Mod.
Royce is an uncredited extra that was actually given a character name, can be viewed during the action in Brighton.

ETHAN A. RUSSELL – Art Director 1973 Album.
Ethan A. Russell worked on the original album as Art Director, which includes the stunning black and white booklet which took five weeks to complete. Russell went on to work on many other projects including, writing, producing and directing the 1996 documentary, The Life and Times of Rickie Lee Jones.

KEN RUSSELL – Potential Director.
Born: 3rd July 1927   Died: 27th November 2011.

Having done the Directorial honours for Tommy and also working with Roger Daltrey on Listzomania in 1975 it is likely that Ken Russell's name was discussed at some stage. Pete Townshend, however, made it clear that he was not in any rush to work with him again!

S

ANDREW SANDERS – Assistant Art Director.
Sanders has worked on a variety of films as either Art Director or Production Designer, his first film in 1970, Ned Kelly, saw him combine the former with that of actor. The eighties saw him involved in the following productions, Shock Treatment 1981, Privates on Parade 1982, Merry Christmas, Mr Lawrence (starring David Bowie) 1983, The Hit 1984, Castaway 1986, The Last Temptation of Christ 1988 and Crusoe in 1989. Into the nineties, and Sanders renewed his acquaintance with Franc Roddam for the 1992 film, K2, the decade also saw him work on Sense and

Sensibility 1995. Recent work has included The Golden Bowl and I Dreamed of Africa in 2000, Possession 2002 and Spider in 2003.

GARY SANDERS – (Mod extra at Brighton).
Gary was a member of the Modrapheniacs Scooter Club and was in Brighton for around a week as an extra. Gary was also one of many whose faces appeared on the inside cover of the soundtrack album, and later went on to marry fellow extra, Angie Mulvey.

ANDY SAYCE – Kenny the Mod in Brighton Scenes.

MARTYN SCULLY - (Mod extra at Brighton).
Scully was a member of Barnsley Vikings scooter club and landed a part of an extra in Brighton, having been recruited at the Southend scooter rally. Martyn is seen in the following photograph (during a break in filming) sitting on scooter, with behind him left to right: - Steve Orridge, Bingo? Fleagal? Kevin Lawn and Kevin Lawton

SIMON SCULLY – (Mod extra at Brighton).
Almost certainly the brother of Martyn (above) and a member of the same scooter club.

GARY SHAIL – Spider.
Born; 10th November 1959

Gary Shail was born in Hendon, North West London and went on to attend the Arts Educational Stage School from the age of fourteen. Fortunately, on 28th February 1975 Gary decided to alter his route to school, a decision that may have saved his life as his usual train would have been caught up in the tragic Moorgate Tube Disaster in which 43 people lost their lives!

He was to spend four years at the school, during which time he earnt his first professional acting role when he played Michael Elphick's son (Elphick was only 27 himself!) in an LWT show called, Holding On. Upon leaving Stage School he embarked on an acting career, although he was also showing very early promise in composing and writing music, which he has always considered his first love!

Shail has always had many interests, one of which was Karate, at which he was quite accomplished and even had to turn down an exhibition in Switzerland to land the role in Quadrophenia. In fact, Franc Roddam thought that the young Shail looked too week to make a convincing fighter, something that angered him, but after a brief exhibition of his martial arts talents he won himself the role of Spider. A very accomplished stuntman, he was even asked to join Peter Brayham's organisation, Special Action Services. The audition that Gary Shail attended was the same one that Toyah and Johnny Rotten were present at, although on this occasion they did not share any scenes together!

The character was originally going to be called Finger, and indeed that is the name that remained in the novel. Spider is one of the few Mods that does not wear a Parka, and instead is seen in a green trench-coat, which was actually Shail's idea. After filming the famous green coat somehow ended up in the possession of John Altman, but over thirty years later it was returned to its rightful owner, who still has the priceless memento to this day!

Prior to Quadrophenia he worked on the small budget independent film, The Music Machine, which saw him star with fellow Quadrophenia actors, Mark Wingett and John Blundell. The former was to become Shail's good friend and even stayed at his parent's house with him during the Quadrophenia shoot.

Another friendship forged during Quadrophenia was with the late Gary Holton, who along with Jesse Birdsall, played Rockers who had to beat him up. Holton was with his girlfriend Donna at the shoot, and Shail with

Tammy Jacobs who also played his other half in the film (being offered a role when she accompanied Shail to his audition) the two couples got on famously and had something of a party after the filming! Shail and Holton had a common love of music and both hoped to work with each other in the future, alas it was not to happen. As for the other Rocker, Jesse Birdsall, him and Shail didn't get on quite so well, as he lured Tammy away from him, which didn't go down very well at the time! A £700 fee went towards a Yamaha 125 motorbike, possibly having had enough of Scooters for a while!

John Entwistle was another friend made during Quadrophenia, the two talked about the Bass guitar, of which of course, Entwistle was the maestro! Shail was to visit him a few times at his home, where he was invited to cast his eye over his collection of classic bass guitars. In 1980 Phil Davis wrote a song called, Blown It! which Gary Shail went onto release, and saw the Record Company making the very-most of the Quadrophenia connection to promote it!

In 1981 Shail landed the part of Oscar Drill in Shock Treatment, which was the follow up to The Rocky Horror Picture Show. The film has become somewhat of a cult, and has led to Shail attending conventions both in the UK and America.

Shail's acting career was to be sporadic over the intervening years as he was always far happier working on his music, although he was to appear in the ITV series Metal Mickey, in the early eighties. The show was a mainstay for the network early evening slot on a Saturday night, and was regularly watched by audiences in excess of 15 million. Another of his high-profile roles was in the 1988 critically acclaimed TV version of Jack the Ripper, where he played alongside Sir Michael Caine. Following this work, he only appeared in a couple of TV roles before concentrating exclusively on his music.

The musical side of Shail's career saw him release his aforementioned single called Blown It! in 1980 on Elton John's Rocket Label. He then went on to work on various TV and film projects including the 1983 BBC TV series, Johnny Jarvis and the 1984 film Pop Pirates which starred Roger Daltrey. Shail's music eventually took him to America where he worked for The Disney Corporation, and the legendary Motown label, writing for, amongst others, Smokey Robinson.

In 1992 with Shail's acting virtually behind him he set up Natural Sound in London which was responsible for TV and advertising jingles, he remained with the company (now based in Dubai) until 1998.

A life virtually dedicated to music sees Gary composing, playing and writing, and acting as when he is offered a role that interests him.

Shail has a son called Ben who is in his early twenties by his ex-wife, Lindsay. His son was able to pocket a few quid in a bet whilst at school due to his father's fame; nobody believed that the face on the iconic Quadrophenia poster belonged to his Dad until he turned up to collect him one day, much to Ben's delight!

Now living in Portsmouth, Shail has a full life and amongst other things is studying for his pilot's licence. Gary Shail has become one of the most loved characters on the Mod/Quadrophenia circuit as he always puts himself out to support them if he is able, and rightly remains proud of his role in the film!

MISCLEANOUS INFORMATION

Books: I think I'm on the Guest List – Autobiography – New Haven Publishing 2015.

SHAM69 – Musical Connection.
Jimmy Pursey founded the group who failed to make it past their audition with Franc Roddam, in 1976. The inspiration for the group's name came from a piece of graffiti in his home town of Hersham, Surrey which read Hersham 69 (the Her had started to fade!). Pursey enlisted the services of Neil Harris (lead guitar), Johnny Goodfornothing (guitar), Albie Slider (bass) and Billy Bostic on drums.

Sham 69 were predominately known for Glam-Rock covers before the emergence of Punk Rock in late 1976, when they immersed themselves fully in the scene. The group went on to release such tunes as Borstal Breakout, and Let's Rob a Bank, until they reached the top-ten with Hersham Boys in 1979, before splitting the following year. Jimmy Pursey remains in the music business and went on to work with the likes of Long Tall Shorty and The Angelic Upstarts. A recent album was released of some of their previously un-heard work, which included four tracks that were recorded for Quadrophenia.

MIKE SHAW – *Music Co-ordinator.*
Shaw worked with The Who (The High Numbers) in the early days and credits are included on their following albums, Meaty, Beaty, Big and Bouncy, The Greatest Hits and Hooligans. Shaw also appeared in the 2007 film, Amazing Journey – The Story of The Who.

TOMMY SHELLEY – *Advisor to Phil Daniels and Cast.*
Tommy Shelley was a famous London based Mod, who gave Phil Daniels and other cast members advice and guidance on all things – Mod! Scooter riding etiquette being one of his main tasks. A party was subsequently arranged partly as a bonding exercise, but also for the cast to learn dance moves and other 'Mod ways' from Tommy. However, they were all asked to leave as it got somewhat out of hand when an unknown member of the Production team starting handing out some blues!

LOUISE SHORT *(Mod-girl extra in Night Club scenes).*
Louise is an uncredited extra in the Brighton Night Club scenes that were actually shot in London! One of many extras that answered a clarion call that was broadcast on Capital Radio.

GEORGE SIMPSON – *Margate Magistrate.*
George Simpson was the actual Magistrate who delivered the 'Sawdust Caesar' address to the first of forty-four youths that appeared before him following the disturbances in 1964.

THE SKUNKS– *Auditioned for Mod Band in film.*
A young Punk band that were formerly known as Dole Q, but changed their name when Siouxsie Sioux berated it in the NME, they were fronted by Gerry Lambe and Franco Cornelli (both aged just 15). Spotted by Pete Townshend, whilst supporting Generation X, he duly signed them to his Eel Pie label and they auditioned for the role of the band in the film. More than a few people at the time remarked that they were somewhat reminiscent of a young Who!

COLIN SKEAPING - *(Rocker at sea-wall / Stuntman).*
Colin Skeaping played the part of the hapless rocker that was thrown over the sea wall by Peter Fenton following their fight. Skeaping was a

stuntman, who recreated the famous scene that appeared on the front of newspapers at the time. Skeaping has had a busy and varied career in his chosen field, appearing in films such as, Batman, Superman III and Whoops Apocalypse. TV work has included, The Bill, Midsomer Murders and Red Dwarf, but probably his most famous role was as the stunt double for Mark Hamill (Luke Skywalker) in the first three Star Wars films.

JAMES SMART – 1964 Mod.

James Smart was a mere fourteen years of age when he was caught up in a battle with Rockers in Hastings, during the August bank-holiday. Sadly, his life was cut tragically short when he fell from a cliff-top following a fight.

TIMOTHY SPALL – (Harry the Projectionist).

Born: 27th February 1957

Timothy Spall made a small but memorable contribution to the film, before going on to become one of the country's most loved and busiest actors. Born in Battersea in South London his first big role was in another Franc Roddam gem, Auf Wiedersehen Pet as the Brummie electrician, Barry Taylor. It was, a role that had many people believing that he actually, was from Birmingham! Spall learned his craft at the National Youth Theatre and RADA, at which he was bestowed the prestigious Bancroft Gold Medal as most promising actor of his year.

Spall has gone on to enjoy a wide and varied career with a string of memorable performances on both the small and the large screen. A fantastic portrayal of Fagin in the TV version of Oliver Twist was just one example of his versatility. In 1996 Spall was diagnosed with leukaemia, and believed it to have - been caused by stress, he has since led a less stressful life and believes this to be a major cause of his ongoing remission. One of our true gems, he is Ray Winstone's favourite British Actor.

CHRIS STAINTON – Musician on original album.

Stainton played the piano on three tracks on the original album, Dirty Jobs, 5:15 and Drowned prior to Pete Townshend mastering of the instrument. Stainton went on to work with Eric Clapton, and Joe Cocker and appeared in the 1985, Michael Caine film, Water, as a band member.

CHRIS STAMP – Story Consultant and Executive Producer of 1973 Album.
Born; 7th July 1942. Died; 24th November 2012.

Stamp was co-manager of The Who from 1964 until 1974 alongside Kit Lambert. The pair had worked together as Assistant Directors on the 1962 film, The L-Shaped Room which starred his brother, Terence Stamp. Stamp was also responsible for the original draft of the Quadrophenia story alongside Pete Townshend, and worked as Executive Producer on the album and various other projects including Tommy. In 1994 Stamp was credited as Producer of Celebration: The Music of Pete Townshend and The Who. After the end of Track Records, Stamp became a Physcodrama Therapist and addiction councillor in New York, sadly he succumbed to cancer and passed away in his adopted City in 2012.

MISCLEANOUS INFORMATION

DVD: - Lambert & Stamp – Documentary – 2105.

TONY STANHOPE (Mod extra London and Brighton).
Tony Stanhope was an associate of 'Ginger' who was also recruited at a scooter rally.

ADRIAN START – Painter.
Other work within the industry for Start has included, The Elephant Man (1980), Empire of the Sun (1987) and the 2006 production of The Queen.

GEORGIANA STEELE-WALKER – Secretary Ramport Studios.
Georgiana was much more than just a secretary at Ramport Studios when the original album was made in 1972, having to keep all parties happy was in no ways an easy job! Georgiana's contribution isn't and shouldn't be easily dismissed.

MARTIN STELLMAN – Screenplay.

Stellman has continued to write various scripts as well as Producing and Directing in his own right. 1980 saw him renew his acquaintance with Trevor Laird in Babylon, a film in which he was credited as both Screenwriter and Associate Producer. Further projects have included Defence of the Realm 1985 and For Queen and Country in 1989. Stellman was recruited following Franc Roddams decision to fire Dave Humphries; the two re-wrote the script, adding approximately 75% of new material! In 2012 it was rumoured that Stellman had wrote a script for a sequel to coincide with The Who's imminent tour of Quadrophenia!

STERLING SCOOTERS – Scooter Suppliers to Film.

Sterling Scooters were based in West Drayton in Middlesex, and were responsible for supplying some of the bikes used in the film.

STIG? – (Mod extra at Brighton).

Stig was a member of the Modrapheniacs Scooter Club and was used as an extra in the Brighton scenes.

STING (Gordon Sumner) – The Ace Face.

Born; 2nd October 1951, (as Gordon Sumner)

Sting was born in Wallsend in the North East, and the oldest of four children, his father ran a Dairy which meant that he was very used to early mornings, helping him regularly on his round.

He was, indeed, earmarked for a role in his father's Dairy, but Sting had other ideas, and after attending Grammar School moved onto Warwick University, but this proved to be a short-lived affair as he would skip lessons to watch bands and returned to the north east after just one term. Various jobs followed such as bus conductor, and builder's labourer, before moving onto a Teachers training College. He subsequently, after qualifying, went onto work at St. Paul's First School in Cramlington, but combined his time there working as a part-time musician.

During this period, he appeared on stage with the Phoenix Jazzmen in a black and yellow jumper looking like a Bumble Bee, thus earning the nickname of 'Sting'!

Frustrated by the lack of opportunities that came his way in his aim to make this his chosen career he moved to London in January 1977 with his then actress wife, Frances Tomelty. Very soon after arriving in London Sting met Stewart Copeland and Henry Padovani (later to be replaced by Andy Summers) and a band was formed by the name of The Police.

He was discovered by A+M Records whilst playing with The Police, but they would find success elusive in those early days, even after releasing 'Roxanne' and 'I can't stand losing you'. It still wasn't happening for the group, and unbelievably both songs were not hits at the time! Luckily enough for both the group and the record company, it was decided to stick with The Police, with A+M convinced that their goal was not that far away.

The Police would go onto to have world-wide number ones in a career that was to see them sell out stadiums all over the planet!

Around this time, Sting decided to move into acting, and as relatively unknown was cast as 'The Ace Face', in Quadrophenia, it was a role that Garry Cooper (Pete Fenton in the film) had previously been up for, he had also appeared in a small role in The Great Rock and Roll Swindle, although his part would later be edited out.

Sting delivered a superb performance in the film; however, for such a pivotal character in the film his dialogue was almost non-existent! With the highlight being his offer to pay his fine in the courtroom by cheque! Sting had trouble mastering the Mod dances, hence being filmed from the waist up during the nightclub scenes; he was also less than an accomplished scooterist coming off more than once! On one of the early days of filming a call-sheet appeared with Sting's real name on it, Gordon, which led to him being serenaded by members of the cast with the song, Jilted John by the group of the same name and which includes the line 'Gordon is a Moron'. At the time of the film's release The Police were at last starting to get the credibility that they deserved, which gave the film's makers the ideal opportunity for Sting's face to front much of their advertising.

His wife at the time, Frances Tomelty, seemed to resent the fact that he was getting a lot of attention for the role, stating at the time, 'All that attention he got from a small role in Quadrophenia when really good actors like Phil Daniels were ignored'

After the film's release Sting went on to become a worldwide star with The Police, and later as a solo-artist, he continues to occasionally flirt with acting, with notable roles in 'Brimstone and Treacle' and an all too brief cameo in 'Lock Stock and Two Smoking Barrels'.

Sting's music remains critically acclaimed both sides of the Atlantic, indeed globally and was rewarded with a CBE in 2003 for his services to the British music industry.

In February of 2007 Sting reformed The Police for a reunion tour that would take them to all four corners of the world, and would see them on the road for the best part of a year.

MISCLEANOUS INFORMATION

Books: Broken Music – Autobiography – Simon & Schuster 2003

Sting – Demolition Man – Christopher Sandford – Little Brown & Co 1998

Websites: www.sting.com

JOYCE STONEMAN – Wardrobe Supervisor.
Extremely experienced in her chosen field, other work has included the 1985 Terry Gilliam production of Brazil, an ambitious project that starred amongst others, Robert DeNiro. Other work has included Absolute Beginners 1986 and the 1978 film, The Class of Miss MacMichael starring none other than Phil Daniels.

THE STRANGLERS – Musical Connection.
The Stranglers were at the very forefront of the Punk and New-Wave movement in the late seventies, and were fronted by Hugh Cornwell. However, he was replaced for a very, very brief period by none other than Phil Daniels, this was due to Cornwell's brief stay in Prison.

STRAIGHT 8 – Auditioned for Mod Band in film.
Originally formed in 1976 Straight 8 were rejected by Roger Daltrey as he said they were too good! Straight 8 were quite an accomplished Rock Band, but lacked the rawness for the type of band they were looking for. However, the audition bought them to the attention of Pete Townshend

who promptly signed them to his Eel Pie label; where they went on to record three albums, supporting the likes of Queen and Slade on tour before splitting up in 1983. Lead vocalist and guitarist, Rick Casson went on to work with Pete Townshend as well as providing the music for TV adverts before re-forming the band in 2015.

THE STYLE COUNCIL – *Musical Connection.*
The group which was Paul Weller's first project following the demise of The Jam saw him joined by Mick Talbot late of another Mod band, The Merton Parkas. The group enjoyed a successful post Mod-revival career, with one hits being, Solid Bond in Your Heart in 1983 which was promoted by an inspired video said to be their mini-homage to Quadrophenia.

THE SUPREMES – *Musical Contribution.*
Formally known as The Primettes this Detroit based girl group originally comprised of Diana Ross, Mary Wilson and Florence Ballard. They went on to enjoy early success in 1964 with, Where Did Our Love Go? This was followed up by a further six USA number one's within a year, and another half-dozen before the turn of the decade.

In 1964 their biggest hit this side of the Atlantic was Baby Love (which is heard during the scene set at The Goldhawk) and became the only number one scored by an American group or artist that year. They very soon became established as a sound that many would try to copy, with Diana Ross becoming the group's star, indeed they soon became Diana Ross and the Supremes. It was widely thought that it was actually Florence Ballard that was the better singer, however, Berry Gordy of Tamla Motown preferred the former and pushed her into the lead role.

In 1967 Ballard was to leave the group, she had become resentful at the emergence of Ross as the group's star, and began to drink heavily which led to her becoming extremely unreliable. Motown sacked her and gave her a $139,000 golden handshake, her life was to become one of sorrow and misery before she died at just thirty-one in February 1976. Many blamed Diana Ross for Ballard's descent into misery, which led to a drug induced heart failure; the former was even booed at her funeral by onlookers.

Motown still own the group's name and a totally unrecognisable line-up still exists today! The curse of The Supremes seems to have fallen upon Diana Ross who was admitted to a mental ward after a nervous collapse in 2002. This followed her failed marriage and a faltering musical career.

DEREK SUTER – Clapper Loader.

Has also worked within the industry as both a cinematographer and electrician, with credits on the following films, The Eagle Has Landed and The Man Who Fell to Earth both 1976, Love and Bullets 1979, Superman III 1983, The Hit, and A Private Function both 1984, Guilty 1993, Thief Takers 1995 and Happy Birthday Shakespeare in 2000. Suter has also worked as a Cinematographer on such TV shows as, Cadfael and Happy Birthday Shakespeare.

JAMES SWANN – Special Thanks.

Swann who was given a special mention in the credits has worked as Associate Producer on the following films, Caesar 1970, Straw Dogs 1971, and The Edge of Sanity 1989. Swann also played the role of Gerard in the 1988 film Mad About You a light-hearted comedy which also featured Adam West Aka Batman. Swann had a friend on the Board of Directors at Brighton & Hove Albion F.C., who in turn, was friends with the local head of police. Much smoozing was done to allow filming, with the police eventually saying as long as no laws are broken they would allow it, of course on day one of filming hundreds did just that by riding through the streets of Brighton with no safety helmets!

NEIL SYKES – Air Cadet in Brighton.

An unplanned appearance was made by 11-year-old Neil Sykes who was a new member of the Brighton Air Cadets, so new in fact that he didn't have his uniform yet! Neil still lives in the area and runs the Modern World Gallery in Brighton a mecca for all things Mod! www.modernworldgallery.com Neil is viewed in the white jumper in the following picture.

T

MIKE TAYLOR – Film Editor.
Mike Taylor was not to see the project through to the end, as he was sacked by Franc Roddam who was not happy with the way the film was being edited and was subsequently replaced by Sean Barton. Taylor worked in the same role in the 1980 film The Long Good Friday, which starred Bob Hoskins, and also The Sailors Return 1978. Television work includes the 1975 television production of The Naked Civil Servant, and Summer of my German Soldier in 1978. In 1987 Taylor had a small acting role in the 1987 production of Concrete Angels.

PHIL TERRY – (Mod at Brighton).
Phil was a Yorkshire based Mod who was used as an extra in some of the filming in Brighton, getting paid more to use his own scooter.

SIMON THOMPSON – Hairdresser.
Three notable films that Thompson has worked on include, Emma 1996 and Titanic 1997, which starred Leonardo DiCaprio and Kate Winslet, and saw him nominated for an Oscar. Other contributions include, Sliding Doors 1998 starring John Hannah and Gwyneth Paltrow. Thompson also worked on Who is Killing the Great Chefs of Europe 1978, and the 1986 production of Shanghai Surprise.

TIGGER? – (Rocker on Road to Brighton).
Tigger was an associate of Tom Ingram, and joined the production with his girlfriend, Bonnie for scenes shot on the road to Brighton.

CLAIRE TOEMAN (Mod girl at Brighton).
Appearing briefly within scenes predominately at the Brighton Ballroom, this young actress was to go on and appear with fellow Quadrophenia actors regularly. Billy the Kid and the Green Baize Vampire saw an appearance alongside Trevor Laid and its star, Phil Daniels. Television credits include, Cats Eyes alongside Lesley Ash, and with Ray Winstone in Robin of Sherwood.

PAUL TOWNSHEND – Mod in 1973 album booklet.
Pete's younger brother was a young Mod in a Seer Sucker jacket in the original albums accompanying booklet. The Who were later to appear as themselves in The Simpsons, with Paul playing the part of his older brother alongside Roger Daltrey and John Entwistle!

BRIAN TUFANO – Director of Photography.
Brian Tufano has worked as either a Director of Photography or Cinematographer extensively within the British Film Industry over several years. Early work with the BBC included the Stephen Frears production, Three Men in a Boat and Alan Parker's, The Evacuees both 1975, later TV work included Silent Witness and Middlemarch. Notable projects on the big screen have included the 1989 production of War Party, which was Directed by Franc Roddam, and the critically acclaimed 1999 film, Tube Tales which starred Ray Winstone. Further films of note that Tufano has worked on are, Shallow Grave 1994, Trainspotting 1996, Life Less Ordinary 1997, East is East 1999, Billy Elliot 2000 and Last Orders 2002.

Tufano returned to the Quadrophenia project in 1997 when he worked on enhancing film that was used for its re-release. A truly outstanding career was capped in 2001, when he received a BAFTA for outstanding contribution to British Film and Television.

KEN TUOHY – Production Assistant.
Tuohy is now a film producer in his own right, and works extensively in Northern Ireland with his recent projects including, Puckoon in 2000 and Soldier and Midnight Children 2001, the former starring Elliott Gould and Richard Attenborough. Earlier projects have included Krull 1983, Bellman and True 1987, Nil by Mouth 1997 and the 1999 production of Mansfield Park.

STUART TURTON (Mod at Brighton).
After a small role in the film Turton appeared in a few episodes of Tales of the Unexpected in the eighties, as well as an appearance in The Bill in 1990.

U/V

GENE VINCENT – Musical Connection.
Kevin is heard giving his rendition of Be-bop-a-Lula during the bathing scene. The song was originally released by Gene Vincent and his Blue Caps in 1956 reaching number 16 in the UK charts. Gene Vincent died at just 36 years of age in 1971 of a stomach ulcer.

W

DAVID WADDINGTON (Mod extra at Brighton).
David Waddington was a member of a Scooter club who was involved in some of the Brighton scenes.

GILLI WAKEFORD – Make Up Artist.

Sometimes credited as Gillian Wakeford she has previously worked for Thames Television notably on The Benny Hill Show, The Bill, George and Mildred and Shelley.

PETE WALKER (Mod extra at Brighton).

Pete Walker was a member of The Barnsley Vikings Scooter Club, and is seen during the action in Brighton, and sits behind Jimmy in the courtroom scenes.

MARY THERESA WALSH-PAMMEN (Mod girl extra in party and club scenes).

Mary Theresa played 3 separate roles in the film during the party scene and also the Goldhawk and Brighton club scenes. Mary was used as a special extra for 3 weeks, and changed her appearance on each scene with the aid of a wig. She is now a Director of her own company in Essex. The following picture shows Mary Theresa in a scene from the house party.

JOHN WARDZINSKI (Mod extra in Brighton).

John Wardzinski was an extra used in the Brighton scenes and was the owner of Jimmy's Lambretta which was subsequently bought by the film's makers. Picture below (courteous of Robin Williams) shows John Wardzinski in union-jack t-shirt next to Williams, also pictured is Colin Hawker leaning on sign extreme left.

MITCH WAX – Tailor for Phil Daniels.
Mitch is part of the Wax family from Dave Wax Outfitters in Hammersmith, and had the honour of making Phil Daniels suit that he proudly wore to Brighton. The suit took approximately 7- 10 days to make. Wax also made the replica suits in the film, Birth of the Beatles in which John Altman took the role of George Harrison.

TERRY WELLS – Property Master.
Wells has an impressive list of films to his credit including the 1996 Walt Disney production of, 101 Dalmatians starring Glen Close. Other work has included the following, The Elephant Man 1980, In the Name of The Father 1993, Interview with a Vampire 1994, Braveheart 1995, The World is Not Enough and The Mummy both in 1994.

KEN WHEATLEY – Set Director.
Wheatley has worked as either Set Director or Art Director on the following films, Babylon 1980, Absolute Beginners 1986, Dealers 1989 Children of the Corn III 1994 and the 1999 production of The Debt Collector. Wheatley also works in Special Effects and Make-Up.

BENJAMIN WHITROW – Simon Fulford.
Born: 17th February 1937

Born in Oxford, Whitrow went on to attend RADA and has always been at home in a more classic role, eventually joining the Royal Shakespeare

Company in 1981. Other film work includes, Clockwise, and Pride and Prejudice, for which he received a BAFTA nomination.

Phil Daniels revealed that he met him at a Golf Day and was asked 'what was the name of that awful film we appeared in together'? He also believes that he took it personally when he told him to poke his job!

THE WHO.
What is there left to say about The Who that hasn't already been said? The classic line up of Pete Townshend, Roger Daltrey, John Entwistle and Keith Moon first played together in 1964 at The Oldfield Tavern in Greenford, Middlesex. In fact, in over fifty years of existence the band have actually only had two other official members, Doug Sandom the original drummer before Keith Moon's arrival, and Kenney Jones who was Moon's replacement following his death! However, during that period many individuals have become members of the groups touring and recording outfit, notably, Simon Townshend, Zac Starkey, Pino Palladino and John 'Rabbit' Bundrick.

Roger Daltrey, was in-fact the first person to bring about the birth of the embryonic band that would later become The Who, when he noticed school mate John Entwistle, carrying a bass guitar and invited him to join his new group, The Detours. A little later in the summer of 1961 on the suggestion of Entwistle, they recruited a certain Pete Townshend, with Harry Wilson on drums and at the time Colin Dawson acting as the group's singer (Daltrey was lead guitarist at the time!). The Detours were very much a covers band, playing both popular music as well as trad-jazz, with Daltrey regarded very much as the bands leader! In 1962 Harry Wilson, would be replaced by Doug Sandom, who although a few years older than his counterparts was a very proficient drummer, and thus a very early version of The Who was born!

Ultimately Coin Dawson left the band following a series of disagreements with Daltrey, and was for a short while replaced by Gabby Connolly, until he also left! With just four members remaining Daltrey was persuaded to take over the singing duties, and Townshend moved up to lead guitarist. In 1964 the band learnt of a group with a similar name and at a brainstorming meeting which included Townshend's pal, Richard Barnes a new one was discussed. The Hair was one suggestion, but it was The Who that Barnes thought was ideal for them, and the following morning a 'democratic' decision was made by Daltrey that it should indeed be The Who!

Around this time The Who were starting to be considered as a serious band and were building a sizeable local following playing regular dates at the likes of the Goldhawk Social Club in Shepherds Bush. With a new manager, Helmut Gorden in control they secured an audition for Fontana Music with a view to landing a recording contract. At the audition, they were told that Doug Sandom's drumming was not up to scratch after which a row ensued predominately between him and Townshend, which resulted in Sandom walking out, never to return!

The Who still had many commitments to fulfil, so used various stand in drummers until that fateful day in April 1964 when a certain Keith Moon who was drummer with another local group called The Beachcombers walked into The Oldfield Tavern in Greenford. Moon asked if he could play a few numbers with them in their second set, and was duly given permission to borrow the present incumbent's kit. After witnessing the whirlwind that is Keith Moon's drumming he was persuaded to ditch The Beachcombers and join Daltrey and company. The classic line up was now complete and would remain intact for another fourteen years!

During a regular gig at The Railway Tavern in Wealdstone, the band were approached by Kit Lambert and Chris Stamp who wanted to feature them in a film they were making. Lambert and Stamp subsequently became the bands management team, who had been persuaded by Mod-Guru and Manager Pete Meaden to embrace the burgeoning Mod-scene and they went onto release what was billed as the first 'authentic Mod single' – a double A side containing, Zoot Suit and I'm the Face! During this period the band were briefly renamed as The High Numbers before very quickly reverting to The Who.

In late 1964, a song heavily influenced by The Kinks, I Can't Explain, was recorded, and released the following year, followed by, Anyway, Anyhow, Anywhere and their anthemic My Generation, which towards the end of the year was followed by the album of the same name. Into 1966 other singles such as Happy Jack followed, but with the Mod movement in its dying days they looked to prove their longevity by casting their musical nets further afield and toured America for the first time. This followed on from a triumphant and legendary debut at the Monterey Pop Festival. The tour of the USA was to support Herman's Hermits, who despite their clean-cut image proved to be perfect allies for Keith Moon who celebrated his 21st birthday during the tour by losing a tooth, and helping to rack up hotel room repair bills in excess of $20,000! The following year Lambert and Stamp set up Track Records, with distribution coming via Polydor and in 1968 The Who were to release its seminal album the rock-opera, Tommy! Nothing for The Who would ever be quite be the same again! Tommy sold in its millions, and was the first album to make The Who some serious money, it was also the album which saw Roger Daltrey truly find his voice and become one of the all-time great front men! The Who's power as a live outfit was never displayed better than their iconic appearance at Woodstock in August of that very year.

With the band, seemingly unable to do any wrong they performed and recorded Live at Leeds in 1970, which is still lauded as one of the best live albums ever, and was followed the next year with Who's Next after the failure of Pete Townshend's, Lifehouse project. In 1972 the album Quadrophenia was recorded, and released the following year, shortly after which Lambert and Stamp were replaced by Bill Curbishley as the bands manager.

Into 1974 saw The Who move into the movie industry for the first time when they transferred Tommy to celluloid, Daltrey took the lead role with Townshend and Entwistle heavily involved in the films score. After a massive word tour in 1976 the group concentrated on their next big screen offering the documentary entitled, The Kids are Alright. Unbeknown at the time, the documentary featured the last live appearance of Keith Moon with the band. After a long battle with the bottle Keith had been taking medication to conquer the effects of alcohol withdrawal, and following a party promoted by Paul McCartney to celebrate Buddy Holly's birthday on 6th September 1978 he returned home and overdosed on clomethiazole tablets. The legend that is Keith Moon fell into a coma and passed away during the small hours of the next day, and the world was robbed of the most unique musician to ever to hold a drumstick!

With the death of Keith Moon the Quadrophenia film project was in doubt for a short while, however the remaining members of the group let it be known that it was their firm intention to carry on. A couple of months on from Moon's death he was replaced by old Mod counterpart, Kenney Jones who actually went onto play on a couple of numbers for the new soundtrack. The film was released in 1979 around the same time of The

Kids are Alright. Later on in the year on 3rd December tragedy sadly struck the group once again. The Who played at the Riverfront Coliseum in Cincinnati where 11 fans were tragically killed in a crowd-rush. With the band, unaware of the unfolding tragedy they played on and were not told of the gravity of the events until the gig had finished!

During 1980 Daltrey worked on McVicar in which he took the lead role, and although the soundtrack was officially a solo album it features both Entwistle and Townshend. During this period, Townshend was busy working on his own solo album, Empty Glass, but was also facing a tough battle with both drink and drugs. Over the next two years the band released two more albums, Face Dances in 1981 and It's Hard the following year. Pete Townshend had become disillusioned with touring whilst the rest of the band wanted to carry on, which led inevitably to problems within the band and one that ultimately saw a period of inactivity from The Who for a few years!

In 1985 The Who played Wembley Stadium as part of the Live Aid concert, and three years later were awarded the Lifetime Achievement at the 1988 Brits. A short set was played in what proved to be Kenney Jones last outing with The Who. Kenney Jones was a fine drummer of great pedigree but was probably never really accepted by his fellow band mates and fans alike, so departed to pastures new! The following year the band toured to celebrate their 25 years together with a new drummer, Simon Phillips being bought in to replace Jones. However, since then the band has never had any other full-time members, with various musicians added to the touring line-ups as and when required!

In 1996 the three remaining members of band reunited to deliver a performance of Quadrophenia for the Prince's Trust in Hyde Park. Although not officially billed as The Who it reinvigorated the trio who had by this time added Zac Starkey, Simon Townshend and Pino Palladino to the line-up. A tour followed which went into 1997 and was a great success, with Quadrophenia at last being performed to the bands complete satisfaction! The Who were back! Triumphantly they graced the biggest venues both sides of the Atlantic, but of course this is The Who and things never run smooth and yet more heartbreak was lurking just over the horizon!

The Who played a few UK dates in early 2002 in readiness for an American tour, but on 27th June, the evening before their first date in Las

Vegas, John Entwistle suffered a heart attack at the Hard Rock Hotel. The Ox was just 57 years of age but in true rock-star style his liking for cocaine was thought to have been a major contributory factor! Entwistle had also been enjoying the services of a prostitute at the time of his death! The great bass player had recently been acknowledged as the best in his craft in a vote to find the Bassist of the Millennium. Rightly so! There have been many great exponents of the four-stringed beast over the years, but has anyone ever bettered The Ox?

The death of John Entwistle seemed to bring Daltrey and Townshend closer than they had ever been before, with a new-found love and respect that was evident for all to see in the forthcoming tours! In 2006 the first studio album since 1982 was released, Wire and Glass was very well received and made the top ten both sides of the Atlantic. The following year saw them headline Glastonbury in an awesome set that showed what a major force in live music they still are.

2012 saw them tour again, with Quadrophenia performed in its entirety along with the usual favourites, also that year saw them perform the last numbers at the GB Olympic closing ceremony!

2015 saw yet another Glastonbury outing and a stunning performance at a packed Hyde Park, showing that these two men in their seventies could still rock! This was part of a massive world tour which saw many rearranged dates in America due to Daltrey contracting viral meningitis. 2017 sees them back on the road once again, and quite how much longer they will carry on is unknown, but one thing is for sure there will still be plenty of people wanting to see them! The Who live are simply like no other, and I certainly wouldn't bet against them still belting out My Generation in their eighties!

THE WHO FILMS LIMITED – *Production Company.*
The Film Production Company that was set up by the band to oversee, Quadrophenia, The Kids Are Alright and McVicar.

ANDREW WILDE – *Jimmy in White City.*

Andrew Wilde played the part of Jimmy in the 1985 production of, White City, and went on to work in the likes of, Game of Thrones.

TOYAH WILCOX – Monkey.
Born; 18th May 1958 in Birmingham.

Franc Roddam: - *'Toyah was interesting, because she was quite litigious. She was always wanting to sue people, the hairdresser, whoever, she was quite a business girl'.*

Toyah Wilcox, (for some reason credited in the film as Toyah Willcox!) was born into a comfortable middle-class family in Birmingham, but always harboured ambitions to perform both as an actress, and a singer. She has managed to successfully juggle both careers for some forty years.

In May of 1975, she secured her first proper acting job in a BBC2 play about a wannabe pop-star, who breaks into the Top of the Pops studios with her boyfriend, played by Quadrophenia co-star, Phil Daniels. The play, Glitter, was the start of a long and varied career for the young performer.

The early eighties proved to be the pinnacle of her success as a recording artist, soaring high up the charts with hits such as It's a Mystery and I Wanna be free. The success was even more remarkable because she was signed to a small independent label, Safari.

It was during the filming of Quadrophenia that Toyah signed for Safari after being released for the afternoon to audition for them, which involved rushing to the recording studios after a gruelling Scooter scene. At the time, she was also filming with Sir John Mills in what proved to be a hectic schedule, which eventually saw her go down with pneumonia! There were many other Quadrophenia co-stars that were chasing recording deals at the time, and she said that although they were all 'delighted' for her that it had 'developed into a competitive race to see who would be signed first'.

With the impending release of Quadrophenia, Safari were quick to release Victims of the Riddle from her album, Sheep Farming in Barnet. Toyah was also busy touring at the time with a good smattering of Mods appearing in the audience, although her music was to have very little resonance with them!

Toyah was known to have been disappointed with Quadrophenia as a finished product at the time, as she felt the story moved away from the rest of the group, focusing mainly on Daniels character, she takes up the story in her autobiography;

'At the time, I couldn't bear to talk about Quadrophenia, also in more recent years I still couldn't bear to talk about it. I was angry at the result and I was angry at the way we were treated while making it. But it is true time does heal those kinds of wounds, they lose their intensity and eventually you can see a different truth. I was probably as much to blame for what happened to me as anyone else'.

Toyah claims never to have seen Quadrophenia all the way through as she walked out during the premier, and does not like seeing herself on the screen. At the 2008 Quadrophenia convention she even introduced the film at the special cinema showing, but still couldn't bring herself to watch what is generally acknowledged as a very solid performance. She is now, however, more than happy to acknowledge Daniels brilliance in the film, and very proud to have been part of it.

Toyah now speaks very fondly of her time on the film, and feels that the young raw ego's that were about actually gave Quadrophenia a far better creative result in the end.

Other notable work from Toyah has included being re-united with Quadrophenia co-stars in the following films;

1984   Murder, the Ultimate Grounds for Divorce.

Toyah played the part of Roger Daltrey's wife, with Lesley Ash playing his mistress.

1989   Little Pig Robinson.

Toyah played alongside Timothy Spall, although they had never actually shared a scene in Quadrophenia.

Toyah was also up for the lead role against Kate Bush in the 1981 production, Breaking Glass that starred Phil Daniels and Mark Wingett. The lead role finally went to her friend and fellow singer/actress Hazel O'Connor.

Toyah continues to be a much sought after musician, actress, presenter and writer who takes very little time off from work. She also has a very impressive world-wide property portfolio, but is predominantly based in Worcestershire with her husband world-famous guitarist, Robert Fripp.

In May 2008, she turned fifty, and typically at the time was recovering from a charity walk through the Gobi Desert!

MISCLEANOUS INFORMATION

Books (2000)	Living Out Loud – Autobiography – Hodder & Stoughton
Websites	www.toyah.net

KATE WILLIAMS – *Mrs Cooper.*
Born 1941

Kate Williams was born in East London during the Second World War, and harboured a wish to be an actress from an early age; however, her first job was that of a secretary. Kate had always been a bright pupil during her school days, and was probably directed towards a more stable career; however, her heart was ultimately allowed to rule her head when she left to join drama school at the East 15 Acting Academy.

Upon leaving drama school she joined a reparatory company before landing her first television role in the mid-sixties in the long running serial, Newcomers.

Kate has always been a busy actress with her earlier career tending to lean towards light comedy, which is where she really came to light in the seventies sitcom, Love Thy Neighbour. Kate played the role of Joan Booth in a show about a white couple living next door to a black couple. It was a show very much moulded in the seventies, and would certainly never be made today; indeed, Kate has talked about how bigoted the show looks today! Kate's role was that of peacemaker between her husband and the black couple next door, and in-fact saw her mostly in a positive light.

She was in-fact not the original choice as Jimmy's mother and was bought in at very short notice to replace Amanda Barrie who had been sacked by Franc Roddam. Roddam described her as 'perfect', and it is to Kate's eternal credit that she delivered a fantastic performance, with her character and Daniels' largely improvised scene towards the end of the film one of its true gems!

Kate is still busy and has appeared in Family Affairs and EastEnders (opposite Phil Daniels in one scene!) in recent years.

ROBIN 'YOB' WILLIAMS (Mod extra at Brighton).
Robin Williams was (and still is!) a member of the Modrapheniacs Scooter club, and landed a part of an extra in Brighton. 'Yob' had hired his Scooter to the Production Company, so took part on a borrowed machine which was not seen on film as it was actually a 1970's model! Williams is seen looking dapper in the following picture in this suit, with Scott Willis. (Photo courteous of Rob Williams)

SCOTT WILLIS (Mod extra at Brighton).
Scott Willis (in the following picture) was also a member of the Modrapheniacs Scooter club, and was in Brighton for around a week's filming.

Scott Willis and Robin 'Yob' Williams during a break in filming.

AMY WINEHOUSE – Potential Female Lead in Stage Version.

The multi-award winning singer/songwriter was once mooted as a possible female lead in a stage production of Quadrophenia. The extremely talented songstresses led a troubled life that saw her die of Alcohol Poisoning in 2011 at just twenty-seven.

MARK WINGETT – Dave.
Born; 1st January 1961.

Mark Wingett was born in Melton Mowbray in Leicestershire, but spent his early years in a small village outside Portsmouth where his Father was stationed with the Royal Navy. He was a fan of Punk Rock in its formative stages, and would travel up with pals from Hampshire to see bands such as The Clash in London. Wingett was educated at Horndean in Portsmouth, and quickly developed an interest in Drama, starting acting at nine years of age. Hampshire County Council offered him a Junior Exhibition in Drama, which was quickly followed by the offer of a place at the National Youth Theatre, and so the seeds were sewn for what was to be his chosen career. It was the inspiration of his Drama teacher, Mr Green that forced him to follow his dream, following a meeting with his careers officer he'd been told he would make a very good Zoo Keeper! Wingett's time on Quadrophenia was not without a few problems who at the time was a Punk Rocker, as well as the youngest member of the primary cast, which meant that he was sometimes a bit headstrong and earned him the nickname 'Brain Damage'. Indeed, he even walked off the set saying that he was not going to continue in the film, he had been rebuked for turning up on set with a big love bite on his neck. This caused the Producers continuity problems, and a row ensued! However, Franc Roddam had the ideal item with which to bribe him back, he had in his possession a shirt that was once owned by his hero, Johnny Rotten. The said garment complete with Rotten's vomit all over it was presented to a delighted Wingett who was very quickly back on board!

During filming in London, Wingett became a house guest of Gary Shail, and after filming shared a flat with Trevor Laird for a while in Stoke Newington.

Following on from Quadrophenia a couple of minor TV roles followed before being re-united with Phil Daniels in the 1980 film, Breaking Glass alongside Hazel O'Connor. Wingett then settled in to a role of a jobbing actor, before his next big break in 1983. Thames Television produced a storyboard production entitled, Woodentop (the slang phrase for uniformed policemen), this later evolved in to The Bill.

Wingett was initially given a one month contract but went on to play the part of Jim Carver for another twenty-four years, clocking up almost 800 appearances! It was a role that was to keep Wingett busy, playing the part of a uniformed officer who would later make it to DC, however, the continuing success of the show meant that he had little time to pursue other roles. It was also a very demanding schedule that in no small part contributed to his personal problems, which saw him getting drunk on a regular basis. Wingett even got hooked on a lethal Antiguan Rum which was 150% proof, before finally admitting he must stop drinking or suffer the ultimate consequences! The death of his co-star, Kevin Lloyd and the insistence of his partner Sharon Martin was enough to make him give up his addiction, which he says is still an ongoing journey! Happily, Mark is now able to enjoy life to the full without the need for a drink!

After he gave up the bottle he entered a long-term affair with an extra from The Bill which was eventually revealed in graphic detail by a Sunday tabloid newspaper. The revelation saw him separate from Sharon for almost two years, before they happily re-united.

In 2007 in a shock announcement it was revealed that Wingett was to leave The Bill, a move that was not popular with show's legions of fans, the show had gone through many changes, and was becoming less and less recognisable from its early days. After leaving The Bill, Wingett had a short spell in EastEnders, even sharing the occasional scene with Phil Daniels.

Wingett seems to be at last losing his DC Carver tag, with several projects due to come to fruition soon, including a Quadrophenia related short-film called, Being.

Outside of work Wingett is a very keen and accomplished scuba diver who enjoys searching sunken wrecks out at sea, which has led to documentary work for cable channels. It was an obsession that began in 1984 as a way of winding down from the hectic filming schedules of The Bill, he was persuaded to give it a try with some friends and has never looked back, completing dives all over the world! Wingett lives in London with his wife, Sharon who is a make-up artist and their teenage daughter, Jamelia; he also has a step-son, Benny.

MISCLEANOUS INFORMATION

Websites: - http://www.markwingett.com

RAY WINSTONE – Kevin Herriott.
Born: 19th February 1957.

Ray Winstone has become one of the country's acting treasurer's and is now one of the most sought after in his field, with his name virtually seemingly a guarantee of success! Born in Hackney, East London his family moved to Edmonton when he was young, where he developed a love for the Cinema, but also had an aptitude for Boxing and began fighting at the age of twelve. Winstone went on to box for the next ten years winning 80 of his 88 bouts! But it was acting that was to be his first love. On leaving school he gained just one CSE, predictably in Drama, which was enough to convince him that his future lay in acting, so he enrolled at the Corona Stage Academy. The stay at the Corona proved to be quite a fraught experience that culminated with him being expelled! However, the school did give him his first professional role at The Theatre Royal Stratford East, in What a Crazy World, which in turn led to a minor role in The Sweeney.

After his expulsion from the school he attended an audition for the BBC play, Scum which was directed by Alan Clarke. It was to prove a watershed in Winstone's career as he landed the lead role of Carlin in the tough no holds barred depiction of life in a Borstal. The play earned him the princely sum of £385, but was made and subsequently banned by the BBC before it was even screened, eventually airing on the small-screen in 1991.

However, shortly after Quadrophenia was in the can the cast of Scum were back in the studios to completely remake the play as a feature film. It was a film that was to shape Winstone's career for many years to come, and saw him able to exact his revenge on co-star, Phil Daniels in the infamous snooker balls in the sock scene! It also landed Winstone with the catch phrase of 'who's the Daddy?' that will be forever associated with him. His reprisal of the role of Carlin was slightly more lucrative, with his fee this time being £1800. Although not in any of the Brighton scenes, he was actually there at the time of filming, having gone down there to get fitted for his costume!

Following on from Scum, Winstone went on to make another film, Last Summer, where he met his soon to be wife, Elaine. The couple have been together since and have three daughters, with the two oldest, Lois and Jaime both following him into the acting business.

A variety of TV roles was to follow in programmes such as, Fox, Auf Wiedersehen Pet, Minder, Robin of Sherwood and Boon. Perhaps not surprisingly Winstone has tended to be offered the hard-man roles, but has attempted to show his softer side with fine performances in the likes of Fanny and Elvis and There's Only One Jimmy Grimble. But, undoubtedly, his finest work has been in such gems as Nil by Mouth alongside Kathy Burke and the 2000 film, Sexy Beast, which was widely acclaimed by fans and critics alike! Another must see film of Winstone's is the 1997 production, Face in which he co-starred with none other than Phil Davis, it is not one of his more talked about pictures, but both he and Davis deliver fine performances in what is essentially a good old gangster romp.

Winstone has continued to mix work on both the large and small screen, enjoying success in the later in recent years in the likes of, Vincent and Henry VIII.

Recent movie projects include Beowulf in 2007 and Indiana Jones and the Kingdom of the Crystal Skull in 2008.

Winstone lives in Essex and is now regarded as one our country's finest, he has seen hard times along the way suffering two cases of bankruptcy and even a very brief spell in a Yorkshire jail. In 1986 an edition of the BBC show, Crimewatch featured an identikit of a wanted man bearing an uncanny resemblance to Winstone, which was enough for the Police to pay him an unwanted visit and ended up with him being incarcerated whilst the misunderstanding was resolved! Winstone and his wife had been watching the show and joked about the likeness, he later joked 'that the police had watched too much telly, thinking that he was a real villain'. Nine years later he was again on the wrong side of the law when he went for a drink with Phil Daniels in the Green Room in Westminster, and an altercation with a fellow drinker, Karl Draper was to follow. Winstone was charged with ABH but later acquitted!

Winstone is an avid West Ham and England supporter, and during the 2006 World Cup in Portugal acted as an official fans ambassador.

WILLIAM WOODHOUSE – Scooter Consultant.
Woodhouse was a member of the Vespa Club of Great Britain, and was retained as a consultant to source Scooters and spares. The VCB160 registration on Ace Face's scooter was his homage to his beloved Scooter Club.

WORD NORTHAL – Distributors of Film in USA.
Distribution Company in the USA, who also had the responsibility of a similar role for Scum the following year.

CHRISTIAN WRANGLER – Sound Mixer.
Christians film work has included, Gumshoe and Get Carter both 1971, Pulp 1972,Bloody Kids 1980, which starred amongst others Jesse Birdsall, The Hit 1984, East is East 1997, and Two Brothers due for release in 2004. He also worked on the 1977 Franc Roddam directed TV drama, Dummy.

X/Y/Z

ROBERT ZIEGLER – Conductor for Pete Townshend's Classic Quadrophenia.
American born, a resident of the UK, Robert Ziegler has conducted both the Royal Philharmonic and BBC Concert Orchestra's on many occasions. Work has also included many forays in the film industry including Hugo in

2011, as well as Sense and Sensibility in 1995. Ziegler was an excellent choice to conduct Classic Quadrophenia having previously worked with the likes of Radiohead, and David Gilmour.

CHAPTER 2

QUADROPHENIA LOCATIONS.

QUADROPHENIA FILM LOCATIONS - Scene by Scene.

All Brighton locations can be comfortably visited within a few hours and are easily accessible from the nearby Brighton National Rail Station. Most London locations can be visited by Public Transport, however expect a long day with plenty of walking! Please also respect the fact that some locations are residential addresses, which have been included as they are widely available on the internet anyway!

* It is assumed that when the film starts with Jimmy walking into shot at Beachey Head that we look back at the previous eventful fortnight in his life. This is assumed by the evidence that is given during the film – although in various interviews it is mentioned that the film covers a period of ten days in the life of Jimmy Cooper! I have divided this section up into scene numbers that make it easier to identify that location. This is *by no means an official guide to the amount of and number of the said scenes. **

All now photographs below are from the authors collection unless they are credited otherwise

QUADROPHENIA FILM – BRIEF STORY.

The film starts with Jimmy walking away from Beachey Head, and then cuts to him riding through the streets of London on his scooter on-route to the Goldhawk Club.

At the club, he scores some pills from an acquaintance, Ferdy, before heading inside and meeting up with his pal Dave, the pair ogle longingly at Steph who is dancing with Peter Fenton.

Jimmy then heads home and borrows some scissors from his sister to add another newspaper cutting to his shrine of all things Mod on his bedroom wall.

The following day Jimmy is at the public bath, when his tranquillity is disturbed by the occupant of the bath next door singing a Gene Vincent song! Jimmy retaliates with his version of The Kinks – You Really Got Me. The pair argue, before recognising each other as old friends.

Later Jimmy and Kevin are re-united at the local pie and mash shop, much to Jimmy's disdain Kevin turns up dressed in his Rocker attire. Jimmy is shocked at first, but accepts him, until that is, some fellow Mods turn up! An embarrassed Jimmy then makes a hasty exit.

After meeting his pals at a local Pub, they all head off to gate-crash a party. Jimmy has a fumble with Monkey and is rewarded with some pills. He notices that Steph has seen this, as she dances with Pete. He breaks this up by putting My Generation on the record player. Steph and Pete leave, and the various couples pair off, however a lone Jimmy decides to have his fun in another way, he destroys the party host's front garden with his scooter.

He heads to the tranquillity of the canal to sit and contemplate in the pouring rain!

The following day Jimmy is seen at work where he is struggling to overcome a serious hangover! Later that night he is carrying out some repairs on his scooter when he is visited by Kevin, the two discuss their respective movements.

The next day he is again at work and seen playing cards with some workmates. He is later sent to deliver some photographs to an office in Town, but detours via the record shop where he looks at his delivery package and helps himself to one of the glamour photographs.

Jimmy later picks Steph up from work and gives her a lift home as the two discuss the forthcoming trip to Brighton. That evening the group are hanging out at Alfredo's café when they decide to head off to The Goldhawk Club. On-route Spider's scooter breaks down, he says to the rest of the group that he will catch them up, however as he is carrying out the repairs him and his girlfriend are attacked by some rockers. On hearing this Jimmy and co set off for some revenge and catch a couple of Rockers at Shepherds Bush Market, one gets away but the other (who turns out to be Kevin) takes a severe beating. On arriving home Jimmy enters an argument with his Dad, who accuses him of having a mental problem.

The following day Jimmy throws a sickie, and goes off in search of pills for the weekend. Following a lead from Pete, Jimmy along with Dave and Chalky buy some from a local gangster. The pills turn out to be fake, and in desperation Jimmy, Chalky and Dave rob a Chemist, which provides them with enough to keep them all happy!

The next day Jimmy and co are all up early to head to Brighton, on-route Chalky is ridden off the road by some Rockers!

On arriving in Brighton, they meet up with various friends and watch in admiration as the Ace-Face arrives on the scene. Later that night the group are all at the local dance hall, unhappy with the attention Steph is giving the Ace-Face, Jimmy decides to upstage him by jumping from the balcony into the crowd, he is duly thrown out. Jimmy ends up on the beach, as Dave and Chalky find their sleeping quarters, which happen to be inhabited by some Rockers.

The next day the group meet at a Café before heading along the promenade.

Later Jimmy and the group head along the promenade, where he is joined by a receptive Steph. Jimmy seems to be euphoric as he is with his mates as well as the girl he loves. Chalky spots some Rockers and exclaims that they were the ones that rode him off the road the previous day. The group run on-masse to confront them in a Café where they dish out a severe beating.

The Mods then retreat to the beach where a fight ensues with a group of Rockers. A massive beach fight follows, after which Jimmy escapes with Steph. Further disturbances follow in a side street whilst Jimmy disappears with Steph where they cement their union with a quickie!

Back on the side street, Jimmy is caught by the police and carted off. He is soon joined by the Ace Face in the police van. The two are held overnight to attend a special court sitting the next day.

Jimmy then returns to London and a less than warm welcome from his Mother, who has found out what he has been up to during the weekend, as well as finding his stash of pills. An even colder reception awaits him at his work place; a row ensues when he is asked why he didn't show the previous day. The argument sees the two-part company!

Jimmy then pays a visit to their local Café where he learns that Steph had now got together with his mate Dave, after a fight Jimmy drives off into the night. A row follows with his Father, before he roars off again!

The following day Jimmy returns to an empty house to pack a bag and head off, after a less than welcoming conversation with Steph he collides with a GPO van where his beloved Scooter is destroyed!

He decides to head back to the scene of his greatest adventure, Brighton. After drinking Gin and taking pills he arrives in Brighton revisiting the places that meant so much to him, including the alleyway the scene of his union with Steph.

Jimmy then spots the Ace Face's pristine scooter and believes he has found a kindred spirit, until it is revealed that he is nothing more than a bell boy at the Grand Hotel, no longer the cool and swaggering icon!

A totally dejected Jimmy steals the prized scooter and heads off to Beachey Head; he struggles to come to terms with how his life has changed in the space of a few days, and seems to contemplate suicide. However, the only death is to be that off the Ace Face's GS scooter in a symbolic rejection of his Mod ideals.

SATURDAY AM

Scene 1
Set: -Beachey Head.
Jimmy is seen walking into shot away from the cliff-edge in a disgruntled state, the camera then pans to the sun which links this and the next scene.

Location - Beachey Head Visitor Centre, Beachy Head, Sussex, BN207YA.

Nearest Station: -Eastbourne National Rail.

The pure white cliffs are some 162 metres above the English Channel below, and an iconic location that is quintessentially British! Offering the highest chalk cliffs in the country, Beachey Head is some twenty miles east of Brighton. Just to the west of Eastbourne it offers fantastic views of points of up to seventy miles away on a clear day.

Beachey Head is constantly eroding, and recedes up to one metre per year (although some six metres were lost in certain areas in 1999), which means that the precise area that was used for filming has long since disappeared into the sea! The area is left completely undeveloped to protect its landscape value, with the natural erosion of the sea helping to leave a gleaming white chalk surface. Indeed, the actual erosion meant that the Belle Toute Lighthouse (not the red and white one viewed in the film) was moved further back inland in 1999.

Beachey Head has long had a notorious reputation as a suicide spot, with many people travelling hundreds of miles to end their life there; the area is littered with floral tributes, as well as notices for people considering suicide from the Samaritans.

SCENE FROM ORIGINAL FILM.   **AS IT LOOKS TODAY.**
(LP)

FRIDAY PM

Scene 2
Set: - Opening Titles – road to The Goldhawk Club.
Jimmy is seen looking content on his way to the Goldhawk Club despite a brief act of derision by some Rockers en-*route*.
Location - King Street, Hammersmith, W6 9JH and
Lots Road, Chelsea, SW1 0RN.
Nearest Station: -Hammersmith Underground
and Fulham Broadway Underground.
King Street in Hammersmith is very near the Hammersmith Odeon and it is likely that Jimmy was riding towards the way the following picture is taken, however the exact part of this street is extremely hard to determine! Look out for the clever editing technique that sees the sun merge into the headlight of Jimmy's scooter. Also, the strategically placed London Taxi that tails Jimmy, it was used to save on the almost completely spent budget as its headlamps provide the only form of lighting! The scene was shot on the sixtieth and last day of filming. The opening titles then appear on the screen in a sickly yellow, something that Franc Roddam says is the only thing he wished he'd changed.

Lots Road is an area very near to Chelsea Football Club, the location where Jimmy is seen en-route to The Goldhawk Club has changed very little. Although filming was carried out at night it is still instantly recognisable. The pictures below show Lots Road which is only a matter of yards away from the famous Chelsea Harbour, home of many of the rich and famous including a certain female star of Quadrophenia!

SCENE FROM ORIGINAL FILM.   AS IT LOOKS TODAY. (LP)

FOLLOWING PICTURE - KING STREET HAMMERSMITH AS IT LOOKS TODAY. (LP)

Scene 3

Set: -Across the road from The Goldhawk Club (exterior)
Jimmy arrives, and after parking his Scooter does a deal for some French Blues with Ferdy.

Location - Junction of Langley Street and Shelton Street, Covent Garden, London, WC2.
Nearest Station: -Covent Garden Underground.
London Film School, 24 Shelton Street, WC2H 9UB.
Jimmy is seen approaching the Goldhawk Club along Langley Street where he passes the London International Film School, included as a personal homage by Franc Roddam as it is where he studied his craft.

SCENE FROM ORIGINAL FILM.   **AS IT LOOKS TODAY.**
(LP)

Scene 4
Set: - The Goldhawk Club (interior)
Cross Section perform 'High Heal Sneakers' followed by 'Dimples'. Jimmy takes some pills and watches Steph and Pete dancing, whilst Dave attempts to wind him up about his feelings for her.

Location - Shelton Street, Covent Garden, London, WC2.
Nearest Station: - Covent Garden Underground.
The real Goldhawk Club is obviously in Shepherds Bush, but this location is some miles away in Covent Garden, now a very trendy area, boasting a vast array of shops and restaurants, as well as the world famous former fruit market.

Eagle-eyed viewers will notice the graffiti on a pillar behind Phil Daniels which reads, Chelsea F.C. Is it a mere coincidence, or a bit of mischief by Mr Daniels maybe? Cross Section were Roger Daltrey's choice for the band having auditioned many others for the role. This followed an advert in the music press looking for prospective new and young bands who fancied their chances! The actual interior scenes were filmed here at a long since disappeared club and is now part of The Belgo Restaurant, one of the capitals largest restaurants that seats up to 420 diners. Belgo is accessed via its entrance on the parallel Earlham Street (50 Earlham Street, WC2H 9LJ). Once inside the restaurant, the pillars that are prominent in the scene are still in-situ making it much easier to recognise!

Filming for this scene was carried out the same day as the interior scenes for the Brighton Night Club, with cast and extras bussed between the two venues. Just across the road from this venue is The London Dance Centre where DJ Jeff Dexter coached members of the cast for the Dance scenes.

SCENE FROM ORIGINAL FILM.   *AS IT LOOKS TODAY*
(REVERSE ANGLE. (LP)
PICTURES OVER - SCENCE FROM ORIGINAL FILM AND AS IT LOOKS TODAY (with thanks to The Belgo Restaurant website)

Scene 5
Set: - Jimmy's Home (exterior)
Jimmy arrives home and puts his scooter away for the night in the shed.

Location - 75 Wells House Road, North Acton, London, NW10 6ED.

Nearest Station: -North Acton Underground.

The location of Jimmy's home has been a subject of much debate over the years, with Kate Williams even claiming that it was a now demolished home somewhere in South London.

However, as you will see in the picture below, 75 Wells House Road is the one! If you stand with your back to the door you will see the view of a small garage opposite, this is the same one viewed later during the row between Jimmy and his mother. The venue was further confirmed by residents. Unbelievably it looks like the actual door that Jimmy had slammed in his face is still there! The house was empty whilst filming took place, and was about to be refurbished, but in the end remained derelict for several years. *Quadrophenia* souvenir hunters would regularly break in and help themselves to anything that took their fancy. One individual was even seen leaving with the fireplace! Houses in this road are currently changing hands for more than £500,000!

SCENE FROM ORIGINAL FILM.   **AS IT LOOKS TODAY.**
(LP)

Scene 6
Set: - *Jimmy's Home (interior)*
Jimmy en-route to his sister Yvonne's bedroom briefly listens to his parents arguing. Inside Yvonne's he borrows her scissors as she sits in front of a sun lamp much to the derision of Jimmy.

Location as per scene 5.
In the novel and script there is a bit more meat put on the bones of Yvonne, but in the finished film this is sadly her only appearance.

Scene 7
Set: - *Jimmy's Bedroom*
Jimmy fixes a newspaper article to his wall and sits back to contemplate the forthcoming events in a state of contentment. 'Cut My Hair' plays in the background.

Location as per scene 5.
Franc Roddam purposely pans the camera in to display a picture of Pete Townshend over Daniels' shoulder, displaying in his opinion the likeness of the two.

SATURDAY AM / DAYTIME

Scene 8
Set: - Public Baths
Jimmy is seen soaking at the public baths when the singing of a Rocker in the next bath disturbs his peace, the singer turns out to be his old pal, Kevin Herriott.

Location - The Porchester Centre, Queensway, London, W2 5HS.
Nearest Station: -Bayswater Underground.
A visit to the public baths was a common occurrence before inside bathrooms became commonplace in houses. Jimmy meets an old pal, Kevin in this one, which is in the city of Westminster and was originally built in 1929. The building is now known as The Porchester Centre and boasts a swimming pool, spa and Turkish baths. Franc Roddam remembers Phil Daniels being more relaxed about his nudity scene than Ray Winstone.

SCENE FROM ORIGINAL FILM.   **AS IT LOOKS TODAY.**
(LP)

Scene 9
Set: - Pie and Mash Shop

Jimmy is next seen at the Pie and Mash shop where he is joined by Kevin, cutting short his meal when he is spotted talking with him by John and another Mod.

Location – A. Cookes, 48 Goldhawk Rd, London W12 8DH
Nearest Station: -Goldhawk Road Underground.
The traditional London eatery was handily placed just a few feet along from the entrance to Shepherds Bush Market. Obviously, non-period vehicles were impossible to avoid as is witnessed by a modern liveried Royal Mail van passing by as Jimmy orders his food. Although the interior had been modernised it was still easily recognisable and possible to sit in Jimmy's chair and enjoy his food of choice right up until its closure in July 2015. The site had been home to a Pie and Mash shop since 1891, with its owners at the time of closure being in situ since 1934. It was a sad day for this part of West London when it closed due to the landlords wish to redevelop, however Cookes now have an online presence and offer home-delivery. Over the years there had been many other Quadrophenia related projects filmed there such as an interview with Pete Townshend.

SCENE FROM ORIGINAL FILM.   AS IT LOOKED PRIOR TO CLOSURE (PHOTO - SHAWN LEE)

EXTERIOR VIEW JUST PRIOR TO CLOSURE IN JULY 2015 (LP)

Scene 10
Set: - Tailors.

Jimmy is next seen when he enters the Tailors to pay an instalment on his suit, Danny and fellow Mod, Lou are also there, the former being fitted for his suit.

Location - Masala Zone, 80/82 Upper Street, Islington, London, N1 0NU.

Nearest Station: -The Angel Underground.

The interior of Dave Wax's tailor shop was used when Jimmy goes to pay for his suit. It was a natural choice as they were responsible for making the new suit that Jimmy wears with such pride to Brighton, however it was made by Mitch Wax at their other shop in Hammersmith (still there today!) The filming in this location was all done in one day. The shop in Islington was demolished and re-built a few years ago, and now incorporates an Indian Restaurant and some offices so is completely unrecognisable! However, the back to front shot of the shops opposite when Jimmy enters give the game away and indeed confirm this location. The location is directly next door to the famous Screen on the Green Cinema, how many people have previously watched the film there completely unaware that filming was carried out just a few feet away?

SCENE FROM ORIGINAL FILM.   DAVE   WAX'S HAMMERSMITH SHOP AS IT LOOKS TODAY. (LP)

SCENE FROM ORIGINAL FILM.   *AS IT LOOKS TODAY. (LP)*

THE FORMER SITE OF DAVE WAX TAILORS TODAY (LP)

Scene 11

Set: -Steph's Workplace
Jimmy next visits Steph at her workplace (a supermarket), where he is informed that she hates Saturday's! Jimmy tells her about his new suit.

Location - Brewdog, 15 Goldhawk Road, London, W12 8QQ.

Nearest Station: -Goldhawk Road Underground.

Steph's workplace is now a bar/restaurant called Brewdog which opened in 2013, but was formerly Ashkens a small independent supermarket. Ashkens was used for both interior and exterior shots; however, the inside is now completely unrecognisable having taken on the persona of a lively bar that is popular with local office staff during the daytime, as well as purveyors of craft beers and ales. Eagle eyed viewers will notice Steph checking out various items that were not available in 1964, and it was here that she gives Jimmy the iconic smile that was captured so perfectly by Roddam for what was to become a widely-used shot. On the DVD directors cut Franc Roddam also remarked how much he loved the acting of the woman behind Jimmy who is attempting to get served whilst he is carrying out his chat-up line. The exterior of Brewdog is instantly recognisable and next to it there is a small dead end road, Bamborough Gardens, it is at this Junction with Goldhawk Road that Jimmy is seen waiting on his scooter for Steph at the end of her shift. The shoot was done during daylight hours, so it would appear, that the shop remained open whilst filming took place.

AS IT LOOKS TODAY (LP)

SATURDAY EVENING

Scene 12
Set: - Jimmy's Bedroom
Jimmy is getting ready for his night out to the sound of 'Zoot Suit'.

Location as per scene 5.

Scene 13
Set: - Pub Toilets
Chalky and Spider are seen for the first time, along with Dave and Jimmy. Dan informs them about a party in the Kitchener Road. Michael is seen comatose by drugs and/or drink on the floor in the corner.

Location - The Alma Public House, 499 Old York Road, Wandsworth, SW18 1TF.

Nearest Station: -Wandsworth Town National Rail.

The Alma pub was the venue used for the groups' get-together prior to heading off to the house party. The exterior wasn't used in the film, but the interior was utilised during closing hours, in what was a largely improvised scene. A regular told me that although the pub had been decorated it was much the same as it was during filming.

SCENE FROM ORIGINAL FILM.   **AS IT LOOKS TODAY.**
(PHOTO - SHAWN LEE)

Scene 14
Set: - Pub Bar
The Mods prepare to leave and Steph accepts an offer to tag along with Jimmy before Pete returns with other ideas. Jimmy leaves alone, to the ridicule of his pals.

Location as per scene 13.

AS IT LOOKS TODAY FROM THE OUTSIDE. (LP)

Scene 15
Set: - Kitchener Road Party (exterior)
The group arrive, only to be refused entrance, following which an argument ensues with the host's boyfriend, before John diplomatically does the honours.

Location - 66 Clarendon Gardens, Wembley, Middlesex, HA9 7LE.

Nearest Station: - North Wembley National Rail and Underground.

A quiet suburban residential area is the ideal location for what is supposed to be a middle-class house party. This part of Wembley is more affluent than certain other parts of the Borough, and is handily located for would-be commuters as well as closely accessible to Wembley Stadium. Clarendon Gardens is also extremely close to Fountain Studios, which had added appeal for the film makers. The location took some tracking down as there are many houses that look the same, but it can be confirmed that the above was indeed the one used in the film for all exterior shots as well as some interior. Interior filming created lighting problems in such a small place with the rest being filmed in the studio.

The party was said to have been based on many that Franc Roddam had attended in his youth, and was one that featured a few brief glimpses of future big names including; Ben Elton(?) and Peter McNamara. Roddam used both hand held cameras and ones on dollies to capture his shots on a specially created dance-floor that allowed the actors to move freely. He says that he particularly enjoyed the segment that sees Phil Daniels put his cigarette in the mouth of a wall mounted ethnic mask. It is also rumoured that Mark Wingett played his love scene for real with his on-screen girlfriend played by Katherine Rogers. Relating what happened to the author Katherine laughed and said they were very young at the time and there was a lot of Champagne flowing! Indeed, there were at least a couple of crates of Champagne as well as plenty of other Alcohol to 'help' the cast get into character! However, not all the filming in this location was to go quite so smoothly! Trevor Laird is seen in the earlier scenes being shadowed by an actress called Linda (?) with whom it was intended he would pair off with, however when the bedroom scenes were being shot the two along with Phil Davis were told they were not required and sent to the dressing rooms with some alcohol. Trevor Laird brooded in the dressing room about the fact that he had been dropped so decided to confront the Assistant Producer, John Peverall, and was told that the film was due to be released in South Africa, and a shot of a black guy with a white girl would not go down well! A row erupted involving Roddam and the film's producers, and although he fought for Laird's inclusion he was ultimately forced to reluctantly accept the decision.

SCENE FROM ORIGINAL FILM.   AS IT LOOKS TODAY.
(LP)

TREVOR LAIRD IS SEEN BRIEFLY TALKING TO LINDA (?) BEFORE BEING REMOVED FROM THE REST OF THE PARTY SCENES.

MARK WINGETT AND KATHERINE ROGERS IN A CONTINUITY PHOTOGRAPH FOR THE ABOVE SCENE.

Scene 16

Set: - Kitchener Road Party (downstairs – interior)

'Be My Baby' is playing as the group split up and look in the various rooms. Jimmy ends up in the front room and exchanges a kiss with Monkey for some French Blues with 'Rhythm of the Rain' playing on the record player. Jimmy notices Steph and Pete dancing intimately which provokes him into ruining their moment. 'My Generation' replaces the previous song on the record player thanks to Jimmy. Pete and Steph decide to leave the party.

Location - as per scene 15 and Fountain Studios (formerly Lee International Studios, 128 Wembley Park Drive, Wembley, Middlesex, HA9 8HP.
Nearest Station (studios): -Wembley Park Underground.
Some of the interior shooting was done in Clarendon Gardens, with the rest being carried out at nearby Lee Studios (now Fountain Studios). The studio is now a thriving entity with shows such as *The X Factor* being filmed there. However, it has had somewhat of an indifferent past changing hand many times since its opening in 1926 as Wembley Park Studios.

It was used as the base for Redifusion Television in the sixties when *Ready Steady Go!* was made there, later becoming the home of London Weekend Television until 1972. In 1978 the Lee Brothers purchased the building which had been empty for some years and thus Lee International Film Studios were born! Films such as *The Elephant Man* and *Yentl* were made there but in 1986 the Lee Brothers left the site to concentrate fully on their larger Shepperton Studios that had been purchased a couple of years previous.

The studios were also the base for *Quadrophenia's* production staff, with Roddam carrying out many of his screen tests and casting interviews there.

AS IT LOOKS TODAY FROM THE OUTSIDE. (LP)

Scene 17
Set: - Kitchener Road Party (exterior)

Pete pushes Michael (the drugged/drunk Mod from the pub toilets) over onto some milk bottles before heading off on his scooter with Steph. Jimmy's mood is dented as he sees them ride off into the night, he pops some pills.
Location as per scene 15.

Scene 18
Set: - Kitchener Road Party (upstairs – interior)
Jimmy returns to the party sometime later and most people have paired off with each other, Dave and John are asked what they are up to, doors are left open and general chaos ensues before Jimmy leaves the scene.

Locations as per scene 15 and Fountain Studios, Wembley Park Road, Wembley, Middlesex.
Nearest Station (studios): -Wembley Park Underground.

Scene 19
Set: - Kitchener Road Party (exterior)
Dave looks out of the bedroom window to see Jimmy on his scooter riding around the front garden destroying everything in his path. Dave shouts his support to him before Jimmy drives through the fence and almost collides with a car that turns out to be the parents of the party's host.

Location as per scene 15.

Scene 20
Set: - Canal Foot Path/ Halfpenny Steps Footbridge.
Jimmy is seen sitting in miserable contemplation at the side of the canal. He spots a couple about the same age as his parents kissing. He rides towards them screaming in an attempt to frighten them before riding off. 'I'm One' play's in the background.

Location - Canal Bridge, adjacent: - Halfpenny Steps Health Centre, 427/9 Harrow Road, London, W10 4RE.
Nearest Station: - Westbourne Park Underground.
The middle-aged couple seen kissing below the bridge were actors that Franc Roddam had used in his TV play, *Dummy*, with the female wearing the same leopard-skin coat as worn by Geraldine James. At first glimpse the female actress could be mistaken for Kate Williams who played Jimmy's mother. The best way to access this location is by tube to the above station then walk approximately 2 minutes to the Canal Bridge below the Great Western Road (which could easily be mistaken as the

bridge used!) then turn left along the canal path and walk the few hundred yards to the one used! Although a new Health Centre has been built, the area to the west of the bridge is easily recognisable by the buildings that remain.

SCENE FROM ORIGINAL FILM. *AS IT LOOKS TODAY.*
(LP)

SUNDAY
No action is seen for this day on the film, but the events of the following morning would suggest another heavy night for Jimmy.

MONDAY AM/DAYTIME

Scene 21
Set: - Jimmy's Work (interior)
Jimmy is seen at work delivering the mail to the various departments within the advertising agency.

Location - 20 Eastbourne Terrace, Paddington, W2 6LE.
Nearest Station: - Paddington National Rail and Underground.
A major refurbishment of this 18-floor office block was carried out on this and adjacent properties a couple of years ago, so both the exterior and interior now bear very little resemblance to when filming was carried out. However, the view in location 26 below remains much the same.

EXTERNAL SHOTS OF THE OFFICES TODAY (LP)

Scene 22
Set: - Jimmy's Work – Toilets
Jimmy is heard being sick in a cubicle whilst Mr Fulford and Michael discuss their latest project. They finish shaving as Jimmy lunges towards the sink, neither party acknowledge each other.

Location as per scene 21.
Many years later Phil Daniels met Benjamin Whitrow who played the part of Mr Fulford at a Golf day, the film obviously made little impact on him as he couldn't remember what it was called!

MONDAY EVENING

Scene 23
Set: - Jimmy's House (interior)

Jimmy arrives home late from work after falling asleep on the train. Burning his hands on his steaming dinner he has a brief row with his mum in the living room as she watches Television. Originally it was planned to see Jimmy asleep on the underground train but London Transport refused permission to film! Jimmy's father sleeps only to wake briefly as Jimmy slams the door. The TV show being viewed by Mr and Mrs Cooper is in fact an edition of The Avengers called, The Frighteners which was originally broadcast on 27th May 1961, and is one of only three episodes that remain from the first series. Briefly viewed are Willoughby Goddard as the Deacon and Philip Locke as Moxon.

Location as per scene 5.

AS IT LOOKS TODAY FROM THE OUTSIDE. (LP)

Scene 24
Set: - Jimmy's Garden Shed

Jimmy is carrying out a repair on his scooter when the sound of a motorbike coming down the alleyway startles him. The visitor turns out to be Kevin Herriott.

Location as per scene 5.
The shed which backs on to the railway line has long since gone.

TUESDAY
No action is suggested for this day during the film.

WEDNESDAY AM/DAYTIME

Scene 25
Set: - Jimmy's Work – Projectionist's Booth
Jimmy plays cards with Des and Harry whilst Mr Fulford and Michael view the advert along with their client for 'the people like you' film.

Location as per scene 21.
This scene involved Timothy Spall and Patrick Murray who were used for just one days filming.

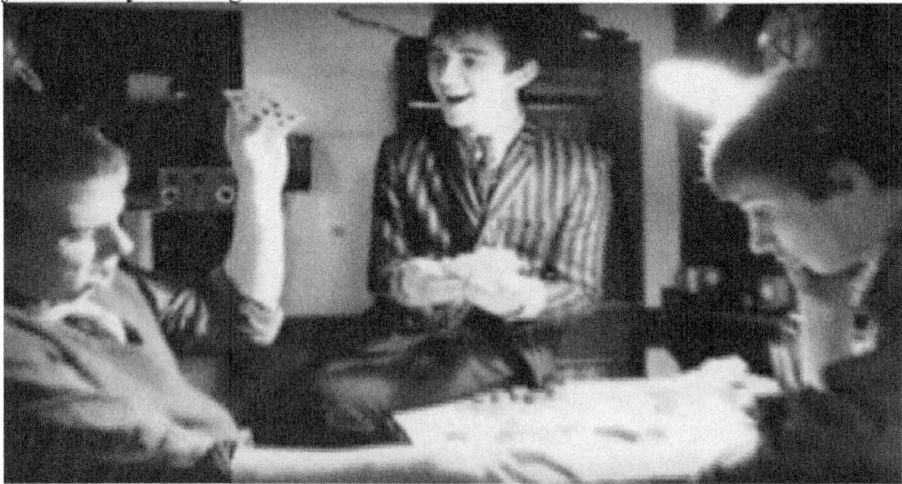

STILL FROM THE ABOVE SCENE.

Scene 26
Set: - Jimmy's Work (interior)
Jimmy collects some photographs that need to be delivered, he is told that he was an hour late and called a 'tacky Herbert'.

Location as per scene 21.

SCENE FROM ORIGINAL FILM. *AS IT LOOKS TODAY.*
(LP)

Scene 27
Set: - Record Shop (interior)
Jimmy, en-route to deliver his photographs stops off at the record shop and listens to 'Anyway, Anyhow, Anywhere' in a booth. He views the pictures whilst the youth in a GPO uniform listens to 'Wishin' and Hopin' in the booth behind him.

Location – as yet unknown.
Watch out for former EastEnders star, Carol Harrison and note the GPO boy who keeps his crash helmet on to hide his peroxide blond hair. Once inside Jimmy enters a listening booth, these mini listening rooms were a staple in most record shops at the time!

Scene 28
Set: - Steph's Workplace (exterior)
Jimmy waits outside the Supermarket where Steph works and offers her a lift home.

Location as per scene 11.

This scene concentrates on the Supermarkets exterior which is on the junction of Goldhawk Road and Bamborough Gardens.

SCENE FROM ORIGINAL FILM.   AS IT LOOKS TODAY.
(LP)

Scene 29
Set: - Road to Steph's Home – Shepherds Bush
Jimmy drops Steph home after cruising through the streets of Shepherds Bush, as they talk about the forthcoming weekend.

Location - Goldhawk Road, London, W12.

Nearest Station: -Goldhawk Road Underground.

A stroll the length of the Goldhawk Road will follow the route that sees Jimmy giving Steph a lift on his scooter from her workplace. The two are seen going past the railway bridge, and are clearly on a trailer, at this point you will notice a young cyclist, Michael Barry, who frantically tries to keep up with them on his push bike. Lesley Ash also revealed that they were being pelted with things by young passers-by as they made their merry way along the Goldhawk Road.

SCENE FROM ORIGINAL FILM.   AS IT LOOKS TODAY.
(LP)

A BREAK IN FILMING IN THE GOLDHAWK ROAD – NOTE THE PASSERS BY IN THEIR SEVENTIES ATTIRE!

WEDNESDAY EVENING

Scene 30
Set: - Alfredos Café (interior)

Jimmy, Dave, Chalky and Spider are all seen discussing the forthcoming weekend around the pinball machine before the proprietor throws them out. 'Night Train' plays in the background.

Location - Meat People Restaurant, 4-6 Essex Road, Islington, London N1 8LN.

Nearest Station: - Angel Underground.

Alfredos café was established in 1920 by the Deritis family who hailed from Italy, and the café was to remain in their hands for some eighty years! Vince Deritis was keen for his son to take over the running of the business but says that 'he wasn't cut out for the catering game', therefore Alfredos was boarded up and closed in early 2000. Islington council were none the less keen to protect the buildings original heritage and gave it grade II listing status, and in December 2002 it was open for business again. S&M (The Sausage and Mash restaurant chain) stepped in, with Director, Kevin Finch restoring it to its former glory largely as a labour of love. The Formica tables and Thoret chairs were all restored and once again became a traditional eating place (although slightly pricier than its old Alfredos days!) It has since changed hands again and is now called Meat People. The café is a must for a visit as the exterior is almost completely unchanged, although the original sign was to turn up on e-bay in early 2003, the inside also remains much the same as featured in the film. Alfredos was also used for *Mojo* the 1997 film that was set in the 1950's and heavily criticised for its constant use of the F and C word, and went on to be widely used in various photo-shoots for projects that required a 60's style café. The café was also a favourite eatery of the former associate of the Kray twins, Frankie Fraser, and became a popular place for fans of the film to pay homage to. Vince Deritis was also heavily involved with Edgware Town Football Club for many years, where the author of this book had many dealings with him, and it was here that he was happy to talk openly about the filming on many occasions. Deritis recalled that filming would take place during night time and into the early hours. The film makers would turn up make a few minor changes like installing a pinball machine and burn incense and charcoal to give it a smoky atmosphere! This would mean that the whole café needed washing down after each night. Alfredos was used for three days filming, whilst Deritis and his daughter would watch the goings on from their window in the flat above, Vince Deritis' father was also present and was none too pleased with some of the language being used! Two weeks later the film crew returned for another night's shoot, and this time left behind a packet of dummy cigarettes that Mr Deritis senior later sold in error to an unsuspecting customer. The crews return to Alfredos also saw a minor skirmish for real when some local youngsters were caught red-handed breaking in and stealing from the electrical van. Vince Deritis could not remember exactly how much he received for allowing them to use his premises, but does say that the follow-on business that it created was most welcome!

SCENE FROM ORIGINAL FILM.   AS IT LOOKED c2010 WHEN IT WAS S&M. (PHOTO - SHAWN LEE)

Scene 31

Set: - Alfredos Café (exterior)

The boys all gather outside the café before heading off to The Goldhawk on their scooters.

Location as per scene 30.

Scene 32
Set: - Road Outside The Bramley Arms Pub
As the group head towards the Goldhawk Club Spider and his girlfriend run into some engine trouble. Spider tells them that he will be along shortly and attempts to repair the problem. For the serious scooter enthusiasts Spider is riding a Spanish made LI 150 Eibar series 3 Lambretta.

Location - Junction of Bramley Road/Freston Road, W10 6ZZ. Nearest Station: - Latimer Road Underground.

The exterior of The Bramley Arms is viewed when Spider encounters problems with his scooter and is subsequently beaten up by some passing Rockers. The Bramley Arms has also featured in *The Lavender Hill Mob, Steptoe and Son* and *Sid and Nancy*, in the later the pubs name was changed to The Old Mahon and although no longer a pub is still instantly recognisable from outside. The building has since been converted into flats, with the *Quadrophenia* link still loosely in evidence as one of its residents is none other than Franc Roddams' son.

SCENE FROM ORIGINAL FILM.   *AS IT LOOKS TODAY.*
(LP)

Scene 33
Set: - The Goldhawk Club (interior)
Jimmy and Dave are seen sitting on the edge of a stage whilst various other members of the group are seen dancing to 'Da Doo Ron Ron'.

Location as per scene 4.

Scene 34

Set: - Road Outside The Bramley Arms Pub
As he attempts to repair his scooter some passing Rockers set upon Spider and his girlfriend.

Location as per scene 32.
The unforgettable scene which primarily featured Gary Shail, Tammy Jacobs, Jesse Birdsall and Gary Holton, was filmed when the pub closed although the lights are on to give it the effect that it is open! Whilst the scene was being set Shail and Holton along with his then girlfriend took hostel in the bar, the two men were big music fans (going onto work with each other) and chatted about their respective tastes as they enjoyed a few beers. Holton, went onto enjoy more than a few, and was well on the way when it came to go for a take (the first of many!), indeed it is evident in the finished film as he struggles to start his bike.

At the time of filming the area surrounding the pub was full of squats whose inhabitants had christened the area, Frestonia. The Frestonians even enforced its own rules and laws, and Roddam was required to seek their permission to film. The above location is a must for any fan of the film as it looks almost the same!

AS IT LOOKS TODAY. (LP)

GARY SHAIL AND HIS THEN GIRLFRIEND, TAMMY JACOBS IN THE ABOVE SCENE.

Scene 35
Set: - The Goldhawk Club (interior)
Chalky enters the club and lets Jimmy and Dave know of Spiders beating, they hastily leave to seek revenge.
Location as per scene 4.

Scene 36
Set: - The Goldhawk Club (exterior)
Jimmy and the group chat with Spider briefly before heading off on their scooters.
Location as per scene 4.

Scene 37
Set: - The Goldhawk Club (interior)
The action cuts to the inside of the Goldhawk where remaining members of the group continue dancing.

Location as per scene 4.
Look out for John Altman who suddenly re-appears after setting off to exact out revenge on the Rockers, in what is quite clearly a continuity error.

Scene 38

Set: - Goldhawk Road Underground Station / Shepherds Bush Market – Tea Stand.

Jimmy and his mates spot two Rockers eating at the Tea Stand and rush towards them.

Location - Goldhawk Road, Shepherds Bush, London, W12 8EG

Nearest Station: -Goldhawk Road Underground.

Shepherds Bush is thought to have been named after its common land area which was a resting place for Shepherds and their cattle. The famous market has changed little over the years and still retains its unique charm, with a mixture of traditional and ethnic food and items available. The market is featured in the scene in which Jimmy and his fellow Mods chase two unsuspecting rockers, one of whom turns out to be Jimmy's' old pal, Kevin Herriot. The market area had been deliberately hosed down prior to filming so that the camera could pick up the glare of the scooter and motorbikes lights, as its operator followed them in a converted Citroen 2cv. Ray Winstone was keen, and allowed to perform his own stunt when his bike crashed into some boxes at the side off the wall, although he later said it was probably an act of bravado that comes with youth. It is also interesting to note that Winstone's father used to run a fruit and veg stall at this market. Royston Edwards a much-used extra is amongst the group of Mods that accompany Jimmy on their plight for revenge!

SCENE FROM ORIGINAL FILM.   AS IT LOOKS TODAY.
(LP)

GOLDHAWK ROAD UNDERGROUND STATION TODAY (LP)

Scene 39
Set: - Shepherds Bush Market
In pursuit of the two Rockers Jimmy and co give a severe beating to one of them (who turns out to be Kevin Herriott) who has come off his motorbike (registration plate number VFC77 – which would no doubt be worth a nice few quid now!) Jimmy realising that the Rocker was in fact Kevin urges his pals to stop the beating before screeching off on his scooter.

Location as per scene 38.
During this segment the lighting equipment is briefly glimpsed, a retake was ordered, however as it was not as good, and the original take was used! Also, very briefly viewed is a dark-haired male in a dark uniform (almost certainly a member of the crew) who runs away from the scene, getting a little too close to the oncoming scooters!

A PRODUCTION STILL SHOWS THE CAST PREPARING FOR THE ABOVE SCENE – NOTE THE CONVERTED CITREON ON THE LEFT OF PICTURE.

Scene 40
Set: - Shepherds Bush Market
Kevin Herriott is seen in a bloodied mess among the rubbish bags and boxes in the market.

Location as per scene 38.

Scene 41
Set: - Jimmy's House – Alleyway
Jimmy is seen in a distressed state on his scooter.

Location as per scene 5.

Scene 42
Set: - Jimmy's House – Downstairs Hall/Lounge
Jimmy's entrance to the house is met with extreme rage from his Father who belts him as he attempts to walk up the stairs. Jimmy and his Father's argument continue into the lounge. It ends with a light-hearted moment between the two, when his Father blames all Jimmy's problems on his Mother's family.

Location as per scene 5.
A superb interplay between Daniels and Elphick is capped by the story of his uncle drowning in a well in his own garden, a true story having happened to a relative of Franc Roddam's.

Scene 43
Set: - Jimmy's House – Bedroom
Jimmy pleasures himself whilst looking at one of the photographs he was supposed to have delivered earlier.

Location as per scene 5.
The face used in these pictures and the commercial belonged to a Czechoslovakian model, whose scenes with Daniels in the lift sadly ended up on the cutting room floor!

STILL FROM AN UNUSED SCENE FEATURING THE CZECHOSLOVAKIAN MODEL.

THURSDAY AM/DAYTIME

Scene 44
Set: - Jimmy's House – Bedroom
Jimmy's bedside clock shows the time at 8.45am he is still fully clothed from last night. His mother enters the room in an unsympathetic manner to learn that Jimmy is feigning illness.

Location as per scene 5.

An excellent performance by Kate Williams as a wholly unsympathetic Mother!

Scene 45
Set: - Dave's Workplace – Refuse Tip
Jimmy is seen talking to Dave about their problem in obtaining some drugs for the forthcoming weekend.

Location - Abbey Road Refuse and Recycling Centre, Abbey Road, Park Royal, NW10 7TJ.
Nearest Station: - Hanger Lane Underground.
Watch out for Dave's boss called George, an actor called, Eric Kent he crops up time and time again in shows from the seventies, particularly The Sweeney. This site now bears little resemblance to the time when filming was carried out, but Eagle eyed watchers will spot the nearby Guinness factory in Park Royal (since closed) in the background. As Jimmy leaves the yard the reversing Dust-Cart appears to be a little bit too close for comfort!

SCENE FROM ORIGINAL FILM.   *AERIAL VIEW OF SITE TODAY.*

Scene 46
Set: - Pete's Workplace – Car Breakers Yard
Opposite Bramley Arms.
Jimmy is seen talking to Dave about their problem in obtaining some drugs for the forthcoming weekend.

Location - Junction of Bramley Road/Freston Road, W10.

Nearest Station: - Latimer Road Underground.

Peter Fenton's workplace is opposite The Bramley Arms, but is no longer a breakers yard, and was only in recent years swallowed up by The Chrysalis building. The building below has recently been demolished,

SCENE FROM ORIGINAL FILM.   **AS IT LOOKED 2015.**
(LP)

THURSDAY EVENING

Scene 47
Set: - Ferdy's House – Front Steps
Jimmy, Dave and Chalky arrive at Ferdy's home to purchase some drugs but are told that he is not in. 'Burnin' Fire' plays in the background.

As yet unknown location, thought to be in the area of Portobello Road, Notting Hill Gate, London, W11.

Scene 48
Set: - Pete's Local –(interior)
Peter Fenton is called to the phone, and is angry when he learns that it is Dave.

Location as yet unknown.

Scene 49
Set: -Telephone Box – (interior)
Jimmy, Dave and Chalky are crammed into a telephone box; Dave demands the details of his supplier.

Location as yet unknown.

Scene 50
Set: - Pete's Local – (interior)
The scene cuts back to Pete who reluctantly gives them the details.

Location as yet unknown.

Scene 51
Set: - Albert Bridge
Jimmy, Chalky and Dave are seen on their scooters crossing the famous bridge en-route to their rendezvous with Harry North.

Location - Chelsea/Battersea London, SW3 and SW11
Nearest Station: -Sloane Square Underground.
The film's makers used this iconic bridge for Jimmy and co.'s journey to Harry North's pub as it is lit up at night, which added to the atmosphere. Regarded, by bridge enthusiasts as the prettiest to span the Thames it was originally opened in 1873.

SCENE FROM ORIGINAL FILM.   AS IT LOOKS TODAY.
(LP)

Scene 52
Set: - Harry North's Pub (The Wellington) – (exterior)
The three lads are seen outside the pub as Jimmy readies himself to go into the pub to obtain the drugs.

Location - Wellington Service Station (Esso), Junction 513 Archway Road, Highgate, London, N6 4HX.
Nearest Station: -Highgate Underground.
The Wellington Pub was demolished in the early nineties, and is now the Esso garage which has honoured the ex-pub by using its name. The gymnasium was, for many years, used by the famous trainer, George Francis who guided such stars there as John Conteh and Frank Bruno. The site is completely unrecognisable now and is situated on the busy A1 heading north. The pub started to suffer as the main road became even busier, and as the area became more affluent the locals would drift into nearby trendier Hampstead.

Franc Roddam recalls that this shot was done around 3.00am with John Bindon enlisting the help of some of his friends from the underworld to add some realism to the scene. Look out for Bobby Ramsey the referee who was an ex-associate of The Krays, and provided security for the films leading actors!

Scene 53
Set: - Harry North's Pub (The Wellington)– (interior)
Jimmy is seen at the bar where he asks to see Harry North claiming to have been sent by Charlie Fenton (Pete's uncle). He is ushered into a boxing gymnasium at the rear of the bar.

Location as per Scene 52.
Watch out for Jimmy totally oblivious of the admiring glances of the Judy Gleeson lookalike blond actress on his left!

Scene 54
Set: - Boxing Gymnasium (The Wellington) – (interior)
Jimmy claims to be the nephew of Pete's uncle, Charlie. Harry North talks with him and easily agrees to supply him some French Blues.

Location as per Scene 52.

Jimmy is introduced to a character called, Teddy, who is played by a yet as unidentified actor who crops up in many cameo roles in seventies TV shows. Harry North, who was played by John Bindon, was shortly after involved in the murder of Johnny Darke in Putney. Darke was stabbed 9 times after which Bindon fled to Ireland. However, on his return he was acquitted of the murder with the help of his character witness a certain, Bob Hoskins!

Scene 55
Set: - Harry North's Pub (The Wellington) – (exterior)
Jimmy is seen walking towards a mk2 Jaguar with Harry North's crony, Teddy. He is handed a bag of French Blues in exchange for a £10 note. The delighted lads decide to have one for the road only to discover they have been supplied with fakes. The lads in their anger decide to wreck the Jaguar after which they speed off on their scooters as they are briefly chased by some of the people inside the Pub. Incidentally tracking down the identity of the actor who played Teddy has been fruitless, if you know his name please let the author know. Franc Roddam could not remember his name but says 'I remember thinking he was very good, and played his part well'.

Location as per Scene 52.
Always hard to watch such a beautiful car being smashed to pieces!

SCENE FROM ORIGINAL FILM.   AS IT LOOKS TODAY.
(PHOTO - SHAWN LEE)

Scene 56
Set: - Chemist Shop Front – (exterior)
The front of the Chemist shop is shown whilst a street cleaning vehicle drives past.

Location - Jays Chemist, 442 Uxbridge Road, Shepherds Bush, London W12 0NS.
Nearest Station: - Shepherds Bush Market Underground
This scene which is probably the funniest in the entire film was written by Martin Stellman. Phil Davis completely owns it, with not only the Durex's on his fingers but also the improvised part where he steals some Talcum Powder for his Mum. It was also one that Franc Roddam got the three actors involved to improvise at his home. The location is still a Chemist although not trading as R.H. Kerr anymore, however the briefly glimpsed Venables Newsagents next door is still operating under the same name.

SCENE FROM ORIGINAL FILM.   AS IT LOOKS TODAY.
(LP)

Scene 57
Set: - Chemist Shop Rear – (exterior) and (interior)
Jimmy, Dave and Chalky carry out their break in to the Chemist shop.
The lads finally locate some drugs before being disturbed by the ringing of the telephone that is attached to the alarm.

Location as per scene 56.

SCENE FROM ORIGINAL FILM LOOKING TO REAR OF CHEMIST, AND AS IT LOOKS TODAY (LP)

Scene 58
Set: - Alfredos Café – (interior)
The lads arrive at the café with Jimmy telling Monkey about the robbery, after which he soon moves his attention to Steph who asks him to give her a lift home later.

Location as per scene 30.

Scene 59
Set: - Steph's House – (exterior)
Jimmy and Steph are seen kissing after he has given her a lift home.

Location - Orchid Street, Wormholt Estate, Acton, London, W12 0SY.
Nearest Station: -Shepherds Bush Underground.
A very brief glimpse is all that's afforded of Steph's house after Jimmy has given her a lift home.

ORCHID STREET AS IT IS TODAY (LP)

FRIDAY PM / EARLY EVENING

Scene 60
Set: - Jimmy's Work – Post-room
Jimmy is virtually bouncing with anticipation of the forthcoming weekend as he sings 'You Really Got Me'. He is paid and rebuked for his sickness the day before.

Location as per scene 21.
Note the superb little vignette from Hugh Lloyd as he disappointedly awaits a reply from Jimmy when he wishes him a 'nice weekend'.

STILL FROM THE ABOVE SCENE.

Scene 61
Set: - Barber Shop – (interior)
Jimmy is seen having his hair cut and enjoys some friendly banter involving himself, Dan, and the barber.

Location - Hammersmith Station, Hammersmith & City and Circle Line, Beadon Road, London, W6 7AA.

The Barber cutting Jimmy's hair was a friend of some of the production crew, and joined them in Brighton to help with costumes and extras, but as far as I can see is not visible in any scenes! The middle Barber may well have been one of the actual staff at the shop, watch him inadvertently stare straight at the camera!

The Barber shop used was that of Alexander's, which had been at this location since 1911, however in 2013 the owners were told that due to refurbishment of the station entrances they were about to be evicted! The decision causing local uproar, the shop had been serving the community for over a century! Nicos Pavlou, and his partner Stavros Christoudolakis were therefore forced to relocate from their spiritual home, the former's father; Demetris was there at the time of filming and included the likes of Kevin Keegan amongst his clients. However, good news was to come two years later, when The Money Shop closed Alexander's moved back just 10 yards from their original home, and is now thriving again back where it belongs!

AS IT LOOKS TODAY – THE ALEXANDER BARBER SHOP ONCE OCCUPIED THE TWO NEWLY MADE ENTRANCES BELOW THE STATION SIGN. THE NEW PREMISES IS VISIBLE JUST BEHIND LAST VEHICE ON RIGHT. (LP)

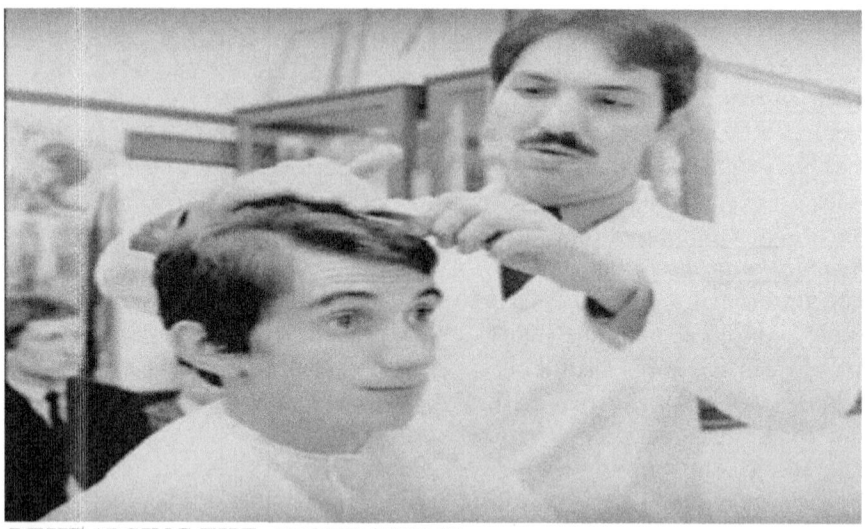

REHEARSING THE ABOVE SCENE

Scene 62
Set: - Jimmy's House – Kitchen
Jimmy is seen searching for newspapers in his wet Levis as his father reads the newspaper and his mother is busy in the kitchen. The sound of *Ready Steady Go* echoes from the living room.

Location as per scene 5.
Before pre-shrunk Jeans were readily available sitting in the bath with your new Levis like Jimmy was a common occurrence in many homes!

Scene 63
Set: - Jimmy's House – Living Room
'Anyway, Anyhow, Anywhere', is playing on the television set as Jimmy attempts to enjoy the music of The Who whilst his father criticises their musical capabilities.

Location as per scene 5.
Ironically the episode of *Ready Steady Go* that Jimmy was enjoying would have been made at the same studios in Wembley used for *Quadrophenia*!

SATURDAY AM/DAYTIME

Scene 64
Set: - Jimmy's House – Bedroom
Radio London plays in the background as Jimmy prepares for the weekend.

Location as per scene 5.
The inimitable Dave Cash sets the scene for the coming weekend in a specially recorded link.

Scene 65
Set: - Journey to Brighton
Jimmy and the fellow Mods are seen en-route to Brighton, as are a group of rival Rockers.

Location - Southlands Road/Willetts Lane, Denham, Bucks, UB9 4HE.
Nearest Station:-Denham National Rail.
(and) - TRL Test Track, Nine Mile Ride, Crowthorne, Berks, RG40 3GA.
Nearest Station: - Crowthorne National Rail.
Approximately 17 miles west of Acton, and straight down the A40 this would prove to be an ideal country-like location. At the time of filming the area surrounding it was occupied with Gypsies who demanded a rental for the area's usage. When this was not forthcoming old cars were dumped to cause havoc and many injuries, including a broken leg for Stuntman, Gareth Milne, however, two days later he was back on set! There was also a lot of damage done to Scooters, which required extensive repairs. When it was evident that the local police were on their way a consignment of helmets was quickly made available. This location is almost the same as when filming took place and well worth a visit. A very brief part of the footage for this scene was filmed at the TRL Test Track in Crowthorne, however it is completely unrecognisable and impossible to define exactly where. This site is also due to have more than 1000 homes built on it soon! It has been used previously in, The Omen, and The Sweeney.

SCENE FROM ORIGINAL FILM.   AS IT LOOKS TODAY.
(LP)

Scene 66
Set: - Road to Brighton
Chalky is seen speeding off from the main group and is caught up by some Rockers who ride him off the road. Jimmy and co finally catch up with him and after realising he is ok leave him in the lay-by. 'Get out and Stay out' plays in the background.

Location as per scene 65.
To this day, Franc Roddam and Phil Davis remain disappointed with the scene that sees Chalky crash his scooter, neither believe that stuntman, Gareth Milne was hidden well enough! Indeed, as Davis points out look out for 'the dodgy wig' that gives the game away!

Scene 67
Set: - Road to Brighton
A group of Rockers are viewed en-route to Brighton with the sea in the distant.

Location - Beachey Head Road, Beachey Head, Sussex, BN20 7YA.
Nearest Station: -Eastbourne British Rail.

As the group of Rockers ride into shot they pass a view purporting to be Brighton, it is in fact Eastbourne.

AS IT LOOKS TODAY. (LP)

Scene 68
Set: - Brighton Beach
A deckchair attendant is seen setting out chairs in readiness for the day ahead.

Location area to the west of Brighton Pier.
Another steal from Roddam who films a real deck chair attendant preparing for the day ahead in a little snippet that adds reality to the forthcoming events.

Scene 69
Set: - Road to Brighton
Jimmy and company stop to admire the distant view of Brighton.

Location - Beachey Head Road, Beachey Head, Sussex, BN20 7YA.
Nearest Station: -Eastbourne National Rail.
The iconic shot that sees Jimmy and co admiring the view, and with him stating "That is Brighton my sons" is a bit false. The actual view that they are all enjoying is of Eastbourne looking down from the Beachey Head Road. This was one of the first scenes to be filmed. The original script also called for a scene where non-scooter riding Mods arrive in large numbers at Brighton Station, but this idea was later dropped.

SCENE FROM ORIGINAL FILM.   **AS IT LOOKS TODAY.**
(LP)

Scene 70
Set: - Madeira Drive
The camera pans up and down the mass of assembled Mods and their scooters.

Location - Madeira Drive, Brighton, BN2 1TW.
This area is instantly recognisable as the meeting place of the Mods on their arrival in Brighton, which was very much the case in the sixties. The location is in front of some shops, bars and cafes in an area that is supported by concrete pillars, and still looks very much the same, apart from the fact that the paving area has been extended to the position of where the scooters had been parked. The area is also a very popular viewing point for the various London to Brighton runs that take place every few weeks in the area.

This is a scene where many extras are used following Franc Roddam's clarion call for Mods on scooters to turn up; they are all here on view! Later, in this segment look out for when Jimmy meets up with Steph, only for her to be whisked away by Pete, prompting him to say "where'd the bird go", somewhere at fierce speed by the looks of things! Wherever she went she would have been easily identifiable. Also, keep a close eye on The Ace Face's scooter as you will notice a walking cane wedged into the spare-wheel housing. This was being used by Sting as he had fallen off and had damaged his ankle! His somewhat awkward riding stance is also due to his reticence to use the clutch properly as it gave him pain, he therefore appears to be a somewhat awkward rider! Gary Shail remembers these as some of the first scenes filmed and the problem of being on set early was overcame by not actually going to bed! Unbelievably, after the local council had initially blocked filming, both Scarborough and Weston Super-Mare were considered for filming but Jimmy Swann managed to convince the people that mattered that it should be Brighton.

AN UNUSED SCENE FROM ORIGINAL FILM. AND AS IT LOOKS TODAY. (LP)

Scene 71

Set: - Madeira Drive, Brighton
A mass of excited noise accompanies the arrival of Jimmy and the group as they walk up and down admiring the mass of Scooters and Mods.

Location as per scene 70.

This is allegedly the scene where Nicholas Lyndhurst puts in an extremely brief appearance (is this him in the following picture?)

SCENE FROM ORIGINAL FILM.   **AS IT LOOKS TODAY.**
(LP)
BELOW NICHOLAS LYNDHURST IN THE ABOVE SCENE?

Scene 72
Set: - Madeira Drive, Brighton
Pete and Steph arrive, with Jimmy paying her attention just as the Ace Face and his crew arrives.
Location as per scene 70.

SCENE FROM ORIGINAL FILM.   AS IT LOOKS TODAY.
(LP)

Scene 73
Set: - Madeira Drive, Brighton
Chalky belatedly arrives to join the group much to the amusement of all those around him.
Location as per scene 70.

A BREAK IN FILMING SEES A YOUNG BOY RECEIVE AN ICE CREAM FROM HIS MOTHER BEHIND THE ACE FACE'S SCOOTER – PHOTO COURTESY OF MIKE McGARRY.

SATURDAY EVENING

Scene 74
Set: - The Brighton Ballroom (interior)

The group is seen inside the Ballroom admiring the Ace Face's dancing. Pete is busy chatting up an American girl. 'Green Onions' plays as Jimmy and Steph who are by now dancing have an argument. Jimmy is next seen attracting the ballroom's attention as he dances away to 'Louie, Louie' on the balcony high above the dance-floor prior to jumping into the baying crowd. The bouncers evict Jimmy.

Location - PureGym Health and Fitness Centre (formerly The Royalty Ballroom), Winchmore Hill Road, Southgate, N14 6AA.
Nearest Station: -Southgate Underground.

The Interior scenes for the Brighton Ballroom were filmed in the old Royalty Ballroom, which has been a fitness centre for a few years now, and is completely unrecognisable on the inside. London's Capital Radio was used to advertise for extras to appear in the scenes, which proved successful as the films makers were inundated with offers; Leslie Ash remembers these scenes with great fondness, although they were filming right up to 5 am. The production was held up for a while when Stings jacket was stolen during a break in filming, but after many frantic pleas the item turned up and allowed the filming to continue. Indeed, these sorts of events weren't uncommon, and if you look closely at the lead cast's Parka's you will notice that they had blue zip's, this was to distinguish them between those of the extras. Although, Jeff Dexter done a sterling job of whipping him and others into shape Sting was known to have struggled with the Mod dances so in these scenes he is largely shown from the waste up! Look out for the clever technique when Jimmy jumps from the balcony into the awaiting crowd, the jump was carried out by a stunt man with Phil Daniels crouched beneath them only to emerge from them as if he had carried it out himself. Closer inspection of some of the girls will show a few ill-fitting wigs! On the day of filming, 19th October 1978 the location was further utilised when a TV studio was mocked up by the Art Department to film Tim Brinton reading the News and reporting on the events in Brighton, this was either abandoned or edited out as it doesn't obviously appear on the finished print. The venue when it was still a Ballroom hosted the likes of Slade and Bill Hailey around the time of filming and became something of a Rockabilly Mecca!

SCENE FROM ORIGINAL FILM.   A SIMILAR INCIDENT AT THE ROYALTY BALLROOM OCCURRED JUST PRIOR TO FILMING - WITH THE FILM'S MAKERS NO DOUBT TAKING INSPIRATION (unknown source from internet)

THE OLD ROYALTY BALLROOM – NOW A HEALTH AND FITNESS CLUB, THE ABOVE PICTURE SHOWING IT'S EXTERIOR PRIOR TO A NAME-CHANGE (LP)

Scene 75
Set: - The Brighton Ballroom (exterior)

Jimmy heads away from the Ballroom having been thrown out, he then heads off to find a place to sleep for the night.

Location - The Sea Life Centre (formerly Brighton Aquarium), Marine Parade, Brighton, BN2 1TB.

Originally opened in 1872 the Aquarium was designed by Eugenius Birch who was also responsible for the West Pier. It was a very popular attraction in its early days with a conservatory and a roller-skating rink on its terrace above, this is where the iconic photograph of the main cast as used on the film's poster, was taken.

The ballroom sign was hung over the aquarium sign and the area still looks the same. However, it was purchased some years ago, by the Sea Life Company who have kept the traditional feel of the old aquarium inside but have replaced its much-criticised tanks with more environmentally friendly ones.

To the left of the main entrance is the previous one to the Florida Rooms, a venue that The Who played back in the sixties. Look out for Spider's mate, Paul Curbishley, who was afforded a role in the film thanks to his brother, Bill. For many years it was in fact thought that this was another brother, Alan, the former footballer and manager of West Ham United. The tunnel towards the beach now sports a mural of musicians with local connections, amongst others there is one of The Who. Pete Townshend would have walked down this tunnel to the Beach when The Who had played there and witnessed the many Mods congregated, perhaps a subconscious seed was planted in his head for what would later become, Quadrophenia!

Scene 76
Set: - The Brighton Ballroom (interior)
Steph and the Ace Face are seen dancing to 'Wah-Wahtusi'.

Location as per scene 74.

Scene 77
Set: - Brighton Beach
Jimmy is seen crouched down on the beach in a pose used for the 1997 re-release. He stares out to sea.
Location - Area to the west of Brighton Pier.

Scene 78
Set: - The Brighton Ballroom (exterior)

The Ballroom empties with the male members of the group discussing sleeping arrangements. Steph and her friend (who we learn is called Shirl) say that they are off to their Bed & Breakfast.

Location as per scene 75.

SCENE FROM ORIGINAL FILM.   **AS IT LOOKS TODAY.**
(LP)

THE TUNNEL FROM AQUARIUM TO BEACH AND MURAL AS IT LOOKS TODAY. (LP)

Scene 79
Set: - Arches Below Pier

Chalky and Dave are seen checking out potential sleeping opportunities. They finally find a fisherman's storeroom that is already inhabited. Later we learn the inhabitants are in fact a group of Rockers.

Location - Beneath Brighton Pier, Brighton Beach Front.

The old fishing storerooms beneath Brighton Pier (formerly The Palace Pier) were used as a temporary accommodation by Dave and Chalky in a hilarious scene. The actual scene was based on a real-life event that happened to some friends of Alan Fletcher who had penned this part of the script. Originally a nearby Beach-Hut was going to be used for this scene, and a minor part of it was one of the few filmed back in the Studio.

SCENE FROM ORIGINAL FILM.   AS IT LOOKS TODAY. (LP)

Scene 80
Set: - Brighton Beach
The scene cuts briefly to Jimmy as he sits solitary on the beach.

Location as per scene 77.

Scene 81
Set: - Amusement Park.
The Ace face and his group are seen riding on their scooters.

Location - Amusement Park – Esplanade off Madeira Drive, Brighton, BN2 1TW.

The Ace Face and posse are seen in the area known as Peter Pans Amusements, which is on the esplanade between Volks Railway and the Beach Café. The area has changed somewhat over the years but is still recognisable with the giveaway being its crazy golf course, which still remains.

SCENE FROM ORIGINAL FILM.   **AS IT LOOKS TODAY.**
(LP)

SUNDAY AM/DAYTIME

Scene 82
Set: - Brighton Beach
Jimmy is again seen on the beach this time walking away from the sea.

Location - Area to west of Brighton Pier.
Jimmy is viewed walking towards the Brighton Pier, and logistically would have been somewhat further along the beach with the old West Pier behind him. Watch out for Daniels' unexpected trip as he tries to dodge an incoming wave. Also, Roddam was lucky enough to unexpectedly capture an incoming fishing boat that comes into shot bathed in the glorious morning sun that really adds to the scene. It was planned to use a lot more of The Pier during filming, but the local council vetoed the idea!

SCENE FROM ORIGINAL FILM.   **_AS IT LOOKS TODAY._**
_(LP)_

Scene 83
Set: - Arches Below Pier

Chalky and Dave awake to discover that they have been sharing their sleeping quarters with a group of Rockers.

Location as per scene 79.

Scene 84
Set: - Beach Café (interior)

Jimmy sits alone until he is joined by the rest of the group who turn up with tales of the previous night's exploits.

Location - Brighton Beach Front. (East of Pier).

The Beach Café was until 2013 still of the same name, and situated just a few feet east of Brighton Pier. The Café which had been redecorated and had new windows was still recognisable, and you can't help thinking that the owners may have missed a trick by not making more of the fact that it was used in the film with maybe a few pictures, or a film poster!

The café was run for many years by George and Betty Wells who were always willing to talk to visitors about the film and happily directed them to Jimmy's chair!

During filming the café became so popular that the cast shunned the recognised catering facilities, so much so, that it eventually took over as the films official caterers. The café owners became firm favourites with the cast and crew, and indeed there was a famous incident when George's Mum, Maureen told Mark Wingett to get his feet off the seat, Franc Roddam liked the little un-planned event so much that he persuaded her to recreate it in the actual film!

Many years later there was uproar when George Wells announced his plans to redecorate the café, with locals demanding that it remain in its original state, which it did until he sold it to the next owners. When the new owners finally redecorated the café Jimmy's chair was saved by local tourist guide, Glenda Clarke, who now has her prized possession at her home. The Beach Café was yet another must visit location in Brighton, although after George and Betty left you would not expect to be served the finest cuisine or indeed receive a particularly friendly welcome! The Café closed and was replaced by a Mediterranean Restaurant and Shisha Bar in 2013, later to be replaced by a Sea-Food restaurant, this had various problems with the local Health and Hygiene Department, and was soon after available to lease (see scene 145 for latest picture!)

SCENE FROM ORIGINAL FILM.   **_AS IT LOOKED SHORTLY BEFORE CLOSURE (LP)_**

Scene 85
Set: - Grand Junction Road

A Group of sea cadets are seen marching to the sound of their band as the hordes of Mods begin to gather.

Location - Grand Junction Road, Brighton (Grosvenor Casino, 9. Grand Junction Road, BN1 1PP).
The area to the west of Brighton Pier and in front of East Street is viewed when a group of air cadets march by. This was another stolen moment for Roddam, as they just suddenly appeared adding to the realism of the whole scene when the Mods gather around the cinema entrance, which is now a Casino. As you can see from the picture below the Cinema was at the time showing, Heaven Can Wait which was of course released in 1978 and not 1964, also showing at the time were Convoy, The Silent Partner and Grease! The cinema had originally opened in 1938 and closed to become a casino in 2000. The building was sometimes known as 'The White Whale' due to its white tiled and glazed façade! It suffered from declining business due to the more modern facilities available just up the road at The Odeon Cinema in West Street, which was even used for the Premier of the re-release in 1997.

SCENE FROM ORIGINAL FILM.   **AS IT LOOKS TODAY.**
(LP)

Scene 86

Set: - Brighton Promenade
The group are seen marching along the Promenade, where they are joined by Steph as a newspaper photographer photographs them. Spider leads the chant of 'we are the Mods'.

Location - Brighton Promenade - Madeira Drive leading into Grand Junction Road.
The action starts just west of the Peter Pan's Volks Railway, where Jimmy is reunited with Steph. It then continues as Spider leads the chants of "we are the Mods" which was totally improvised and a press photographer scurries for a photograph, at this point Brighton Pier is clearly visible behind them. However, by the time the photographer gets in front of them to click away, the group are back a couple of hundred yards further down the road with the pier in front of them, only for it to suddenly appear behind them again. The way this scene was edited only eagle eyed viewers will notice the seamless join in action.

SCENE FROM ORIGINAL FILM. FROM ABOVE. (LP) **AS IT LOOKS TODAY**

Scene 87

Set: - Brighton Promenade
As the group march along the action cuts to a Rocker and his passenger as they pass by on their motorbike.

Location - Brighton Promenade, Grand Junction Road opposite Queens Hotel.

Scene 88
Set: - Brighton Promenade
The action cuts back to Chalky who recognises that the passing Rocker was the one who had forced him off the road the previous day.

Location - Brighton Promenade, Grand Junction Road Opposite East Street.

Scene 89
Set: - East Street Café (exterior/interior)
The Rocker and his passenger are seen pulling up on their motorbike and entering the café.

Location - Queens Hotel Corner East Street and Brighton Sea Front, 1-3 Kings Road, BN1 1PP.

The Café in which Chalky spots the Rockers that had ridden him off the road was at the time a separate building, which was part of Forte's Café Chain and surrounded by the Queens Hotel. The café has long since disappeared and has been swallowed up by the Queens Hotel complex, so is now unrecognisable from the outside. There is a Fish and Chip shop that laid claims to being the café used in the film for many years, this being just up the road on the corner of Ship Road, this is not the case! This chippie has been established for over 45 years, and was indeed frequented on occasions by some of the cast. However, it was never actually used for any filming. The café was being patronised by some Rockers when Chalky and co rush in and met out their revenge, with a Rocker extra making a laughable attempt to hold them at bay with the door. Once inside the Mods cause havoc with the main window being put through by Spiders friend, and Jimmy nearly catching the café owner for real with a flying plate, he did however catch some other flying debris and a small cut on his left cheek is just visible. The chaos that ensued was so real that Director of Photography, Brian Tufano ended up losing a tooth!

Following the conclusion of the East Street riot the exterior is viewed again in a memorable scene that catches many extras unaware, as unbeknown to them Franc Roddam had told the cameraman to keep rolling!

SCENE FROM ORIGINAL FILM.   **AS IT LOOKS TODAY.**
(LP)

BELOW ROCKER EXTRA'S RESTING ON THE ROOF OF THE CAFÉ AT TIME OF FILMING.

Scene 90
Set: - Grand Junction Road leading into East Street, Brighton.

The action cuts back to Chalky and the group as they charge towards a confrontation with the Rockers in the café.
Location as per 89.

Scene 91
Set: - East Street Café (exterior/interior)
The Mods are seen charging towards the café and a battle with the outnumbered small group of Rockers.

Location as per scene 89.

SCENE FROM ORIGINAL FILM AND PHOTO OF ROCKER EXTRAS DURING FILMING (COURTESY OF TOM INGRAM – PICTURED FAR RIGHT) NB NOTE PHIL DAVIS EXTREME LEFT.

Scene 92
Set: - Marine Parade/ Madeira Drive
A Rocker is seen running from the group only to be stopped and beaten by Pete.

Location as per scene 70.
In a scene re-enacted from the original riots in 1964 Pete and co force a Rocker (played by stuntman – Colin Skeaping) over the wall onto a steep concrete slope that leads between the two. This is the area above the meeting place of the Mods at the start of their time in Brighton.

SCENE FROM ORIGINAL FILM.   **AS IT LOOKS TODAY.**
(LP)

Scene 93
Set: - East Street Café (interior)
The Café owner is seen on the phone to the police as he shields himself with a tray whilst his premises are being wrecked.

Location as per scene 89.

A PROMOTIONAL PICTURE INSIDE THE CAFÉ FEATURING FRANC RODDAM BEHIND THE COUNTER.

Scene 94
Set: - Brighton Esplanade
Pete and Dave are seen pushing a Rocker over the side towards the beach below.

Location as per scene 92.

Scene 95
Set: - East Street Café (interior/exterior)
The Mods are seen running out of the café and congratulating themselves on their efforts. A police van screeches into shot forcing the group to run towards the beach.

Location as per scene 89.

Scene 96
Set: - Promenade Slope to Beach, Grand Junction Road
The mob is seen running from the café across Grand Junction Road down the slope onto the Beach.

Location as per above.
The slope now has a control barrier at the top but is otherwise the same.

AN UNUSED SCENE FROM THE ORIGINAL FILM FEATURING STING AND EXTRAS INCLUDING ROYSTON EDWARDS ON UNION JACK SCOOTER AND AS IT LOOKS TODAY(LP)

Scene 97
Set: - Brighton Beach
In the prelude to the full-scale riot the Mods are seen goading the Police after knocking a woman out of her deck chair.

Location - Area to west of Brighton Pier.

The location of the main riot scenes involved a lot of choreography. Franc Roddam was unhappy with the first take as he felt that the extra's acting as Policemen were not taking it seriously. Roddam told the Mods to really go for it in the next take, in what was a superb scene. John Altman volunteered to take part in a fight that saw him end up falling into the sea. Look out for the female stuntwoman in a yellow coat who is knocked from her deck chair, and the many members of public watching from the promenade above, an added-bonus for the reality of the scene. Toyah is also seen to be extremely hacked off when she is shoved during a scene in a moment of realism.

The deck chairs that were made into weapons were made from balsa wood, with others being cut with saws to allow them to break easier, and the pebbles that were used as missiles were in fact potatoes. Note the constant change in the footwear of Lesley Ash, understandably she had trouble running in her stilettos so they were substituted for hush puppies. Lesley Ash describes these scenes as 'frightening and realistic', as her and Phil Daniels were required to be at the very front of the charging mob, indeed both were flanked by a couple of bodyguards just in case any extras got a bit too carried away! Indeed, some of this scene was so intense it had Leslie Ash in tears! Toyah also vouches for its realism saying 'we were punching shit out of each other 110%', although Leslie Ash in fact pulled out of a planned fight with one of the female Rockers, Linda Regan. Franc Roddam was very happy with the footage shot on the beach, helped by the kind weather at the time. When he shouted 'cut' he would also tell the cast to rebuild the scenery on their way back to their starting positions. There were understandably several injuries incurred during these scenes, including an extra that needed several stitches in his back after being bitten by a Police dog. These scenes as well as various others required re-dubbing due to poor sound quality whilst filming. Also, note the Rocker with a Motorhead T-shirt, the band were not formed until 1975!

SCENE FROM ORIGINAL FILM AND AS IT LOOKS TODAY VIEWED FROM BRIGHTON PIER (LP)

Scene 98
Set: - Marine Parade
The Police van is viewed en-route to the Beach area.

Location - Marine Parade heading east – junction of Manchester Street.
There is now a large Harry Ramsden's Restaurant, in this area and with the vehicle heading east it is moving away from the trouble! The picture below shows Harry Ramsden's Restaurant, the police van would have had this on its left-hand side heading easterly just past Manchester Street.

SCENE FROM ORIGINAL FILM   AS IT LOOKS TODAY
FROM BRIGHTON PIER (LP)

Scene 99
Set: - Area around Brighton Aquarium
The Mods are seen en-route to the beach. Pete obtains a large flowerpot that is dispatched through the window of a fortune-teller almost hitting its occupant.

Location as per scene 75.
The group are seen running down the steps from Marine Parade towards the Aquarium, there were many promotional pictures taken around this area, some of which appear on the special features section of the DVD. There is a tunnel that leads towards the beach between the Aquarium and fortune teller's premises which is still there and leads out to left of The Beach Café. The fortune teller's premises are still instantly recognisable, although it has changed use many times. The scene in which Pete smashes the fortune teller's premises proved to be somewhat too close for comfort. The lady who played the Palmist was told to keep an eye out for somebody in a red jacket, but missed him and very nearly copped a plant pot in the face.
This area is must on a visit as it is still very much the same as when filming took place.

AS IT LOOKS TODAY. (LP)

Scene 100
Set: - Brighton Beach
The group assembles on the beach almost out of breath relating their stories of beatings that have been inflicted upon Rockers.

Location as per scene 97.

Scene 101
Set: - Promenade Grand Junction Road
A group of Rockers are seen running towards the beach to confront the awaiting Mods.

Location - Promenade Grand Junction Road opposite The Queens Hotel.

Scene 102
Set: - Brighton Beach
The action is fast and furious as a full-scale battle between the Mods and Rockers commence – chaos reigns supreme!

Location as per scene 97.

Scene 103
Set: -West Street
A collection of Police vehicles screech into shot – sirens ringing out their imminent arrival.

Location - West Street leading to Seafront – Phoenix Buildings, 32 West Street, Brighton, BN12RT.
An area of Brighton that was used very little, the Police vehicle passes the 1930 built Phoenix Building heading towards the seafront.

SCENE FROM ORIGINAL FILM.   AS IT LOOKS TODAY.
(LP)

Scene 104
Set: -Brighton Beach
The action cuts back to the Beach area.

Location as per scene 97.

Scene 105
Set: - Brighton Beach Toilets (exterior)
The Ace Face is seen inflicting a beating on two Policemen with the remnants of a broken deckchair.

Location- Toilets/Paved area of Beach to west of Brighton Pier.
The scene where the Ace Face beats up some Policemen is still the same as when filming took place.

SCENE FROM ORIGINAL FILM. AS IT LOOKS TODAY.
(LP)

Scene 106
Set: - Brighton Beach
Masses of Mods are seen running from the police along the promenade towards East Street.

Location - Brighton Beach /Promenade Grand Junction Road leading to East Street.

Scene 107
Set: - East Street
The Mods are seen running up along East Street, only to have their exit blocked by Police.

Location - East Street, Brighton, Sussex, BN1 1NF.
The scene of the running riot that sees Jimmy and the Ace Face eventually arrested. The road is now one way, and whilst still easily recognisable has very few of its original shops still in place. Probably one of the last to remain would be the Wimpy Bar that is spotted and only closed in 2004. The ABC cinema that is spotted had been empty for several years with a nightclub finally opening there in October 2007. There is also an entrance to the building on the seafront which shows posters advertising, The Guns of Navaronne, Grease and Heaven Can Wait during the action.

SCENE FROM ORIGINAL FILM.   **AS IT LOOKS TODAY.**
(LP)

Scene 108
Set: - East Street
The Mods are seen penned in at the other end of East Street as they begin their chanting The Ace Face appears to be bored and throws a wooden box through a shop window.

Location as per scene 107.
The Ace Face is seen smashing a shop window with a wooden crate, which required two takes, and was originally planned to be done with a fibreglass Spastics Society collection box. A rethink meant that a wooden crate was used instead so as not to cause offence to anybody.

Scene 109
Set: East Street / Alleyway
Jimmy and Steph break off from the main group and head up an alleyway into the back entrance of a Chinese restaurant.

Location – Alley off Little East Street (Quadrophenia Alley).

Probably the most visited of all Brighton locations the alleyway is a small passage between East Street and Little East Street, and is still instantly recognisable from the film. It has become something of a shrine for visiting Quadrophenia fans and Mods, and is adorned with various samples of graffiti that are regularly painted over. In 2002 during one of the Quadrophenia tours a committed fan of the film used this venue as the place to propose to his girlfriend! The actual door to the stairwell that was the scene of Jimmy and Steph's brief love scene has been painted over various times, and was at the time of filming the rear entrance to Choy's Chinese Restaurant. The premises were taken over in 2006 by Momma Cherries Soul Food Restaurant who had outgrown their previous nearby premises thanks in no small part to their participation of one of Gordon Ramsay's television shows. However, it is now once again a Chinese Restaurant!

The actual scene was rumoured to have been played for real, something that was denied by all involved! The confines of the location meant that the Director and Cameraman were suspended in precarious positions above the actors on balanced ropes and riggings. Leslie Ash was known to have been extremely nervous about the scene, with her then boyfriend, Peter Buckland who was 15 years her senior phoning her the night before the shoot pleading with her not to go through with it! Indeed, the original script was a lot more graphic. The actual day arrived and she was too nervous and not ready to do the scene so a few precious hours were lost, not a great day for Roddam who rounded it all off by being whacked by a camera! The alleyway, which is even called Quadrophenia alleyway by the local tourist board is probably the most iconic location in the whole film, with a visit an absolute must!

THE ENTRANCE TO 'QUADROPHENIA' ALLEY AS VIEWED FROM EAST STREET (LP)

A GREAT SHOT OF FRANC RODDAM PREPARING FOR THE ABOVE SCENE – AND AS IT IS NOW (LP)

Scene 110
Set: - East Street
The Mods are seen fighting with the Police outside of the Wimpy Bar.

Location as per scene 107.

Scene 111
Set: - East Street / Alleyway
Steph pulls Jimmy towards her as they begin to make love, oblivious of the chaos just a few yards away.

Location as per scene 107.

Scene 112
Set: - East Street
The Ace Face pulls a Policeman from his horse and is joined by other Mods in kicking him to the floor.

Location as per scene 107.

Scene 113
Set: - East Street / Alleyway

Jimmy and Steph are seen in the throes of their lovemaking.

Location as per scene 109.

Scene 114
Set: - East Street
The fighting continues in East Street.

Location as per scene 107.
Scene 115
Set: - East Street / Alleyway
The scene cuts back to Jimmy and Steph.

Location as per scene 109.

Scene 116
Set: - East Street
The fighting continues in East Street.

Location as per scene 107.

Scene 117
Set: - East Street / Alleyway
The scene cuts back to Jimmy and Steph.

Location as per scene 109.

Scene 118
Set: - East Street
The fighting continues in East Street with more mounted Policemen having joined their colleagues.

Location - as per scene 107.

A BREAK IN FILMING (EAST STREET) – EXTRAS RELAXING! NOTE GARRY COOPER EXTREME LEFT – PHOTO COURTESY OF TOM INGRAM.

Scene 119
Set: - East Street / Alleyway
Jimmy and Steph finish their lovemaking and head down the alleyway and back onto East Street.

Location as per scene 109.

Scene 120
Set: - East Street
As Jimmy and Steph return to the now quieter East Street he is grabbed by the Police who throw him into a waiting Black Mariah. Dave grabs Steph and leads her to safety.

Location as per scene 107.

Scene 121
Set: - Police Van (interior)
Jimmy is seen in the back of the van in the company of some Rockers, and is shoved by one of them as he falls towards him when the van breaks.

Location - almost certainly no longer in existence.

Scene 122
Set: - Brills Lane
As the police van breaks to a halt The Ace face is seen being thrown into the back of it.

Location - Brills Lane, Brighton, BN1 1PN.
A small connecting road between East Street and Grand Junction Road, the suggested route of the Police van, would have been virtually impossible, so some editorial licence was employed. Tom Ingram who plays a Rocker is offered a cigarette from the Ace Face's case only to have it closed sharply on his finger. A cut finger ensued that Ingram still talks about today!

THE ACE FACE IS THROWN INTO THE POLICE VAN.

SCENE FROM ORIGINAL FILM.   **AS IT LOOKS TODAY.**
(LP)

Scene 123
Set: - Police Van (interior)
Jimmy is seen taking a cigarette with The Ace Face.

Location - almost certainly no longer in existence.
Look out for Kevin Lawton (Ginger) the reluctant Rocker who does not want to look at the camera, a widely-seen Mod extra that was reluctantly re-cast for this scene with a slight financial persuasion!

Scene 124
Set: - East Street
The remaining group of Mods are viewed some of whom are contained by Police Officers.

Location - as per scene 107.
Franc Roddam left the camera rolling with most the cast unaware, however the astute Trevor H. Laird 'clocked it' and throws in a delightful slight shrug of the shoulders that absolutely steals this impromptu scene!
Indeed, in the Directors commentary, Roddam comments 'He's thinking that because he's the dealer and the only black person, as far as he's concerned the others are just a bunch of cunts'.

IN A SCENE FROM THE ORIGINAL FILM TREVOR H. LAIRD IS THE ONLY ONE AWARE THAT THE CAMERAS ARE STILL ROLLING.

Scene 125
Set: - East Street/ Castle Square, Brighton.
The Police van is seen en route to the Police Station.

Location – East Street junction with Caste Square.
As the Police vehicle heads from the top end of East Street the Brighton Pavilion is just visible behind. The Regent Arcade entrance is also identifiable.

AN INTERESTING PICTURE SHOWS PRODUCTION STAFF LOOKING TOWARDS THE TOP END OF EAST STREET.

Scene 126
Set: - Road Leading out of Brighton
The remaining Mods are seen heading out of Brighton on their scooters with Steph having by now joined Dave. Dave's passenger on the way down was his girlfriend played by Katherine Rogers but is now nowhere to be seen!

Location - as per scene 69.

SCENE NOT ACTUALLY SEEN IN THE FILM WITH MONKEY RIDING AS CHALKY'S PASSENGER AS THEY HEAD AWAY FROM BRIGHTON.

MONDAY AM

Scene 127
Set: - Magistrates Court (interior)
Jimmy and the Ace Face are seen amongst a packed courtroom full of other survivors of the weekend. The Ace Face is handed out a stiff fine and brings the courtroom to its knees with laughter when he offers to pay it by cheque.

Location - Lewes Crown Court, High Street, Lewes, BN7 1YB.
Nearest Station: Lewes National Rail.
The original choice for the Magistrates Court was in Hastings, but after it was visited it was thought to be too modern! Lewes at the time of filming did not actually have a Magistrates Court, so the Crown Court was utilised and thought to be more in keeping with the period! Now all its duties are carried out in Brighton.
It was during this scene that the Magistrate used the famous "Sawdust Caesar" speech. This was virtually a carbon copy of the one used by Dr George Simpson who was chairman of the Magistrates in Margate during troubles back in 1964. Dr. Simpson's address in full is as follows, *"It is not likely that the air of this town has ever been polluted by the hordes of hooligans, male and female, such as we have seen this weekend and of whom you are an example. These long-haired, mentally unstable, petty little hoodlums, these Sawdust Caesar's who can only find courage like rats, in hunting in packs, came to Margate with the avowed intent of*

interfering with the life and property of its inhabitants. It will, perhaps, discourage you and others of your kidney who are infected with this vicious virus that you will go to Prison for three months."

The original script called for a lot more dialogue from Phil Daniels. The scene sees Sting deliver his one true line of the film, when he offers to pay his fine by cheque there and then! This was in fact another line that was based on what a young Mod had said in court at the actual time of his similar punishment.

TUESDAY AM

Scene 128
Set: - Jimmy's House / Downstairs Hallway (interior)
Jimmy is seen arriving home only to be greeted by his extremely irate mother who throws him out.

Location as per scene 5.
In a hastily rehearsed and largely improvised scene, both Kate Williams and Phil Daniels deliver a stunning performance, even more remarkable when you learn that the two had just met! Kate Williams had only been recruited the day before following an audition alongside Michael Elphick; she replaced the sacked Amanda Barrie at short notice, and even had to wear her costumes!

SCENE FROM ORIGINAL FILM.   THE VIEW FROM HOUSE AS IT LOOKS TODAY. (LP)

Scene 129
Set: - Jimmy's Back garden / Shed
Jimmy is seen in an agitated state as he parks his Scooter in the Garden Shed.

Location as per scene 5.

WEDNESDAY AM

Scene 130
Set: - Jimmy's Work / Mr Fulford's Office (interior)
Jimmy is seen facing the music from his boss after returning late to work. After listening for a while Jimmy tells him what he can do with his job.

Location as per scene 21.
In the famous scene where Jimmy tells his boss what to do with his job Phil Daniels believes that Benjamin Whitrow was genuinely shocked and took it personally! Certainly, there is a genuine look of disbelief as he reels back into his chair following Daniels' outburst. Many years later the two actors played golf together, with Whitrow asking "what was that bloody terrible film we did together?"

WEDNESDAY EVENING

Scene 131
Set: - Alfredo's Café (interior)
Jimmy is seen at the café where he realises that Steph is now with Dave, he buys a bag of pills from Ferdy, and informs them of his resignation.

Location as per scene 30.

Scene 132
Set: Alfredo's Café (exterior)
Jimmy has a pop at Steph and Dave, and after a snide remark from his ex-pal head-butts him. A fight ensues before being broken up by Ferdy and Chalky, Jimmy then roars off on his scooter.

Location - as per scene 30.
Mr Deritis senior, the proprietor of Alfredos was known to be less than enamoured with the language used during this scene! With the Property

closed and falling into disrepair, thankfully Kieran McAleer had the foresight to contact the owners and rescue the signage. Kieran's actions no doubt saved these iconic signs from the builder's skip! And he is pictured below with them.

AS IT LOOKS TODAY. (LP)   KIERAN MCALEER WITH THE RESCUED ALFREDO'S SIGNAGE.

<u>Scene 133</u>
<u>**Outside Jimmy's House / Exterior and Road**</u>
Jimmy is seen on his scooter before banging on the door and shouting abuse at his father. His father tries to chase him up the road as he roars off on his scooter.

<u>Location - as per scene 5.</u>
Another largely improvised scene in which Phil Daniels endears himself with his screen dad by calling him an 'old spunker'.

SCENE FROM ORIGINAL FILM.   ROAD AS IT LOOKS TODAY. (LP)

Scene 134
Set: - Canal Toe Path
Jimmy is seen in a distressed state as he sits on his Scooter in the pouring rain.

Location - as per scene 20.

AS IT LOOKS TODAY (VIEWED FROM THE BRIDGE LOOKING WEST) (LP)

THURSDAY AM

Scene 135
Set: - Jimmy's Back garden / Shed
Jimmy's father is seen leaving for work by the back door. Jimmy then leaves the shed where he has spent the evening and enters the house via the same door.

Location - as per scene 5.
In the original script, Jimmy, would not sleep in his shed but alongside a Tramp in an old warehouse.

Scene 136
Set: - Jimmy's Bedroom
Jimmy collects some clothing from his bedroom and in a fit of anger rips the various posters and newspaper articles from his wall.

Location - as per scene 5.

Scene 137
Set: - Steph's Road
Jimmy is seen waiting somewhere near Steph's house where he confronts her as she is on her way to work. The pair argue and Jimmy ends up kicking his scooter.

Location - Orchid Street, Wormholt Estate, Acton, London W12 0SY.
Nearest Station: -Shepherds Bush Underground.
The scene of Jimmy's attempt to rekindle his affair with Steph sees him firmly rebuffed; however promotional pictures from these scenes see them in a lot friendlier guise, smiling at each other! This location is still very recognisable and just a short distance from the Goldhawk Road.

SCENE FROM ORIGINAL FILM.　　　**AS IT LOOKS TODAY.**
(LP)

Scene 138
Set: - Roads Around White City

Jimmy is seen in a distressed state as he collides with a GPO van. He argues with the two Postmen before abandoning his scooter.

Location - Gravesend Road, Wormholt Estate, Acton, London W12 and Sawley Road, Wormholt Estate, Acton, London W12.
Nearest Station: -Shepherds Bush Underground.

Jimmy is seen riding down Gravesend Road to the junction with Sawley Road, just a short distance from his meeting with Steph when he collides with a GPO van. This scene sees Daniels at his brilliant best, as most of it was totally improvised "All you fuckin' Mr Postmen" etc. The GPO van driver was a stuntman, who looked genuinely shocked at the way Daniels went for him! Also, look out for a middle-aged man in blue overalls who was passing by and got an unexpected role in the film, as he thought the accident was for real! The locations are still very much the same with the scooters final resting place almost identical. This is one of the films iconic scenes and belongs 100% to the genius of Phil Daniels.

SCENE FROM ORIGINAL FILM.　　　　　**AS IT LOOKS TODAY.**
(LP)

SCENE FROM ORIGINAL FILM.　　　　**AS IT LOOKS TODAY.**
(LP)

Scene 139
Set: - Paddington Station / Platform 1 (interior)
Jimmy is seen to the side of a weighing machine where he takes some pills and swishes them down with some Gin. '5.15' plays in the background.

Location - Paddington Station Praed Street, London, W2 1HQ.
Paddington station was used for filming but would (in reality) have been little use for a journey to Brighton, as it serves the west-country and Wales. Victoria is the actual London station that serves Brighton. Paddington Station has a National Rail service heading west of London and is also served by various London Underground lines.

SCENE FROM ORIGINAL FILM.　　　　**AS IT LOOKS TODAY.**
(LP)

Scene 140
Set: - Train Toilet
Jimmy is seen looking in the mirror as he puts on some eyeliner; he is disturbed by a lady who is given a dirty look before forcing his way past her and two men standing outside. '5.15' plays in the background.

Location - almost certainly no longer in existence.
Franc Roddam said that for these scenes they simply turned up at the Station and boarded a train to Brighton, and that no permission to film was ever sought! Apparently, the type of Train used was not actually around in 1964!

Scene 141
Set: - Train Carriageway
Two schoolgirls watch Jimmy as he opens the window to throw his travel bag out. Jimmy walks along the carriageway where he notices none other than his ex–boss, Mr. Fulford in one of the first-class compartments. '5.15' plays in the background.

Location - almost certainly no longer in existence.

PHIL DANIELS AND CAROLINE EMBLING DURING A BREAK FROM FILMING ABOARD THE TRAIN.

Scene 142
Set: - First-Class Compartment
Jimmy is seen entering one of the first-class compartments, he slumps between two city gents who are obviously not amused. Jimmy is heavily under the influence of drugs. '5.15' plays in the background.

Location - almost certainly no longer in existence.
Look out for the city gent with the handlebar moustache it's the same actor from the original 1973 album booklet. A fact that was confirmed to the author by Ethan Russell, who took the original photographs.

SCENE FROM ORIGINAL ALBUM   ORIGINAL SCENE FROM FILM

Scene 143
Set: - Railway Tracks
The scene cuts to a view of the railway tracks. '5.15' plays in the background.

Location - unknown (somewhere between London and Brighton!)

Scene 144
Set: - Brighton Beach
The scene cuts to a view of the sea off Brighton Beach. '5.15' plays in the background.

Location - Area to east of Brighton Pier.

AS IT LOOKS TODAY. (LP)

FRIDAY AM/DAYTIME

Scene 145
Set: - Brighton Beach Café (interior)
Jimmy is seen smoking and taking some pills as he looks out towards Brighton Beach.

Location as per scene 84.

SCENE FROM ORIGINAL FILM.   **AS IT LOOKED PRIOR**
TO IT'S CLOSURE (LP)

AS IT LOOKS TODAY. (LP)

Scene 146
Set: -Brighton Beach
The scene cuts to a swimmer in the sea off Brighton Beach.

Location - Area to west of Brighton Pier.
Peter Brayham the stunt arranger is viewed in an orange and white swimming cap in the bracing sea (protected slightly by grease and oil) to the west of the pier.

Scene 147
Set: - Brighton Beach
Jimmy is seen crouching on the beach in a contemplative mood as the sea foams in to dampen his Parka in what is a highly poignant scene. 'Love Reign O'er Me' plays in the background.

Location - Area to west of Brighton Pier.
Clever use of The Who's 'Love Reign O'er Me' is used in this scene. The view of Daniels crouched on the shingle looking out to sea has been a much-used picture over the years.

ORIGINAL SCENE FROM FILM   AS IT LOOKS TODAY
VIEWED FROM THE SLOPE ON TO BEACH (LP)

Scene 148
Set: - Brighton Esplanade
Jimmy is seen walking along Brighton Promenade and briefly looks at some elderly and disabled people.

Location - Opposite Queens Hotel, Brighton Esplanade.
The same deck chair attendant as seen earlier is viewed, as well as some disabled people who get an unplanned part in the film.

AS IT LOOKS TODAY LOOKING FROM QUEENS HOTEL. (LP)

Scene 149
Set: - East Street Alleyway
Jimmy visits the scene of his and Steph's union, before leaving he kicks the door.

Location - as per scene 109.

SCENE FROM ORIGINAL FILM.   **AS IT LOOKS TODAY.**
(LP)

Scene 150
Set: - Brighton Grand Hotel (exterior)
Jimmy is delighted to see The Ace Face's scooter to the side of the hotel. His joy is short-lived as he views his former hero acting as a junior porter; he rushes towards the entrance of the hotel. 'BellBoy' plays in the background.

Location - Kings Road, Brighton, Sussex, BN1 2FW.
The Grand is a five-star hotel with spectacular sea views and was originally built in 1864; however, a major rebuild was required in 1984 following an IRA bomb. The bomb was directed towards the Conservative Government who were in Brighton for their annual conference, with the 201-room hotel not being re-opened until 1986. It was rumoured that some senior members of the production staff stayed there during filming, and in 1997 a post film party was held in its downstairs club to celebrate the film's re-release. A truly iconic location in Brighton, and well worth treating yourself to a stay there!

AS IT LOOKS TODAY. (LP)

Scene 151
Set: - Brighton Grand Hotel – Entrance and Foyer (interior)
The Ace Face is seen carrying some suitcases into the foyer towards the lift. Jimmy rushes towards the doorway where he shouts out 'BellBoy'. 'BellBoy' plays in the background.

Location - as per scene 150.

Scene 152
Set: - Brighton Grand Hotel (exterior)
Jimmy runs towards The Ace Face's scooter, which he manages to start, and speeds off. 'BellBoy' plays in the background.

Location - as per scene 150.

SCENE FROM ORIGINAL FILM.   *AS IT LOOKS TODAY.*
(LP)

Scene 153
Set: - Road to Beachey Head Cliffs
Jimmy is seen leaving the road towards the cliffs on his stolen scooter.

Location - as per scene 1.

Scene 154
Set: - Beachey Head Cliff-Tops
Jimmy is seen riding the scooter along the cliff-top before turning and revving it up in a final ride towards the edge. 'Love Reign O'er Me' is heard playing loudly during this scene.

Location - as per scene 1.
The filming at Beachey Head was done on the first of sixty days shooting, which Phil Daniels believed was useful as it gave him a firm idea in which direction his character was heading. Daniels along with stuntman, Gareth Milne where used for the filming of this sequence, with the former being warned by Ray Corbett not to get so close to the edge of the cliffs, Daniels said he was touched by his concern, but was quickly told that he was more concerned about the problem of having to re-cast him!
The finished shoot is the subject to a couple of the film's most famous continuity errors, with the evidence of tyre marks along the cliff top from previous takes, something that today would have been easy to have removed by computer trickery in the editing stage. Also, watch for the fly screen on the Vespa appearing then disappearing!
The close-ups of Daniels on the scooter were achieved with him being strapped on to a scooter fitted to the rear of a specially converted Citroen 2cv, Daniels face in these shots is absolutely, priceless!
The overhead shots for these scenes were achieved using a helicopter, which proved to be quite an event apparently, the Pilot had a somewhat warped sense of humour and relished in perching the craft on the edge of the cliff whilst rocking it back and forth!
The scene in which the Vespa is sent heading over the cliff was cleverly calculated with a specially built ramp so that they would know exactly where it would land, however, somebody had got their calculations wrong and the trajectory of the scooters flight was such that it hurtled through the air just a few feet away from the hovering helicopter, with amongst others Franc Roddam on board! Roddam says that his original idea was to see Jimmy going over the cliff with the scooter, but he changed his mind (perhaps a sequel was in somebody's mind!)

STUNTMAN GARETH MILNE DOUBLES FOR PHIL DANIELS DURING THE PENULTIMATE CLIMACTIC SCENE.

Scene 155
Set: - Beachey Head Cliff-Bottom
The Ace Face's scooter is seen spinning through the air before smashing on to the rocks below before the closing credits appear on the screen. 'Dr Jimmy' plays.

Location - as per scene 1.
As the Vespa hits the bottom and smash into a thousand pieces the end-credits begin, Roger Daltrey screams 'You stop Dancing' in what is a fitting finale to the film!

SCRIPT DEVIATIONS.
As is known the script was not used as a definitive document with plenty of improvisation and bits added and removed along the way. Some notable changes are as follows: -
1. Jimmy's original name was Jimmy Haines, but changed late on to Cooper by Franc Roddam as homage to a character in his 1975 documentary, Mini.
2. In scene 23 Jimmy is asked why he is late by his Mother and says that he fell asleep on the train and woke up in 'bloody Neasden'.

This was going to be used as a scene but London Transport refused to sanction the filming!
3. After scene 44 when Jimmy throws a 'sickie' he was originally going to be seen having breakfast in Alfredos.
4. In or around scene 45, Jimmy was originally going to be quizzed by Dave as to why he disappeared at the time of Kevin's beating.
5. As is known Franc Roddam was originally planning to send Jimmy over the cliff with the Vespa. The film would have ended with a shot of Jimmy's bedroom wall and a close-up of a newspaper heading which reads 'MOD DEATH DIVE'.

QUADROPHENIA ALBUM LOCATIONS

LONDON LOCATIONS

The House on Front Cover

Shaftesbury Park Estate, (enter via Grayshott Road), Battersea, SW11.

Nearest Station: -Clapham Junction National Rail.

No exact location for this is known, but it is thought to be somewhere in the above area!

The House with Overturned Car.

1-3 Wycliffe Road, Battersea, SW11 5QR.

Nearest Station: -Clapham Junction National Rail.

The houses featured on pages 17 -20 have changed from 'ugly ducklings' to 'beautiful swans' in what is now a very desirable place to live! (the following picture shows it in July 2106 – LP)

Queenstown Road/ Battersea Power Station.

116 Queenstown Road, Battersea, SW8 3RZ.

Nearest Station: -Queenstown Road (Battersea) National Rail.

The above address is probably the best in which to replicate the scene on page 6 of the brochure which sees Jimmy riding down Queenstown Road with the iconic Battersea Power Station behind him. The Battersea Power Station is undergoing a major renovation, so at the time of the photograph below only one of the four chimneys had been replaced. (Pictured below in July 2016 - LP)

Hammersmith Odeon

Now, Eventim Apollo, Off Fulham Palace Road, Hammersmith, W6.

Nearest Station: -Hammersmith Underground.

The iconic building pictured in the album booklet pages 23/24 (apart from the signage) still looks the same. In the original picture the members of The Who are pictured leaving the venue as Jimmy looks on. (the following picture is from July 2016 LP)

Greenwich Foot Tunnel.

(Northern Entrance) Island Gardens, Ferry Street, Isle of Dogs, E14.

Nearest Station:-Island Gardens Docklands Light Railway.

As featured on page 10 of the brochure the Greenwich Foot Tunnel crosses beneath the River Thames. The Tunnel links the Isle of Dogs in East London to Greenwich on the South of the River. Originally opened in 1902, it was built to make commuting from Greenwich to the old East London Dockyards easier for its employees. The iconic Tunnel has featured in many films and TV shows over the years, and as it is classified as a public highway is open 24 hours a day! (Pictured over in July 2014 – LP)

Recording Studios

(Formerly Ramport Studios) 115 Thessally Road, Battersea, SW8 4EJ.

Nearest Station: -Battersea National Rail.

The Who paid £15,000 for the old St. Andrews church hall, which was one of the few remaining buildings that remained after severe bomb damage in the area. The studio was surrounded by the newly built Patmore estate, with its inhabitants having to get used to the constant noise and drunken escapades that surrounded the making of the album in 1973. The building is now a Doctors surgery. (Pictured below July 2016 –LP)

Waterloo Station.

Waterloo Rd, London SE1 8SW.

The entrance to Waterloo Station is pictured on page 27 as Jimmy heads off to Brighton. (Pictured below July 2016 –LP)

BRIGHTON LOCATIONS

Palace Pier

Now Brighton Pier, Brighton Seafront, Brighton, West Sussex.

Nearest Station: -Brighton National Rail.

Long since renamed Brighton Pier the iconic Pier was recently purchased by a Pizza Restaurant magnate. (Pictured over 2016 – LP)

West Pier

Derelict Structure, Brighton Seafront, Brighton, West Sussex.

Nearest Station: - Brighton National Rail.

The picture below shows all that remains of The West Pier, having long since been demolished by fire. (LP)

The Grand Hotel

Kings Road, Brighton, Sussex, BN1 2FW.

Nearest Station: -Brighton National Rail.

As per 150 of Movie Location Section.

MISC LOCATIONS.

1996/7 QUADROPHENIA TOUR.

Dudley Hotel, Lansdown Place, Hove, BN3 1HQ.

Nearest Station: -Brighton National Rail.

The above hotel was used as the Ace Face's place of work in the backdrop for the Quadrophenia tour. The Grand Hotel refused permission so, The Dudley Hotel in Hove was utilised. Sadly, the hotel faced some hard times and after a name change was finally closed in 2013 after 150 years of business with plans to turn the building into private apartments. The picture below shows the building when still known by its original name.

CHAPTER 3.

QUADROPHENIA – THE MUSIC

Below all the songs are detailed, I hesitate to call it a review as I have always found it very subjective as to what one person likes, and another doesn't! I personally love every song from the Quadrophenia cannon, admittedly, though, some more than others! The original 1973 album versions, and those of the soundtrack are treated as one of the same, as the latter is usually a remix or a direct reworking of the original. John Entwistle was the man responsible for remixing the soundtrack version, Roger Daltrey was known to be less than happy with some of the original versions as he thought his vocals sometimes got lost! In Entwistle's reworking's Daltrey's voice is certainly more to the fore as is his own Bass work, some of which were completely re-recorded!

<u>Original Album – reached number 2 in charts</u>
<u>Album – TRACK 2657 013 – (originally released 16th November 1973)</u>
<u>Double Play Cassette – TRACK 3526 001</u>
<u>8 Track Cassette – TRACK 3876101</u>
<u>CD – POLYDOR 531 971 – 2 (1996)/ DIRECTORS CUT –POLYDOR 2777841 -2 (2011)</u>
<u>all the following tracks are performed by The Who unless otherwise stated*</u>

Play list:

1.	I am The Sea	2.09
2.	The Real Me	3.21
3.	Quadrophenia	6.13
4.	Cut My Hair	3.44
5.	The Punk and The Godfather	5.11
6.	I'm One	2.38
7.	The Dirty Jobs	4.30
8.	Helpless Dancer	2.34
9.	Is it in my Head?	3.44
10.	I've Had Enough	6.15
11.	5:15	5.01
12.	Sea and Sand	5.02
13.	Drowned	5.27
14.	Bell Boy	4.55
15.	Doctor Jimmy	8.36
16.	The Rock	6.37
17.	Love Reign O'er Me	5.58

NB; on 8track cassette tracks 11 and 15 are separated into parts 1 and 2 respectively.

I AM THE SEA

Plays at the very start of the film as Jimmy Cooper walks into shot from the cliff edge at Beachey Head contemplating his recent adventures. The song represents the four themes of the members of The Who, and links together brief snippets of, Helpless Dancer (Roger Daltrey's theme), Is It Me (from Doctor Jimmy) – (John Entwistle's theme), Bell Boy (Keith Moon's theme), and Love Reign O'er Me (Pete Townshend's theme).

The sound of the sea's crashing waves onto the shores is the back-fall to a line from each of the above songs. The sound effects that were used for this song were recorded in Cornwall, and fit in perfectly with the four themes, which has a very special knack of teasing you into anticipation of what is about to come.
It links delightfully with The Real Me, which steps from it shadow, before literally exploding onto the screen!

I am the Sea is the perfect piece of music to introduce you into the world of Quadrophenia.

Other versions: -

Classic Quadrophenia: - If anybody has any doubts that Quadrophenia doesn't lend itself to an orchestrated version they only need to listen to this opening track. Robert Ziegler conducts the Royal Philharmonic Orchestra in a superb rendition of the opener, which although remaining faithful to the original, gives a broader interpretation of Townshend's piece, which you would indeed expect with a full orchestra!

THE REAL ME

If I am the Sea introduces you to Quadrophenia, then it is surely The Real Me that drags you into the film, in what is a particularly strong number. This track is quite simply the perfect one for this particular part of the film, it is played as Jimmy rides his scooter towards the local Mod hangout, The Goldhawk Club, and sets the scene for the forthcoming events. When you hear The Real Me, you just know that you are going to enjoy the film.

The vocals of Daltrey and Moon's sublime drumming (for which he was unbelievably criticised by some!) are the two strong features of the track.

The original 1973 version features Daltrey ending the song with an echoed version of the song's title, however this doesn't appear on the 1979 reworked version, which was produced by John Entwistle and is the better of the two.

The song was released as a single in Japan, America (reaching just number 92 in the charts!) France and Belgium and was covered in an interesting way by Fastball on the covers album, Substitute

The NME at the time said 'it has a sound that's simultaneously and uncompromisingly violent as a boot disintegrating a plate glass window at 4am, and as smooth as a night flight by 747'. The Real Me, is and will remain forever one of The Who's many gems!

Other versions: -

Classic Quadrophenia: - Alfie Boe makes a game effort on this, and with such a voice its always going to be a great version. However, this is primarily a rock song, and Daltrey's vocals do this song more justice than the former. Personally, I found Boe's live performance better than his recorded version!

Directors Cut/Demos: - When Townshend made the Demos available on the Directors Cut in 2011 it was always going to be interesting to see how these songs began their life. Townshend's vocals on this version make this a very good take on what was to become a great song!

QUADROPHENIA
An instrumental offering from the 1973 album that failed to make it onto the 1979 soundtrack. A very cleverly produced piece of music that appears very briefly during the film. A synthesised section is heard when Kevin is seen lying battered after his beating in Shepherds Bush market. A further section of this track can then be heard as Jimmy sits on the beach looking out to sea during his adventures in Brighton.
Other versions: -
Classic Quadrophenia: - If you were unaware of the original album you may have been fooled in to believing that this version came first! An amazingly well put together piece does the song that gave both the album and film its name justice!
Directors Cut/Demos: - *(Four Overtures)* To call this track a Demo almost feels like you are doing it a disservice! Townshend played all the instruments before Keith Moon and John Entwistle replaced their parts – Stunning!!

CUT MY HAIR
Roger Daltrey said that he felt that some of the problems with the original album were that some of its tracks were too explanatory.
This may, therefore, be the reason that this track is only heard very briefly during the film. It is heard whilst Jimmy returns to his bedroom after a visit to the Goldhawk club near the very start of the film.
Cut My Hair is a song that describes Jimmy's relationship with his parents and both sides respective problems in understanding the other.
It also features John Curle reading a news report at the end of the track which relates to the trouble between Mods and Rockers during the troubles at Brighton. Although it is an interesting addition to the song it works equally well without its inclusion.
Other versions: -
Classic Quadrophenia: - The sheer power of Boe's voice means that Billy Idol is virtually unheard on the recording in what is a particularly strong number from the former!

Directors Cut/Demos: - A great version, and really interesting to hear the song in perhaps its rarest form!

THE PUNK AND THE GODFATHER
Only briefly used at the end of the film, this track sees Daltrey and Townshend share the vocals in what is an interesting if not classic song. The song also makes it onto the soundtrack album, and although not one of the albums gems is still well worth a listen, with the lyrics being of particular interest and definitely worth reading!
Other versions: -
Classic Quadrophenia: - Boe shares a two hander with Pete Townshend, who both combine with the London Oriana Choir to deliver a stunning version.
Directors Cut/Demos: - (Punk) Awesome version which again goes to show how good Townshend's Demos were, great to hear his work on the Bass guitar shining through, which was remodelled in the recorded version.

I'M ONE
One of the real gems from both the album and film, in which Townshend takes the lead vocals. The track is used to great effect when Jimmy sits on his scooter in the pouring rain at the side of the canal. Jimmy had just returned from the party in the Kitchener Road where he had failed to win the affections of Steph, and is seen in a state of miserable contemplation. It is one of them songs that The Who simply get it 'right' on, Drums, Bass, Vocals etc. combine to make I'm One a real treat for all. Of the two versions, i.e. the original and the soundtrack, the latter is the better as Entwistle has re-mixed it to enhance Townshend's vocals which are somewhat echoed and distant in the former. Roger Daltrey who gives way to Townshend for the vocals particularly enjoyed it saying that it said a lot about the way he was feeling at the age of 17 back in London.
Other versions: -
Classic Quadrophenia: - A song that will be forever identified by Townshend's understated vocals was always going to be hard to improve upon. Alfie Boe doesn't try to better the original and gives an interesting take on one of the original albums classics.
Directors Cut/Demos: - The Demo version sees Townshend employ a different vocal tone to the finished track. In his notes, Townshend reveals that this is one of his favourite songs that he gets to sing on his own.

THE DIRTY JOB'S
A rarely heard or performed song that is worth dipping into occasionally! It is a song that was not used on the film soundtrack as it was describing

the 'dirty job' that Jimmy had as a dustman in the original story. Chris Stainton is heard on the piano as Townshend hadn't quite yet perfected his playing! Although this song tends to be one of the albums forgotten tracks it has an interesting if bizarre ending when a rioting Mod gang are heard prior to circus music. In the original 1973 version, there is a mysterious bit of squawking that does not appear on any other versions, this being some recorded footage of a debate in Speakers Corner, Hyde Park which was used to replicate striking miners!
Other versions: -
Classic Quadrophenia: - A song that features The London Oriana Choir, Alfie Boe and the cockney vocals of Phil Daniels shouldn't work, should it? However, it does, very well, in what is a most enjoyable version!
Directors Cut/Demos: - A great version in its embryonic state, which reminds me very much of the version that Simon Townshend put across on Quadrophenia live shows.

HELPLESS DANCER
The first of the four themes to be heard on the album, this one being Roger's. The full version is only heard on the original album with a much briefer rendition heard on the soundtrack release. The track does, however, have the honour of closing the film, as it links into the final credits. Although very briefly used in the movie it is a measure of the strength of this fairly short number that it makes a very big impact at the film's close.
Other versions: -
Classic Quadrophenia: - Much more of a two-hander between Boe and Daniels, in what is another justification in bringing Classic Quadrophenia into being!
Directors Cut/Demos: - *(Russian Dance)* Pete's vocals were added late on in the Demo process, (actually at Ramport Studios) not long before it was re-recorded. This is a song that cries out for Daltrey's vocals!

IS IT IN MY HEAD?
This track is preceded by a brief snippet from 'The Kids are Alright' and 'Doctor Jimmy', and is the first of two tracks that Glyn Johns assisted on the production, the other being 'Love Reign O'er Me'.
Although this track is not included on the soundtrack, its first line is used at the end of the film, and also when Jimmy is carted off in a police van following his arrest in Brighton. This track is one that is typical of Townshend's masterful writing, and stands the test of time very well. This track was originally going to be part of the abandoned project, Long Live Rock – Rock is Dead!

Other versions: -
Classic Quadrophenia: - Boe delivers masterful vocals in a real gem from this particular album.
Directors Cut/Demos: - A delightful softer set of vocals make this a great version, also notable for the fact that it was the first to feature Townshend making use of the Grand-Piano.

I'VE HAD ENOUGH
This track, which is one of the longest on the original album is also one of its best. Townshend and Daltrey share the vocals in what is a very descriptive song. The former has used this track to describe Jimmy's love of style as well as his ultimate questioning of the Mod ethic, and throws in a little bit of 'Love Reign O'er Me' for good measure. The soundtrack version is slightly different as it features Daltrey blasting 'You stop Dancing' at its end. The pure strength of this song meant that Entwistle had a minimal amount of re-mixing to do for the soundtrack, for what is quite simply one of the highlights of both albums and the film.
Other versions: -
Classic Quadrophenia: - Alfie Boe is joined by Billy Idol who plays the part of Ace Face on this track. A real marriage of two different genres works to produce a worthy version.
Directors Cut/Demos: - Townshend goes for a slightly maniacal vocal interpretation in the songs original outing, which is also notable for great use of the synthesizer and banjo. The demo also sports an interesting alternative ending.

5.15
One of The Who's most popular songs at their live gig's. A song that is still as strong as the day it was written, it is strange to note that this 'classic' enjoyed little success in the charts, reaching number 20 in the UK. The length of the track meant that it was not favoured by DJ's wishing to fill their rigid three minute slots.
Both tracks i.e. the 1973 version and also that of the soundtrack are absolute gems, with the former preceded by the noise of a train door slamming and a station announcer. The original version, although the rawer of the two is probably the better. The booklet that accompanies the 1973 album shows Jimmy mk1 in exactly the same scene as Jimmy mk2 some six years later. Unbelievably the moustached city gent to Jimmy's right is the same in both versions, and even appears to have the same tie! This actor therefore has the honour of being the only actor to have

appeared in both versions. A mere coincidence? it is more likely that this artist is well known to somebody close to the group that worked on both.

5.15, delightfully describes one of the most poignantly acted scenes of the whole film, and is right up amongst the bands top hits.
Other versions: -
Classic Quadrophenia: - This much-loved track from the album and film was always going to be a hard act to follow. However, Boe and the London Oriana Choir do it justice in an interesting interpretation of the original.

SEA AND SAND
Daltrey and Townshend again share vocals on a track that is not used in the film version. This track samples not only I've Had Enough, and Helpless Dancer, from the album, but also uses a line from the early hit by The High Numbers Aka The Who, I'm The Face. A decent track all in all with Moon's drumming very evident in the background.
Other versions: -
Classic Quadrophenia: - In a shortened version Boe is once again joined by Billy Idol who takes the vocals of the Ace Face.
Directors Cut/Demos: - A great raw version of another Quadrophenia gem that originally appeared (minus drums) on Pete Townshend's Scoop 3 in 2001.

DROWNED
Chris Stainton is again present on the piano, which he plays with great gusto! A song, which Townshend says is a song about God's love, represented as the ocean made up of drops of water, and represented by every one of us! Another song that failed to make it into the film version. Check out the *30 years of maximum R'n'B* DVD for an excellent live version.
Other versions: -
Classic Quadrophenia: - Alfie Boe is joined by Pete Townshend in a good version of the original. The live version at the Royal Albert Hall was one of its highlights with Townshend's guitar playing impeccable!
Directors Cut/Demos: - Awesome guitar work by Townshend on a song that was conceived three years before Quadrophenia was recorded!

BELL BOY
The second of the themes to appear on the album, this being unmistakably that of Keith Moon. The song tells the story of Jimmy's return to Brighton, when he sees his Mod ideals dashed upon learning that the 'Ace

face' is a bell boy! Within the lyrics for some reason the year of the Brighton troubles are described as 1963!
Roger Daltrey says that Bell Boy is one of his favourites from the album as it brought back so many fond memories of Keith Moon, and that it had so much of his spirit in it!

Keith Moon, obviously steals the song with his superb drumming and comical singing. The song features the classic opening line, A beach is a place………. etc., - absolutely superb!
Both the original and soundtrack versions are absolute gems, with the latter being probably the tighter of the two. The Who and Moon in particular are at their absolute looniest and absolute best in this classic. You are highly recommended to watch the live version of this song which appears on 30 years of maximum R'n'B DVD.

Other versions: -

Classic Quadrophenia: - Great work by Boe, but it is Billy Idol's work as the Bell Boy that makes this such a great version. Hopefully Keith Moon would have approved!

Directors Cut/Demos: - Of course, this song is so identifiable with Keith Moon that it always seems strange hearing anybody else perform it. Indeed, Townshend actually sings it! He later mused that it if Roger Daltrey had sung it would have sounded 'frightening'. Again, interesting to hear the song in its earliest form.

DOCTOR JIMMY

This track, which includes John's theme – Is It Me? plays over the closing credits, and lasts a mammoth eight minutes and thirty-six seconds. Entwistle heavily edited and re-mixed this for the soundtrack version, both versions, however, are excellent but the earlier is probably the better of the two.
Roger Daltrey talked about the track during the films promotion as 'probably the most aggressive track on the album, about the two sides of a drunken man, the drunk and the sober!'
A real diamond within the Quadrophenia box of jewels. Some stunning lyrics can be found from the hand of Mr. Townshend. In the NME review from the release period it was described 'as an obituary for the Mods by the band who did most to define their attitude'

Other versions: -

Classic Quadrophenia: - If somebody told you that one day Alfie Boe would sing the 'F' word accompanied by the Royal Philharmonic Orchestra, you would probably say they were mad! Boe gives an outstanding performance in a great tribute to the original.

Directors Cut/Demos: - Definitely a Daltrey song, however Townshend does not do it an injustice with his vocals. In his Directors Cut notes he says that he felt that one day he would be made to apologise for the lyrics, and says, 'I do so here. Now.'

THE ROCK
The second and final instrumental track on the album features a mixture of various album tracks, and runs for over six minutes. This track has the unmistakable Quadrophenia sound, and has a melodic and soothing rhythm throughout.
Other versions: -
Classic Quadrophenia: - Robert Ziegler conducts the Royal Philharmonic Orchestra superbly in this fine version!
Directors Cut/Demos: - (*Finale*) Hard to believe that this was a Demo, showcases what an absolute genius Townshend is! Stunning!

LOVE REIGN O'ER ME
The 1973 album ends with one of Townshend's undoubted masterpieces, which is the last of the four themes, this being Pete's.
A firm favourite of fans of the group, and the film, and one that is always accepted gratefully at live performances. Indeed, it was part of the four-song set that the group played during the iconic Live Aid Concert at Wembley Stadium, in July 1985.
There is very little left to say about the song other than its lyrics, music, singing, playing and production are as close to perfection as is possible, and that unbelievably it only reached number 76 in the American charts!
Other versions: -
Classic Quadrophenia: - If there is one song on the album that needs to be nailed, then this is the one! Probably the albums most famous track does in fact lend itself very much to a classical version, and Alfie Boe delivers a stunning rendition which was even better live!
Directors Cut/Demos: - A song that Pete Townshend says came about due to a pre-adolescent crush on Shirley Bassey, and was originally destined for the abandoned project, Long Live Rock – Rock is Dead. A great version, however, this really is a song that was tailor made for Daltrey!

QUADROPHENIA – music from the soundtrack of The Who film (various artists)
Album – POLYDOR 2625 037 – (originally released September 1979)

Cassette – POLYDOR 3577 352 – (originally released September 1979)
CD – POLYDOR 543 691-2 – (released 2000)

MUSIC FROM THE SOUNDTRACK OF THE WHO FILM **QUADROPHENIA**

Playlist:
1.	I Am The Sea	2.03	
2.	The Real Me	3.28	
3.	I'm One	2.40	
4.	5.15	4.50	
5.	Love Reign O'er Me	5.11	
6.	Bell Boy	4.55	
7.	I've Had Enough	6.11	
8.	Helpless Dancer	0.22	
9.	Doctor Jimmy	7.31	
10.	Zoot Suit	2.00	The High Numbers
11.	High Heel Sneakers	2.46	Cross Section
12.	Get Out And Stay Out	2.26	
13.	Four Faces	3.20	
14.	Joker James	3.13	
15.	The Punk and The Godfather	5.21	
16.	Night Train	3.38	James Brown
17.	Louie, Louie	2.41	The Kingsmen
18.	Green Onions	2.46	Booker T and The MG'S

19.	Rhythm of The Rain	2.28	The Cascades
20.	He's So Fine	1.52	The Chiffons
21.	Be My Baby	2.30	The Ronettes
22.	Da Doo Ron Ron	2.09	The Crystals
23.*	I'm The Face	2.29	The High Numbers*

(track 23 only appeared on the c.d. version)

THE WHO – songs from QUADROPHENIA. Original Soundtrack
CD – POLYDOR 519 999-2   - (released 1993)

Playlist:

1.	I'm The Face	2.31	The High Numbers
2.	Zoot Suit	2.00	The High Numbers
3.	I Am The Sea	2.03	
4.	The Real Me	3.30	
5.	I'm One	2.40	
6.	5.15	4.51	
7.	Love Reign O'er Me	5.11	
8.	Bell Boy	4.57	
9.	I've Had Enough	6.12	
10.	Helpless Dancer	0.23	
11.	Doctor Jimmy	7.32	
12.	Get Out and Stay Out	2.28	

13.   Four Faces   3.21
14.   Joker James   3.14
15.   The Punk and The Godfather   5.28

ZOOT SUIT – (The High Numbers)
The only single from The High Numbers *Aka* The Who was put together by the then bands manager, Pete Meaden. This track describes exactly what was expected of any self-respecting Mod of the day. The track is heard when Jimmy prepares himself to party on a Saturday night in his bedroom.

HI HEEL SNEEKERS – (Cross Section)
A song that is performed by the excellent Cross Section at the Goldhawk Club when Jimmy first meets the other members of the gang. This song has been covered in the past by many performers including, Elvis Presley, Paul Weller and John Lee Hooker. This version is right up there with all of them, and is performed by a group who could have and should have enjoyed much more success.

GET OUT AND STAY OUT
A song that was specially re-written for the soundtrack, and although worthy of its place within that framework, generally tends to be one of the less favoured from the album. The track is the first to feature Kenney Jones on drums, and if nothing else this track is a vehicle to show how talented he was in that direction.
Directors Cut/Demos: - *(Fill No 1)* In this form the above song did not make the original album, and was planned as nothing more than a short interlude.

FOUR FACES
Another of the new songs that was recorded for the soundtrack. This track is basically an explanation of the mental state of Quadrophenia. It is also interesting to note that it was in fact Keith Moon's drumming that is heard and not that of Kenney Jones, apparently, John Entwistle overlaid Moon's drumming on to the re-worked track, he also added some extra bass and strings.   Townshend takes the vocals on this track which is quite 'Tommyesque', in a song that all in all is fairly decent.
Directors Cut/Demos: - *(Quadrophonic)* A great version that for me is even better than the finished item!

JOKER JAMES
Kenney Jones appears again in place of Keith Moon, with Roger Daltrey at the time claiming this made them a lot tighter, as he felt Jones played with more conviction and energy. The track is quite similar to some of their music from the sixties, although not in the classic sense. Joker James is a strange choice for the soundtrack album as it doesn't appear anywhere on the film.
Directors Cut/Demos: - Pete Townshend revealed that this song began as a Poem in the late 60's. The Demo is an interesting version, however Daltrey's 'attacking' vocals seem to suit this song better.

NIGHT TRAIN – (James Brown)
The Godfather of Soul can be heard belting out this classic number from the jukebox during a scene in Alfredo's café. A much-covered song by such people as Georgie Fame, this, though really is the only version worth listening to. Night Train fits perfectly and extremely authentically within the film.

LOUIE LOUIE – (The Kingsmen)
The Kingsmen cover this track which was written in 1955 by Richard Berry. It was a song that caused controversy in its time as it was adjudged to include pornographic lyrics, but was actually written about a barman called Louie who told Berry about his plans to move to Jamaica in search of true love. Louie Louie, has been covered by various artists including, The Beach Boys, but this version remains the definitive one, and is very much of the period, sounding as good now as when it was first recorded over forty years ago.

GREEN ONIONS – (Booker T and The MG'S)
Another classic song of the era that has well and truly stood the test of time. The track is heard during the dance at the ballroom in Brighton, and was a real Mod favourite that always tends to make it on to any period compilation albums.
Green Onions enjoyed something of a renaissance after the film and was duly re-released thus becoming a top-ten hit all over again. The quality and crispness of this instrumental masterpiece insures that it is in constant demand for adverts and television trailers over forty years from it's original release.

RHYTHM OF THE RAIN – (The Cascades)

Pete and Steph's song at the Kitchener Road party that causes Jimmy so much distress. The song is instantly recognisable and appears on almost every sixties compilation album ever made!

The songs 'classic' status was put at serious risk by a less than capable cover version by Jason Donovan in the late eighties.

HE'S SO FINE – (The Chiffons)

Another song heard on the jukebox during the film. The Chiffons, an all-girl group from New York enjoyed chart success with this catchy tune. However, it will probably be more remembered for being part of a protracted legal battle between its writers and George Harrison. The courts eventually deciding that, He's so Fine was plagiarised for the ex-Beatles solo hit of, My Sweet Lord.

BE MY BABY – (The Ronettes)

This 'classic' of the sixties is heard during the Kitchener Road party, and is perfectly evocative of the period. The Ronettes were from the Phil Spector stable, and enjoyed a top-five hit with this track.

DA DOO RON RON – (The Crystals)

Yet another all-girl group from Phil Spector, The Crystals provide the lyrics for this song that was a hit in 1963, and again some eleven years later. The track is heard playing at the Goldhawk Club when the group set of in revenge for Spiders beating. Another 'classic' of the era that was covered by the larger than life Bette Midler some years later.

I'M THE FACE – (The High Numbers)

Released in early July 1964, this was packaged by the then group's management as the first authentic Mod single. Although the band enjoyed little commercial success at the time with this track it remains one of their favourites over fifty years from its release! *Sea and Sand* from the 1973 album pays homage to the track at its end with a brief lyrical snip.

QUADROPHENIA – DIRECTORS CUT – BOX SET (DEMOS)
Album – POLYDOR 2777843 - 4 – (originally released November 2011)

Play list:
1. The Real Me   4.23
2. Quadrophenia – Four Overtures   6.15
3. Cut My Hair   3.27
4. Get Out and Stay Out   1.20
5. Four Faces – Quadrophonic   4.01
6. We Close Tonight   2.39*
7. You Came Back   3.14*
8. Get Inside   3.08*
9. Joker James   3.38
10. Punk - Punk and the Godfather   4.50
11. I'm One   2.36
12. Dirty Jobs   3.43
13. Helpless Dancer   2.15
14. Is it in my Head?   4.09
15. Any More   3.17*

16.	I've Had Enough	6.19
17.	Fill No 2	1.29*
18.	Wizardry	3.06*
19.	Sea and Sand	4.12
20.	Drowned	4.12
21.	Is it Me?	4.37*
22.	Bell Boy	5.00
23.	Doctor Jimmy	7.25
24.	Finale – The Rock	7.53
25.	Love Reign O'er Me	5.08
26.	Ambition	

** was not included in this package but was offered as an extra via excusive on-line access.

* These Demos do not appear on any of the subsequent Quadrophenia albums and are available only as Demos in this package, although track 6 does appear on the 1974 album, Odds & Sods.

WE CLOSE TONIGHT
A superb song that didn't make the final cut, but appeared the following year on Odds & Sods. This track was designed to put more flesh on the bones of Jimmy's character.

YOU CAME BACK
A song that demonstrates how strong the finished album is, as it also wasn't included. Townshend says that he styled it in 50's Rhythm and Blues style, much like that of the Platters.

GET INSIDE
Would have been a great addition to the album with some great work on the Mandolin by Townshend. Saluted the fact that Jimmy was originally going to have a gypsy heritage!

ANY MORE
A song that was quite simple in its composition with just Piano and Acoustic Guitar, which would have easily been at home on the album. This song was Townshend's attempt to show Jimmy at the very depths of his despair.

FILL NO 2.
A short but sweet beautiful Piano solo from Pete Townshend.

WIZARDRY
Another interesting instrumental, think Prog Rock meets Electropop meets Acid House!

IS IT ME?
Begins with a Hammer House of Horror type introduction, a track that was meant to put more meat on the bones of the Ace Face character, whose Father we learn was an old friend of Jimmy's own Father! A track that could have easily been at home on both Quadrophenia and Tommy.

AMBITION
A track that was originally supposed to have been included as an extra on Q-Cloud. The vocals were actually not added until 2011, and is a track that The Who attempted to record on various occasions, but for one reason or another it never worked. The track is available to view as a live performance by Pete Townshend on Rachel Fuller's In the Attic. You can check this video out on Youtube.

NON – ORIGINAL SOUNDTRACK MUSIC
the following tracks appear within the confines of the film, but are not featured on any Quadrophenia related albums (all songs by The Who – unless otherwise stated)

DIMPLES – (Cross Section)
Sadly, no recording is available of this excellent re-working of the classic John Lee Hooker track with which he enjoyed a big hit back in 1956. The track was also covered by amongst others The Animals, but the brief snatch that we hear on the film is enough to affirm that this would too have been a more than able cover.

ANYWAY, ANYHOW, ANYWHERE
We hear this famous *Who* song twice during the film, once whilst Jimmy is in the record shop booth, and whilst he sits in his wet Levis watching Ready Steady Go. The actual edition of Ready Steady Go!, was probably the one that was aired on 26th January 1965, giving the film's makers an opportunity to exercise a certain amount of artistic licence, because, of course, the film was set the in the previous year. It is said that Townshend was heavily influenced by Jazz musician, Charlie Parker in the writing of this song.

MY GENERATION
What more can be said about this one? Another case of artistic licence was used by the film's makers as this was not released until 1965 when it reached number two in the UK charts. The group have also re-released it on two further occasions. It is the song that usually ends the bands gigs, and has been covered by countless artists including Oasis.
A song that perfectly encapsulates the era is delightfully used in one of the scenes at the Kitchener Road party.

BABY LOVE – (The Supremes)
The classic Motown track is heard during the Kitchener Road party, and is a track that enjoyed massive commercial success, reaching number one in the autumn of 1964.

SWEET TALKING GUY – (The Chiffons)
Another favourite of the sixties compilation album makers. This song is heard on the jukebox in Alfredo's café.

BLAZING FIRE – (Derrick Morgan)
This offering from the legend of ska music can be heard during the lads attempt to score some drugs at Ferdy's house.

5-4-3-2-1 – (Manfred Mann)
As the theme tune of Ready Steady Go!, this track is briefly heard as Jimmy sits down in the living room to enjoy his favourite television show.

BABY DON'T YOU DO IT – (Marvin Gaye)
This song from the late, great, Marvin Gaye, is another juke box offering from Alfredo's during the final group scene's which end with Jimmy and Dave fighting.

WAH-WATUSI – (The Orlons)
Heard during the scenes at the Brighton Ballroom where Ace Face demonstrates his dancing skills. This catchy tune with the hard to follow lyrics was also a hit for The Isley Brothers.

WISHIN' AND HOPPIN – (The Merseybeats)
The Merseybeats formally from the Brian Epstein stable enjoyed a chart hit with this hit in 1964. The track is heard during Jimmy's visit to the record store.

PETE TOWNSHEND'S CLASSIC QUADROPHENIA.

Album – DEUTSCHE GRAMMOPHON – 479-4529 / CD – 479-5284 / DELUXE CD – 479-5057. – released 9th June 2015.

DVD OF LIVE PERFORMANCE – DEUTSCHE GRAMMOPHON/SKY – 00440-073-5225 – released 9th October 2015.

Play list:

1.	I am The Sea	3.52
2.	The Real Me	3.21
3.	Quadrophenia	6.05
4.	Cut My Hair	3.48
5.	The Punk and The Godfather	5.04
6.	I'm One	2.44
7.	The Dirty Jobs	4.27
8.	Helpless Dancer	2.35
9.	Is it in my Head?	3.49
10.	I've Had Enough	6.10
11.	5:15	4.18

12.	Sea and Sand	4.03
13.	Drowned	5.27
14.	Bell Boy	4.53
15.	Doctor Jimmy	8.36
16.	The Rock	6.51
17.	Love Reign O'er Me	5.56

An idea that had been talked about for a while finally came to fruition in 2014, when Quadrophenia was given a classic treatment by Pete Townshend and his long-term partner, Rachel Fuller. Recorded between 21st and 23rd October at the Air Studios in London, the album was orchestrated in the main by Rachel Fuller, with Martin Batchelor doing the honours on three tracks, The Dirty Jobs, Sea and Sand, plus Is it in My Head? It is also interesting to note that Townshend had offered classical takes on the songs to Franc Roddam when they met prior to the film being made. The idea was politely refused as Roddam thought that it would make the film to much like a 'Ken Russell – Tommy type film'!

The album was released by Polydor owned, Deutshe Grammaphon with Alfie Boe turning out to be the perfect choice for the lead vocals of Jimmy, coming with a pedigree in Opera and Classical Music second to none in this country. Billy Idol reprised his role as Ace Face/Bell Boy, with Phil Daniels also returning to Quadrophenia to supply vocals for The Dirty Jobs and Helpless Dancer in which he is credited as Jimmy's Father! The music was provided by the world-famous Royal Philharmonic Orchestra, being conducted by Robert Ziegler, who had previously worked with both them and the BBC Concert Orchestra in the past, as well as such luminaries as David Gilmour. The orchestra and vocalists were superbly aided by the London Oriana Choir, veterans of many productions all over Europe having appeared at the Royal Albert Hall many times since they were formed back in 1973.

The original album was re-recorded with the Classical treatment in its entirety in what some die-hard fans of The Who saw as treason! However, it seems to have eventually won most of them over. This was never designed to compete with Roger Daltrey's interpretation of Quadrophenia, and should be seen as a completely different take on Townshend's masterpiece!

Rather snootily the UK Classical charts deemed it ineligible, and excluded it, which angered Townshend who hit back with the following retort, "Classic Quadrophenia is not allowed in the U.K. classical charts?" "Musical snobbery in the classical elite still alive and kicking then. F—'em." Indeed, Townshend must have been laughing at the embarrassment that this caused the coordinators of the UK Classic Charts as it easily outsold its rivals and would have, and should have been Number 1!

The album was given its world premiere at the Royal Albert Hall on 5th July 2015, and was subsequently broadcast the next day on Sky Arts, before transferring to DVD on general release. The premiere at the Royal Albert Hall was a magical evening, it being the perfect venue for its first live outing, with the sell-out crowd being treated to outstanding work by all musicians and singers alike! Alfie Boe demonstrated why he was the perfect choice for Quadrophenia's classic take, with both Pete Townshend (The Godfather) and Phil Daniels being given extremely warm receptions. As a massive fan of all things Quadrophenia I was looking forward to this anyway, but I must say it well and truly surpassed my expectations!

QUADROPHENIA BY THE WHO ON TOUR

QUADROPHENIA TOUR 1973/4

Following the release of the album in 1973 The Who toured to promote it, in what proved to be a somewhat fraught experience for all involved. The complexity of the album meant that backing tapes and special effects recordings were required; however, there was to be many technical problems that made it a less than enjoyable time for the band.

TOUR SCHEDULE 1973

28TH OCTOBER   TRENTHAM GARDENS, STOKE.

A bad start saw Townshend having to change his guitar on no less than twenty occasions!

29TH OCTOBER   CIVIC HALL, WOLVERHAMPTON.

1ST NOVEMBER   BELLE VUE, MANCHESTER.

2ND NOVEMBER   BELLE VUE, MANCHESTER.

5TH NOVEMBER   ODEON CINEMA, NEWCASTLE.

A disastrous show saw the backing tape go faulty; Pete Townshend argued with Bob Pridden and smashed his guitar before smashing the tapes up. The curtain came down and The Who returned to play other numbers from their catalogue.

6TH NOVEMBER   ODEON CINEMA, NEWCASTLE.

7TH NOVEMBER   ODEON CINEMA, NEWCASTLE.

11TH NOVEMBER   THE LYCEUM, LONDON.

13TH NOVEMBER   THE LYCEUM, LONDON.

20TH NOVEMBER   THE COW PALACE, SAN FRANSISCO.

A somewhat indifferent start to the American leg of the tour saw Keith Moon collapse and having to be carried off the stage twice!

22ND NOVEMBER   THE FORUM, LOS ANGELES.

23RD NOVEMBER   THE FORUM, LOS ANGELES.

25TH NOVEMBER   MEMMORIAL ARENA, DALLAS.

Ironically this concert received much critical acclaim, but Pete Townshend said that it was the weakest of the tour!

27TH NOVEMBER   THE OMNI, ATLANTA, GEORGIA.

28TH NOVEMBER   ST.LOUIS ARENA, MISSOURI.

29TH NOVEMBER   AMPHITHEATRE, CHICAGO.

30TH NOVEMBER   COBO HALL, DETROIT.

This proved to be one of the strongest performances of Quadrophenia, with little or no technical problems.

2ND DECEMBER   THE FORUM, MONTREAL.

3RD DECEMBER   BOSTON GARDENS, BOSTON.

4TH DECEMBER   THE SPECTRUM, PHILADELPHIA.

6TH DECEMBER   THE CAPITAL CENTRE, LARGO.

18TH DECEMBER   SUNDOWN THEATRE, EDMONTON.

Due to the demand for tickets at their previous London dates The Who decided to do a series of four shows (with the first dedicated to Tommy) which went well, and even seemed to please Townshend who felt that they were the best they had played Quadrophenia at anywhere.

13TH DECEMBER   RAINBOW THEATRE, FINSBURY.

19TH DECEMBER   SUNDOWN THEATRE, EDMONTON.

22ND DECEMBER   SUNDOWN THEATRE, EDMONTON.

23RD DECEMBER   SUNDOWN THEATRE, EDMONTON.

TOUR SCHEDULE 1974

9TH FEBRUARY   PALAIS DES GROTTES, LILLE.

Six dates in France were added to the schedule in what was to be the last time The Who played Quadrophenia live until 1996.

10TH FEBRUARY	PALAIS DES EXPOSITIONS, PARIS.
15TH FEBRUARY	LES ARENAS, POITIERS.
17TH FEBRUARY	FOIRE DE TOULOUSE.
22ND FEBRUARY	PALAIS DES EXPOSITIONS, NANCY.
24TH FEBRUARY	SPORTS PALAIS, LYON, FRANCE.

QUADROPHENIA – Hyde Park, 29th June 1996

As part of the MasterCard Masters of Music Concert for the Prince's Trust Pete Townshend, John Entwistle and Roger Daltrey re-united to perform Quadrophenia in its entirety. The Concert was attended by Prince Charles who was joined by amongst others, Leslie Ash and Pele. An estimated crowd of 150,000 attended. Although strictly not billed as The Who it was for all intense and purposes the old firm back together again! Pete Townshend had been constantly annoyed that he had been unable to deliver his masterpiece in its entirety to a live audience. Now with the advances in musical technology Townshend was at last able to perform the piece as he had always intended. The Who at the time were technically no longer a band, so they were performing Quadrophenia as a bunch of un-named musicians, the first time the trio had performed together since 1989. TED as they were dubbed (Townshend, Entwistle and Daltrey) went onto to tour America and Europe eventually reverting back to the name of The Who!

Townshend re-wrote the show to include a superb narration by Phil Daniels (who's every appearance was greeted by cheers!), and included special guests, such as Adrian Edmonson taking the part of the Ace Face. The show was enhanced with footage from the original film and new scenes that were shown on a large screen to add to the event. Roger Daltrey was wearing a Mod target style eye patch following an accident during rehearsals, when Gary Glitter hit him in the eye with a microphone stand. It was a truly memorable event which shared a bill with Bob Dylan, Alanis Morrissett, Jools Holland and his Rhythm and Blues Orchestra, as well as Eric Clapton who put in an awesome performance!

The success of Quadrophenia meant that Townshend had at last got his wish to see his work performed in the way he had always longed for, and the inevitable seeds were sewn for a new full on tour!

THE BAND

Pete Townshend	GUITAR/VOCALS And PIANO
John Entwistle	BASS GUITAR and VOCALS
Roger Daltrey	VOCALS
Zak Starkey	DRUMS
John Bundrick	KEYBOARDS
Jon Carin	KEYBOARDS
Jody Linscott	PERCUSSION
Geoff Whitehorn	GUITAR
Simon Townshend	GUITAR/VOCALS
Billy Nichols	MD/BACKING VOCALS
Sonia Jones, Peter Howith and Suzy Webb	BACKING VOCALS
Neil Sidwell, Simon Gardner, Paul Spong Steve Sidwell and Andy Fawbert	BRASS SECTION

MISC

Pete Townshend	WORDS AND MUSIC
Bill Curbishley	PRODUCER
Harvey Goldsmith	PRODUCER

GUEST APPEARANCES

Phil Daniels	NARRATOR
Adrian Edmonson	ACE FACE
Stephen Fry	HOTEL MANAGER
Dave Gilmour	BUS DRIVER
Gary Glitter	ROCKER
Trevor McDonald	NEWS READER

QUADROPHENIA TOUR 1996/7

TOUR SCHEDULE 1996

16TH JULY	MADISON SQUARE GDN, NYC.

Almost 90,000 fans watched the band perform Quadrophenia over six nights at this iconic venue prior to a three-month break, when the tour resumed. Phil Daniels was used as a narrator for these shows, but later described it as being one of his worst ever jobs. 'I felt as though I was interrupting the crowd's enjoyment – who had obviously come to see The Who'.

17TH JULY	MADISON SQUARE GDN, NYC.
18TH JULY	MADISON SQUARE GDN, NYC.
20TH JULY	MADISON SQUARE GDN, NYC.
21ST JULY	MADISON SQUARE GDN, NYC.
22ND JULY	MADISON SQUARE GDN, NYC.
13TH OCTOBER	ROSE GARDEN, PORTLAND.
14TH OCTOBER	THE TACOMA DOME, WASHINGTON.

Some problems with Pete Townshend's guitar meant that it required the obligatory demolishing on stage! Simon Townshend, Pete's younger brother joined the tour after this date with Pete playing much more acoustically.

16TH OCTOBER	G.M. PALACE, VANCOUVER.
17TH OCTOBER	G.M. PALACE, VANCOUVER.
20TH OCTOBER	SAN JOSE ARENA, CALIFORNIA.
22ND OCTOBER	THE GREAT WESTERN FORUM, L.A.
23RD OCTOBER	AMERICAN WEST ARENA, PHEONIX.
25TH OCTOBER	ARROWHEAD POND, ANAHHEIM.

26TH OCTOBER	MGM GRAND GARDEN, LAS VEGAS.

Unbelievably this was the band's first visit to Las Vegas, although they had all played there before individually.

29TH OCTOBER	McNICHOLS ARENA, DENVER.
31ST OCTOBER	THE UNITED CENTRE, CHICAGO.
1ST NOVEMBER	THE UNITED CENTRE, CHICAGO.
3RD NOVEMBER	PALACE OF AUBURN, MICHIGAN.
4TH NOVEMBER	ERVIN J. NUTTER CENTRE, OHIO.
6TH NOVEMBER	THE GRAND ARENA, CLEVELAND.
8TH NOVEMBER	CIVIC ARENA, PITTSBURGH, USA.
9TH NOVEMBER	MIDLAND ARENA, BUFFALO.
11TH NOVEMBER	US AIR ARENA, LANDOVER.
12TH NOVEMBER	THE CENTRUM, MASSACHUSETTS.
14TH NOVEMBER	THE CENTRUM, MASSACHUSETTS.
15TH NOVEMBER	NASSAU COLISSEUM, LONG ISLAND
17TH NOVEMBER	CORE STATE, PHILADELPHIA.
18TH NOVEMBER	KNICKERBOCKER ARENA, ALBANY.
19TH NOVEMBER	CONTINENTAL ARENA, NEW JERSEY
6TH DECEMBER	EARLS COURT ARENA, LONDON.

A critically acclaimed and triumphant return to the home country.

7TH DECEMBER	EARLS COURT ARENA, LONDON.
11TH DECEMBER	NYNEX ARENA, MANCHESTER.

TOUR SCHEDULE 1997

23RD APRIL					FORUM, COPENHAGEN.

After the winter break the band were back on the road for the next leg of the Quadrophenia tour, this time they were once again billed as THE WHO.

25TH APRIL					GLOBE ARENA, STOCKHOLM.

26TH APRIL					OSLO SPEKTRUM, OSLO.

28TH APRIL					OSTSEEHALLE, KIEL, GERMANY.

29TH APRIL					DEUTSCHLAND HALLE, BERLIN.

1ST MAY						STADHALLE, VIENNA.

4TH MAY						OLYMPAHALLE, MUNICH.

5TH MAY						HANS MARTIN, STUTTGART.

6TH MAY						FASTHALLE, FRANKFURT,

10TH MAY					FOREST NATIONAL, BRUSSELS,

11TH MAY					THE AHOY, ROTTERDAM,

13TH MAY					THE ZENITH, PARIS.

14TH MAY					THE ZENITH, PARIS.

16TH MAY					HALLENSTADION, ZURICH.

18TH MAY					WEMBLEY ARENA, LONDON.

A very successful show was witnessed by the mother of the late-great Keith Moon.

19TH JULY					RIVERPORT, MISSOURI.

A return to America and Canada for the last leg of the legendary tour.

20TH JULY					NEW WORLD THEATRE, ILLINOIS.

22ND JULY					TARGET CENTRE, MINNEAPOLIS.

23RD JULY					AMPHITHEATRE, MILWAUKEE.

25TH JULY					PINE KNOB THEATRE, CLARKSTON.

26TH JULY	DEE CREEK CENTRE, INDIANA.
28TH JULY	MOLSON CENTRE, MONTREAL.
29TH JULY	MOLSON AMPHITHEATR, TORONTO.
31ST JULY	GREAT WOODS CTR, MANSFIELD.
2ND AUGUST	MEADOWS THEATRE, HARTFORD.
3RD AUGUST	PNC ARTS CENTER, NEW JERSEY.
5TH AUGUST	DARIEN LAKE P.A.C., NEW YORK.
6TH AUGUST	BLOCKBUSTER-SONY, NEW JERSEY.
7TH AUGUST	NISSAN PAVILION, VIRGINIA.
9TH AUGUST	AMPHITHEATRE, VIRGINIA BEACH.
10TH AUGUST	AMPHITHEATRE, RALEIGH.
12TH AUGUST	PAVILION, NORTHCAROLINA.
13TH AUGUST	AMPHITHEATRE, ATLANTA.
15TH AUGUST	ICE PALACE, TAMPA.
16TH AUGUST	AMPHITHEATRE, FLORIDA.

TOMMY AND QUADROPHENIA LIVE – 3 DISC DVD BOX-SET.

Released - 7 Nov 2005 - UK: Rhino 0349 70500-2

On 7th November 2005, a 3-disc DVD box-set was released, which was very much the baby of Roger Daltrey, who along with Aubrey Power directed the project. The Quadrophenia disc features all seventeen songs in chronological order, with performances taken from the 1996/97 tour of America, and featuring, Billy Idol and P.J. Proby, there are also special commentary features from both Daltrey and Pete Townshend.

Other extras included photo and souvenir galleries, an interview with Billy Idol, and "The Story of Quadrophenia" as told by Aubrey Powell. The other discs are from a Tommy live performance in Los Angeles in 1989, with the final disc being a best of compilation, recorded live at various venues, with a total running time of 417 minutes.

The disc was warmly welcomed by fans of The Who, with the excellent sound quality of particular note! The performances that are captured are how The Who had hoped to present the album almost a quarter of a century prior!

The release of this eagerly awaited boxset was marked with a premier in a Mayfair cinema with the great and the good from The Who in attendance. A sprinkling of fans (including the author) were also given the chance to attend.

QUADROPHENIA AND MORE – NORTH AMERICA AND EUROPEAN TOUR 2012/13

TOUR SCHEDULE 2012/13 – NORTH AMERICA.

1ST NOVEMBER   BANK ATLANTIC CTR, FLORIDA.

The Who made a glorious return in a tour that saw Quadrophenia played in its entirety, and was followed by some of their big hits, with the shows being lauded by both critics and fans alike!

3RD NOVEMBER	AMWAY CENTER, ORLANDO.
5TH NOVEMBER	GWINNETT CENTER, DULUTH.
8TH NOVEMBER	BI-LOC CENTRE, GREENVILLE.
11TH NOVEMBER	CONSUL CENTRE, PIITTSSBURGH.
13TH NOVEMBER	VERIZON CTR, WASHINGTON D.C.
14TH NOVEMBER	BARCLAYS CENTRE, NEW YORK.
16TH NOVEMBER	T.D. GARDENS, BOSTON.
20TH NOVEMBER	THE BELL CENTRE, MONTREAL, QC.
21ST NOVEMBER	SCOTIA BANK PLACE, OTTOWA.
23RD NOVEMBER	AIR CANADA CENTRE, TORONTO.
24TH NOVEMBER	JOE LOUIS ARENA, DETROIT.
27TH NOVEMBER	TARGET CENTRE, MINEAPOLIS.
29TH NOVEMBER	ALLSTATE ARENA, ROSEMONT.
30TH NOVEMBER	ALLSTATE ARENA, ROSEMONT.
2ND DECEMBER	BRIDGESTONE ARENA, NASHVILLE.
5TH DECEMBER	MADDISON SQUARE GDN, NYC.
6TH DECEMBER	PRUDENTIAL CENTRE, NEWARK.
8TH DECEMBER	WELLS FARGO CTR, PHILADELPHIA
9TH DECEMBER	MOHEGAN RESORT, UNCASVILLE.
12TH DECEMBER	'CONCERT FOR SANDY RELIEF', NEW YORK.

28TH JANUARY	HONDA CENTRE, ANAHEIM.
30TH JANUARY	STAPLES CENTE, LOS ANGELES.
1ST FEBRUARY	ORACLE ARENA, OAKLAND.
2ND FEBRUARY	RENO EVENTS CENTRE, RENO.
5TH FEBRUARY	VALLEY VIEW CENTRE, SAN DIEGO.
6TH FEBRUARY	JOBBINGTON ARENA, GLENDAE.
8TH FEBRUARY	THE HARD ROCK, LAS VEGAS.
10TH FEBRUARY	THE HARD ROCK, LAS VEGAS.
12TH FEBRUARY	PEPSI CENTRE, DENVER.
14TH FEBRUARY	BOK CENTRE, TULSA, OKLAHOMA.
16TH FEBRUARY	KFC YUM CENTRE, LOUISVILLE.
17TH FEBRUARY	SCOTTENSTEIN CTR, COLUMBUS.
19TH FEBRUARY	COPPS COLISEUM, HAMILTON.
21ST FEBRUARY	NASSAU COLISEUM, UNIONDALE.
22ND FEBRUARY	BOARDWAK HALL, ATLANTIC CITY.
24TH FEBRUARY	VERIZON ARENA, MANCHESTER.
26TH FEBRUARY	DUNKIN DONUTS CTR, RHODE IS.
28TH FEBRUARY	'BENEFIT FOR TEEN CANCER' N.Y.

EUROPEAN LEG OF TOUR

8TH JUNE	o2 ARENA, DUBLIN.
10TH JUNE	ODYSSEY ARENA, BELFAST.
12TH JUNE	SECC ARENA, GLASGOW.
15TH JUNE	o2 ARENA, LONDON.
16TH JUNE	o2 ARENA, LONDON.

18TH JUNE	MOTORPOINT ARENA, SHEFFIELD.
20TH JUNE	METRO ARENA, NEWCASTLE.
23RD JUNE	MANCHESTER ARENA.
28TH JUNE	LG ARENA, BIRMINGHAM.
30TH JUNE	ECHO ARENA, LIVERPOOL.
3RD JULY	BERCY CENTRE, PARIS.
5TH JULY	ZIGGO DOME, AMSTERDAM.
8TH JULY	WEMBLEY ARENA, LONDON.

The tour ended appropriately in London with a special charity performance. A hot but memorable night, saw the last (to date) Quadrophenia show given a superb treatment!

QUADROPHENIA LIVE IN LONDON BOX SET

Released in various forms, the ultimate being a 5-disc limited collector's edition, that captured in full the triumphant last show of the Quadrophenia and more tour on 8th July 2013.

The deluxe metal box set included the following: -

• 10-inch Round Metal Mod Headlight Container

• 1 Blu-Ray Disc™: Concert Film

• 1 Standard DVD: Concert Film

• 1 Blu-ray Audio Disc™ Format: Quadrophenia (1973) 5.1 Album Mix – First Time Ever

• 2-CD Soundtrack: Concert Audio

• Mod Headlight Button

• 6" Mod Headlight Sticker

• Booklet with photos and liner notes

Audio CD (June 10, 2014)

THE WHO – DISCOGRAPHY

Section 1 – Studio Albums

My Generation	*POLYDOR*	*1965*
A Quick One	*POLYDOR*	*1966*
The Who Sell Out	*POLYDOR*	*1967*
Tommy	*POLYDOR*	*1969*
Who's Next?	*POLYDOR*	*1971*
Quadrophenia	*POLYDOR*	*1973*
Odds and Sods	*POLYDOR*	*1974*
The Who by Numbers	*POLYDOR*	*1975*
Who Are You?	*POLYDOR*	*1978*
Face Dances	*POLYDOR*	*1981*
It's Hard	*POLYDOR*	*1982*
Wire and Glass	*POLYDOR*	*2006*

Section 2 – Soundtracks

Tommy	POLYDOR	1975
The Kids are Alright	POLYDOR	1979
Quadrophenia	POLYDOR	1979
Quadrophenia (songs from)	POLYDOR	1993

Compilations and Selected Live Albums

Live at Leeds	POLYDOR	1970
Meaty Beaty Big and Bouncy	POLYDOR	1971
Who's Last	MCA	1984
Live at The Isle of Wight 1970	SONY	1996
The Ultimate Collection	POLYDOR	2002
Who's Missing	MCA usa*	1985
Two's Missing	MCA usa*	1987
Who's Better Who's Best	POLYDOR	1988
Join Together	VIRGIN	1990
30 years of Maximum R&B	POLYDOR box set	1994
My Generation: very best of The Who	POLYDOR	1996
The BBC Sessions	POLYDOR	2000
Live at The Royal Albert Hall	SPO	2003
Then and Now	POLYDOR	2004
The Best of The Who	MCA usa*	1999
The Who Collection vol.1	POLYDOR	1985
The Who Collection vol.2	POLYDOR	1985
The Who – The Singles	POLYDOR	1984
The Who – Rarities 1966-72 Vol 1and 2	POLYDOR	1983

Blues to the Bush   MUSIC MAKER   2000

Then and Now   POLYDOR   2003

all the above are original release dates and all are available in cd format - there are literally hundreds of other albums (imports/bootlegs) available. The above is, however a reasonably concise record of their work

CHAPTER 4.
STAGE SHOWS.

Stage shows have surfaced both sides of the Atlantic, these having been sanctioned by Pete Townshend over recent years! The following is the information on the ones that I know about: -

QUAD – LUNA C PRODUCTIONS - LOS ANGELES 2005/6 and 2007.

Bill Schultz had previously worked in the medical field, but was a massive fan of The Who, and decided to re-work his favourite album, Quadrophenia into a stage show. Schultz along with partner's including the founder of KISS; Bill Aucoin financed the show, which opened in Los Angeles in November 2005, with further shows coming over the next two years.

Quad was a celebration of the album consisting of trained musicians playing members of The Who, with a narrative linked through it by actors playing the parts of the story's characters.

Initially there were grand plans for the stage show including taking it to Broadway. Bill Schultz explained his project at the time thus: - "Our production will be very much unlike the movie," "The main character, Jimmy, will come across as more sympathetic. Growing up I related to Jimmy's dilemma and felt a kinship. Our show will journey into his head and present the contents on-stage, from the tenacious arguments with mom and dad, to the fights on the beach between Mods and Rockers, to a yearning for the beautiful girl he can't have. It's basically West Side Story crossed with Romeo & Juliet. This is my way of completing the circle from the first time I heard Quadrophenia."

QUAD
A Spectacular Musical Staging of...
The Who's Quadrophenia

<u>*QUADROPHENIA – ROYAL WELSH COLLEGE OF MUSIC AND DRAMA – THE SHERMAN THEATRE, CARDIFF. – 9TH-17TH FEBRUARY 2007.*</u>

The first Stage Show to happen in the UK was performed with the blessing of Pete Townshend, by The Royal Welsh College of Music and Drama, in February 2007. This version was less of a celebration of the album and more of a direct re-telling of the story paying faithful reverence to the album version of Quadrophenia. Pete Townshend attended the show, and it was felt that this was the nearest he had got to seeing his story of Quadrophenia in the flesh!

Written by Jeff Young and Directed by Tom Critchley its cast consisted of students of the RWCMD, including Rob Kendrick as Jimmy, a role he went on to reprise in a later National tour! This production was immensely important in the evolution of Quadrophenia as a theatrical event. The following is a promotional photograph from 2007.

QUADROPHENIA – STAGE SHOW UK TOUR SUMMER/AUTUMN 2009.

In 2009 Tom Critchley, Jeff Young and John O'Hara who had worked on the RWCMD production two years previously reworked, recast and expanded it with Pete Townshend's full support, and went on to tour it nationally. Bill Schultz who had been involved in the Los Angeles production returned as Producer, with the full touring schedule as follows:-

Plymouth Theatre Royal	May 9th-16th
Birmingham Hippodrome	May 18th-23rd
Edinburgh Festival Theatre	May 25th-30th
Glasgow Kings Theatre	June 1st-6th
Bath Theatre Royal	June 8th-13th
Manchester Opera House	June 15th-20th
Sunderland Empire	July 6th-11th
Cambridge Arts Centre	July 20th-25th
Cheltenham Everyman	July 27th-August 1st
Leeds Grand	Aug 3rd-8th
Nottingham Concert Hall	Aug 10th-15th
Aberdeen His Majesty's	Aug 17th-22nd
Liverpool Empire	Aug 24th - 29th

Brighton Theatre Royal   Aug 31st-Sep 5th

Norwich Theatre Royal   Sep 15th-19th

Wolverhampton Grand   Sep 21st-26th

Coventry Belgrade   Sep 28th -Oct 3rd

Jimmy's Character was played by four actors each taking a facet of his personality, and each delivering a superb performance. In particular, Ryan O'Donnell and Jack Roth were outstanding! O'Donnell gave what proved to be an award-winning performance, and has continued to work heavily on the stage with a role in The Kinks musical, Sunny Afternoon due to hit the road in 2017. Jack Roth, son of Tim has broken into TV, and is a name we will be hearing a lot more of in the future! Sadly, this production never made the West End, but if repeated is a definite must see! The Cast and Crew are detailed below: -

PRODUCTION

Musial, Lyrics and concept by Pete Townshend

Stage Adaption by Jeff Young, John O'Hara and Tom Critchley

Produced by Bill Schultz, Ina Melbach and the Theatre Royal Plymouth

Director – Tom Critchley

Writer – Jeff Young

Musical Supervisor/Arranger – John O'Hara

Set Designer – Sophie Khan

Costume Designer – Carl Perry

Choreographer – Frances Newman

Lighting Design – Ace McCarron

Fight Direction – Kevin McCurdy

Sound Design – Jason Barnes

Musical Director – Elliott Ware

Casting Director – Pippa Ailion

CAST

Jimmy (Romantic) – Ryan O'Donnell, Jimmy (Lunatic) – Jack Roth,

Jimmy (Tough Guy) – George Maguire, Jimmy (Hypocrite) – Rob Kendrick

The Girl - Sydney Rae White

Mum - Kirsty Malone, Dad – John Schumacher

Guardian Angels – Dawn Sievewright, Iris Roberts and Lillie Flynn

Godfather – Kevin Wathen

Ace Face – Ryan Gage

Gang Leader – Tom Robertson

Swing – Daniel Curtis, Sean Croke and Brendan Reece

MUSICIANS

MD and Keyboards – Elliott Ware

Additional Keyboards – Tim Whitting

Guitars – Nick Kendall and James Canty

Bass – Steffan Iestyn Jones

Drums – Greg Pringle

Brass – Owain Harries

Cello – Anna Menzies

Violin – Miriam Davis

QUADROPHENIA – THE ROCK MUSICAL – NK THEATRE ARTS – THE FORUM THEATRE, ROMILLY. 13TH – 16TH MARCH 2013 and THE PALACE THEATRE, MANCHESTER. – 14TH JULY 2013.

NK is an all-inclusive (regardless of Age, Race or Disability etc.) Theatre and Arts workshop in Stockport that encourages everyone to join in! Quadrophenia was devised by Dominic Stanage and Kerry Day, and culminated in a special one night performance at The Palace Theatre in Manchester. Lorded with outstanding reviews, Andy Gregory who took the lead role as Jimmy went on to win the Best Actor award in the 2013 Manchester Music Awards. I have only ever heard good things about this production, and only wish I had been there to have witnessed it!

QUADROPHENIA – MERCURY THEATRE YOUNG COMPANY – THE MERCURY THEATRE, COLCHESTER. – 22ND-24TH AUGUST 2013.

In 2013 The Mercury Theatre set up a new production company for 16 -25 year olds with help from the Arts Council South East, and Quadrophenia was chosen as their debut production.

The adapted story was written by Kenneth Emson, and Directed by Tony Casement, featuring a large cast that delivered a stunning show, which made a mockery of the fact that they were all still very inexperienced and novices to their craft! Chris Connelly (Jimmy) and Lucy Davidson (Monkey) were particularly outstanding in what was a fine tribute to the original story with one or two interesting modifications!

QUADROPHENIA – SPOTLIGHT MUSICAL THEATRE GROUP, BECCLES, SUFFOLK -SUMMER 2017.

In the summer of 2017 a production is planned in Suffolk based on the NK production in Manchester. Having seen this company perform Tommy, it will be well worth watching!

CHAPTER 5.

QUADROPHENIA EXTRA'S.

QUADROPHENIA CAST REUNION'S AND CONVENTIONS.

Film and Comicon is held every year at various venues around the country, and in September of 2007, Franc Roddam and members of the cast reunited in Earls Court. Cast members present were, Phil Daniels, Gary Shail, Toyah Wilcox, Trevor H. Laird, Phil Davis, Garry Cooper, Mark Wingett and John Altman. The two-day event gave fans the chance to meet the stars from the film, and obtain signed souvenirs. There were also replicas of the scooters on show courtesy of, Dave Wyburn and Royston Edwards. Fans also had the chance to attend a special Q & A session. Later in the year a smaller cast event gathered for a similar event in Birmingham. The success of both galvanized Worcester based, Reel Events to organize a full blown convention the following year as detailed below:

TARGET 30 QUADROPHENIA CONVENTION – HOIDAY INN, BRIGHTON, APRIL 5TH – APRIL 6TH 2008.

Tim Evans the proprietor of Reel Events in Worcester was the brains behind the inaugural Quadrophenia Convention, in what was a memorable weekend in Brighton.

Cast members in attendance were, Phil Daniels, Mark Wingett, Toyah Wilcox, Gary Shail, Garry Cooper, Phil Davis, Trevor Laird and John Altman. With special extra Royston Edwards, and former drummer with The Who Doug Sandom also there! The weekend began unofficially on the Friday night, when members of the cast and fans mingled in the bar to get the festivities under way!

The Saturday saw various Q & A sessions with cast members, which were conducted by Dilip Sarkar MBE, an expert and esteemed author on various aspects of Aviation History, however his expertise in his own field made him, perhaps, a strange choice for this particular one! There were also various signing sessions by all the cast in attendance.

Gary Shail had organised a scooter ride past just after lunch with around 100 scooters briefly bringing Brighton seafront to a complete standstill, in one of the highlights of the weekend! After a special gala-dinner it was off to the cinema.

The Duke of York cinema in Brighton was the venue for a special screening of Quadrophenia, which was introduced by Mark Wingett and Toyah Wilcox. This was probably my favourite ever time of watching the film in a cinema, coming on well after 10.00pm both cast and fans alike were all suitably 'refreshed'. The original grainy old X certificated print was shown - with the auditorium a riot of noise and merriment. It was quite surreal to watch the film a few seats in front of Phil Daniels, with him constantly joining in with the laughing and shouting – a truly memorable night!

The Sunday saw Brighton unusually swathed in snow! This and the previous night's events saw things get going a little late, but more tales and anecdotes entertained the gathered throng again, with various other exhibits on show for them also to enjoy! It was planned to repeat the event the following year but various things including the looming recession saw it later shelved. Tim Evans is hoping to organise another Quadrophenia event sometime in the future so keep an eye on their website: - www.thevideodrome.net

The following picture shows cast reunited at the above event in Brighton.

QUADROPHENIA SYMPOSIUM – UNIVERSITY OF SUSSEX - JULY 10-11TH 2014.

In 2014 Quadrophenia was the subject of a special event hosted by The University of Sussex in Brighton.

Here by the Sea and Sand: A Symposium on Quadrophenia, was sponsored by the Centre for Modernist Studies, the Centre for Visual Fields, the Centre for Research into Childhood and Youth, University of Sussex, and the Interdisciplinary Network for the study of Subcultures. The two-day event began with a tour of locations used in Brighton, and was followed by a special screening of the film at The Duke of York Cinema, which featured a Q & A with Franc Roddam and Alan Fletcher. The following day the Symposium moved onto the Lecture Hall at the University, and featured the following Lectures and Presentations: -

Pam Thurschwell (University of Sussex): Introduction.

Paolo Hewitt (the esteemed Mod author) reading from his book The Sharper Word: A Mod Anthology.

Christine Feldman-Barrett (Griffith University, Australia): Beyond Brighton, Beyond Britain: Quadrophenia and the Post-1960s Mod Diaspora.

Suzanne Coker (Birmingham Arts Council): Quad to Run: on Quadrophenia and Born to Run.

Simon Wells (Author of Quadrophenia – A Way of Life): Quadrophenia Fans: A Way of Life

Dolores Tierney (University of Sussex): Quadrophenia as a 'new' cult musical.

Stephen Glynn (De Montfort University, and author of Quadrophenia: Cultographies): "Dressed up Better than anyone": Quadrophenia and the Cult Film Experience.

Andy Medhurst (University of Sussex): From Soho, down to Brighton: Capital, Coast and Quadrophenia.

Keith Gildart (University of Wolverhampton): Class, Youth and Dirty Jobs: Exploring continuity and change in post-war England through Pete Townshend's Quadrophenia.

Sam Cooper (University of Sussex): Heat Wave: The Who, the Mods and the Cultural Turn

Ben Winsworth (University of Orleans): "Who (the Fuck) are you?": Out with the In Crowd in Quadrophenia (1973)

Tom Wright (University of Sussex): 5:15: Mods, Mobility and the Brighton Train

Pam Thurschwell (University of Sussex) "You were under the impression that when you were walking forward, you'd end up further onward, but things ain't quite that simple": Quadrophenia's segues and historical impasse

Brian Baker (Lancaster University): The Drowning Machine: the sea and the scooter in Quadrophenia.

James Wood (Harvard University): Keynote Speech.

FOLLOWING PICTURE SHOWS PROGRAMME COVER FOR THE ABOVE EVENT.

Here by the sea and sand
A symposium on the album and film
QUADROPHENIA

Sponsored by the Centre for Modernist Studies, University of Sussex. Co-sponsored by the Centre for Visual Fields and the Centre for Research into Childhood and Youth, University of Sussex

University of Sussex 10–11 July 2014

Keynote Speaker: James Wood (Harvard University, The New Yorker)
With the participation of Franc Roddam (Director, Quadrophenia)

US
University of Sussex

More information on registration and programme available at
herebytheseaandsand.wordpress.com
or email quadrophenia.symposium@gmail.com

SPECIAL SCREENINGS

Over recent years' special screenings of Quadrophenia have taken place the length and breadth of the country, in places such as the BFI in London, Whitley Bay, Great Yarmouth and Brighton Beach to name but a few! Screenings tend to either be part of a local film festival, or a scooter rally, very often featuring members of the cast or crew, in either a Q & A, or personal appearance. However, this was upped a notch in February 2015 at the Hammersmith Apollo, as detailed below: -

QUADROPHENIA – FULLY IMMERSIVE CINEMATIC EVENT – HAMMERSMITH EVENTIM APPOLLO – 11TH FEBRUARY 2015.

More than 3,000 people packed the (formerly known) Hammersmith Odeon for a very special screening of the film. The show included a full showing of the film, whilst actors recreated various scenes in real-time, including the famous balcony dive from the night club scene. Following the film there was a Q & A with Franc Roddam and cast members, Phil Daniels, Phil Davis, Mark Wingett, Garry Cooper, Toyah Wilcox, Jeremy

Child, Trevor Laird and Danny Peacock. Katherine Rogers was also in attendance. The evening in the Theatre was rounded off by a superb set by top tribute band, Who's Who and a VIP after party.

Although the showing will never beat the one in Brighton for me, it was an amazing night witnessing so many peoples love of the film in this iconic venue! How many films could even think about filling such a large venue?

DOCUMENTARIES

Over the years there have been a number of Documentaries dedicated to both the film and album, which are detailed below: -

TALKING PICTURES – BBC TV – FIRST BROADCAST 7TH SEPTEMBER 1979.

Produced and presented by Gavin Millar, Talking Pictures was a new series of programmes concentrating on a different movie every week, with Quadrophenia featuring in its debut show.

Some great unseen outtakes are viewed, along with interviews by Rosemary Bowen-Jones with Roger Daltrey, Franc Roddam, Jeff Dexter and Sting. The latter was asked 'what is it like playing the Ace Face' with his tongue-in cheek reply stating that is was 'very easy as you can see I'm very debonair'.

Daltrey was viewed auditioning bands for the early scenes at The Goldhawk Club, and was asked about the recently released, Saturday Night Fever his reply stating 'Saturday Night Fever nicked a lot from Quadrophenia, but Quadrophenia will be a better film'.

Millar's view that the 'acting doesn't owe much to traditional drama school acting – more of a vernacular American style', was perhaps, in line with his lack of knowledge of youth culture. He certainly wouldn't have endeared himself to Mods saying that they stuck fur to their anoraks! And that the girls were ugly ducklings!

A documentary, perhaps, very much of its time, it is still well worth a watch, and is currently available on YouTube. Running time 25 minutes.

CAST & CREW – BBC TV – FIRST BROADCAST 22ND MARCH 2005.

Presented by Kirsty Wark, and made by IWC Productions, a company at the time owned by Wark and her husband Alan Clements, and shown on BBC4 as part of an ongoing series.

The programme retrospectively looked at films, reuniting cast and crew and visiting some of its locations. Kirsty Wark was joined in a studio by Franc Roddam, Roy Baird, Brian Tufano, Martin Stellman and Sean Barton to discuss the film, and the impact it has had, drawing similar parallels with other youth cult films such as Train Spotting! Phil Daniels and Mark Wingett were also interviewed separately, with the latter being credited for his role as 'Woody' in the film (somebody hadn't done their homework!)

Franc Roddam also visited some locations in Brighton, in a show that lasted just under forty minutes. Cast & Crew is available to view on YouTube, although, sadly the quality is not great, but still worth a watch. Running time approximately 40 minutes.

ON LOCATION WITH FRANC – UNIVERSAL DVD RELEASE 2006.

Made by Momentum productions as an extra for the re-packaged DVD, released in 2006, this sees Franc Roddam revisit some of the locations used in London and Brighton.

On Location with Franc lasts about fifteen minutes and tells some intriguing stories about how they were sourced and obtained. Interestingly, Franc says that there is not one location he would have changed, however to get them was not always a smooth ride! Roddam had asked the location men to obtain 24, and a couple of weeks later was infuriated when only 2 of them had been confirmed, a fight nearly ensued, in a very heated argument! Eventually all the locations were confirmed, and all parties were happy! On Location with Franc is a most welcome extra to this DVD release.

A WAY OF LIFE – UNIVERSAL DVD RELEASE 2006.

Made by Momentum productions as an extra for the re-packaged DVD released in 2006, this is an in-depth look at how the film was made, and how it is still relevant today! Narrated by Robert Elms, and Directed by Darren Cavanagh, it is split into five chapters; The Who the What and the Why/Parka Life/Brighton Beach Memoirs/This is the Modern Word and Modern Life is Rubbish! Contributions come from, Franc Roddam, Robert Sandall, Phil Daniels, Phil Davis, Mark Wingett, Leslie Ash and Toyah Wilcox. Roddam and the cast relate their memories of filming, and the aftermath of the film, with Roddam revealing how he assembled his company of actors and the methods used, including using the script only as a basis. Towards the end of the documentary we see fans of Quadrophenia watching it in a cinema and relaying their views on it, and its relevance to the youth of today. Roddam says that he realised the film's potential when he went to view the film at Pinewood Studios with Brian Tufano, who was absolutely blown away by it! Running time approximately 60 minutes.

THE WHO, THE MODS AND THE QUADROPHENIA CONNECTION – SEXY INTELLECTUAL PRODUCTIONS 2008.

Narrated by Thomas Arnold, with Production and Direction duties carried out by Alec Lindsell, this Documentary was released by Chrome Dreams Media in 2009. This film centres on the history of the album and film, and the impact Quadrophenia had on the Mod movement, and youth in general. I revisited this DVD having not viewed it for a couple of years and was pleasantly surprised, as I had forgotten how good it was! Although not an official release from The Who, it has some great contributions from the likes of Alan Clayson, Brett 'Buddy' Ascott, Chris Pope, Chris Hunt,

David Edwards, Eddie Piller, Paolo Hewitt, Ron Nevison, Simon Stebbings, Terry Rawlings and Richard Barnes. The latter gives a great insight into the chaos surrounding the recording of the album at the newly purchased Ramport Studios.

The contributor's further talk about the music, fashion and Quadrophenia in general. It also has plenty of archive footage from both the film and Mod events from the sixties. A great addition to anybody's Quadrophenia collection, and available from various sites on-line for between £10 and £15. Running time 94 minutes.

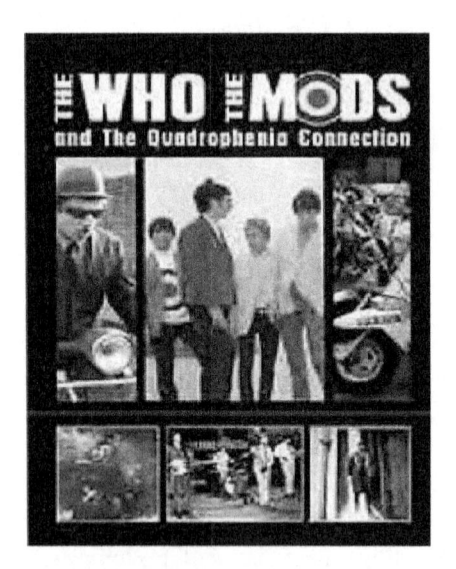

QUADROPHENIA: CAN YOU SEE THE REAL ME? – FIRST BROADCAST 29TH JUNE 2012.

Produced and Directed by Matt Casey, this was first aired on BBC4 to further promote the release of the Directors-cut box-set of the original album. On the night that this was aired, BBC4 had a dedicated Quadrophenia night, later showing the film and a recent performance by The Who at the electric proms.

Made by Glebe Productions in conjunction with The Who, and using Pete Townshend's personal archives, it dissected the album with some particularly revealing interviews with both him and Roger Daltrey. The former was clearly (as it shows) under a lot of pressure to produce an album of quality, having failed to properly get the recently abandoned Lifehouse project off the ground! Other notable contributions came from Bill Curbishley, Ron Nevison, Mark Kermode, Howie Edelson, Richard Barnes, Ethan A. Russell, Irish Jack and Georgiana Steele-Walker. The films maker also tracked down Julie Emson and Maxine Isenman who lived close to the Ramport Studios, and were asked to act as Mod-Girls in the Albums brochure that was produced by Ethan A. Russell. The girls also talked warmly about Terry 'Chad' Kennett, who was dragged from a local pub to play the part of Jimmy. John Entwistle and Keith Moon, are also included in some great archive footage with the later conducting his interview in a Toilet! And in a nice touch the film was dedicated to original Jimmy, Terry (Chad) Kennett.

The Documentary appears every now and then on BBC4, and hopefully will be released on DVD, as at the moment, it is only available on this format in the US. Running time approximately 70 minutes.

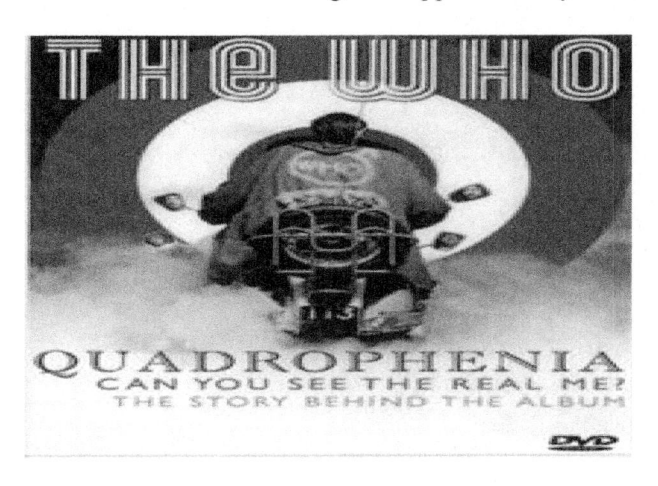

GUIDED LOCATION TOURS.

The available guided tours of locations are detailed below:-

BRIGHTON WALKS – BRIGHTON LOCATION TOUR.

Local tour guides, Damian Partridge and Lyn Neville organise Quadrophenia waking tours every bank-holiday, and are also available to carry them out any other time subject to numbers (speak direct to Damian or Lyn for more information!)

A topless bus tour is also carried out as part of the Mod-Weekender on August bank-holiday. Reviews of these tours are very complimentary, and their contact details are included below: -

Telephone & Fax 01273-302100 Website: - info@brightonwalks.com

Mobile 07775870195

PICTURE BELOW SHOWS TOUR GUIDES, DAMIAN AND LYN WITH GARY SHAIL ON A PREVIOUS TOUR.

SIMON WELLS – BRIGHTON LOCATION TOUR.

Simon Wells, author of the excellent Quadrophenia: A Way of Life carries out Sunday tours (please make contact for upcoming dates!). With Simon's vast knowledge of the film you are guaranteed a great time over a two-hour period, which also shows some sites from the original events of 1964.

For more information check out Simon's Facebook page; Quadrophenia Brighton Tours.

THE QUADROPHENIA LONDON LOCATIONS BUS TOUR – KIERAN McALEER.

In June 2016, Quadrophenia aficionado, Kieran McAleer carried out a mini-bus tour of London locations. There are more planned in the future so contact Kieran's Facebook page for further information:

https://www.facebook.com/kieran.mcaleer6

DREW STANSALL – QUADROPHENIA CLUB NIGHTS.

Drew Stansall, the former saxophonist with The Specials, now fronts a touring club night up and down the country, which first started in Leicester in 2012. The 'Quadrophenia Nights' see Stansall play all the Mod favourites, which is then followed by a live set from a Mod related band such as Whos Next or a Kinks tribute band, all the while the film plays as a backdrop behind them. Details of what is a great night out can be found at the following website: - http://www.quadrophenia.club

EXHIBITIONS: -

There have been, and are, a few exhibitions that will interest fans of Quadrophenia which are detailed below: -

BRIGHTON MUSEUM AND ART GALLERY.

Situated in the gardens of the Royal Pavilions this museum has a few artefacts and displays relating to the troubles in Brighton in 1964. Entrance fees are approximately £5 for adults, with special exhibitions available sometimes during the August Mod-Weekend. Check the following website for more information: - brightonmuseums.org.uk/brighton.

LONDON QUADROPHENIA EXHIBITION 2011/12 – PRETTY GREEN, CARNABY STREET, LONDON W1.

To celebrate the impending release of the Directors-cut box-set, Liam Gallagher's flagship clothing store, Pretty Green in Carnaby Street, held a special exhibition. Running from October 27th 2011 until January 31st 2012, it gave visitors a once in a lifetime opportunity to view Pete Townshend's master tapes, and various previously unseen manuscripts, as well as a plethora of photographs and other exhibits. Pretty Green clothing also released a special limited edition parka to coincide with the exhibition, which was launched by a mass gathering of Mods and Scooters!

THE HORSE HOSPITAL

The Horse Hospital is an arts venue which also hosts exhibitions relating to the media of film fashion, music and art. A specialist in-house hire company, Contemporary Wardrobe, also supplies vintage street fashion, couture items and accessories to the Film, TV and Fashion industries.

Contemporary Wardrobe was originally set up in 1978; by costume designer & stylist Roger K. Burton who was in the same year responsible for sourcing and supplying many of the outfits for Quadrophenia. For more information check out the following Website: - www.thehorsehospital.com

Address: - Colonnade, Bloomsbury, London WC1N 1JD

THE QUADROPHENIA COLLECTION – LITTLEDEAN JAIL, FOREST OF DEAN, GLOUCESTERSHIRE.

In November 2007 Dave Wyburn, avid collector of Quadrophenia memorabilia, and owner of two scooters; one of the Vespa's used by the Ace Face, and a full replica of Jimmy's Lambretta sold his collection to Andy Jones the curator and owner of Littledean Jail. In April of the following year these items were added to their own exhibits to create a unique and superb collection that any fan of the film will want to see! You will get to view countless signed items of memorabilia, including a copy of the script, and original parkas used in the film. The Quadrophenia collection is only a small part of this unique Museum which was once a working prison, and houses some intriguing artefacts (some of which are not for the feint hearted!) The Quadrophenia collection and Littledean Jail are well worth a visit, with tickets currently around £10. Website: - www.littledeanjail.com

Address: Church St, Littledean, Nr. Cinderford GL14 3NL. Tel: 01594-826659.

QUADROPHENIA THEMED HOTEL ROOM – BRIGHTON.

The Hotel Pelirocco has various themed rooms one of which is called the Modrophenia suite. This pop-art Mod themed double room is its homage to both the film and Modernism in general. Its walls are adorned with prints of The Who, and stills from the film, whilst your bedside tables are made from cut-down scooters, and the quilt is a specially made one in the style of a parka! Picture below shows the Modrophenia room. Website: - www.hotelpelirocco.co.uk

Address: - 10 Regency Square, Brighton BN1 2FG. Telephone: - 01273-327055.

COLLECTABLES:-

With the continued interest in all things, Quadrophenia there are an absolute raft of official and non-official items available, with the on-line auction sites usually the best way to track them down. Here are just some of the items that are out there: -

SIGNED ITEMS.

Up until only recently signed items of memorabilia were hard to obtain, however pre-printed/copied signatures were used extensively to sell a plethora of items such as 10"x8" stills from the film. There is absolutely no point in buying these now, as most cast autographs are widely available anyway! Sting, and Leslie Ash, are usually the hardest to track down, but they do still crop up on eBay fairly regularly. For the rest of the cast (including Phil Daniels) you can usually pick up a signed item from between £10 and £20.

ORIGINAL ITEMS RELATED TO FILM.

Anything such as clothing or props used in the film are highly collectable, but vary rarely become available. I obtained the briefly glimpsed union-jack parka some years ago, (picture below) and paid less than £40 for it. However, I have never seen anything in that price range since! Also, very occasionally copies of the script become available, it took me years to get my hands on one, and you can expect to pay at least £100 for one!

FILM POSTERS / STILLS AND LOBBY CARDS.

Original posters from the film can fetch over £400, but reproductions can be obtained for around £15, and when it's framed on your wall who knows the difference? Original film stills are very collectible but copies can be purchased for as little as £3.00. Lobby Cards are regular visitors to the online auction sites, both as complete sets and as separate items. Try to obtain a complete set if you can, and expect to pay in the region of £50 for them.

BOOKS

Virtually all of the cast have released autobiographies over the years, and there are also plenty of books that include Quadrophenia, but the ones featured below are those that are dedicated solely to it: -

Quadrophenia – The Novel by Alan Fletcher (Corgi 1979 – 055211183X)

The original Novel is now a much sought after item, and is interesting as it puts a little bit more flesh on the bones of one or two characters. Original price £0.95p, expect to pay between £20 and £30 on eBay.

Chasing the wind: A Quadrophenia Anthology – by Gary Wharton (Lushington Publishing 2002 – ISBN 0-9542187-0-10

Gary Wharton has gone on to self-publish several other books, with this being his first. An interesting read that predominately centres on the film version of Quadrophenia. Price £14.95 plus postage from the following; –

Lushington Publishing, 7 Kewstock Avenue, Llanrumney, Cardiff, Cf3 4DB. E-mail: - garywha@yahoo.com

Quadrophenia – Cultographies - by Stephen Glynn (Wallflower Press 2014 – ISBN 10: 0231167415)

Stephen Glynn is an associate research fellow at De Montfort University (UK), and released this book as part of a Cultographies series. Perhaps more of an essay type book, that although not revealing many unknown facts about the film is interesting, in that it approaches the film in a totally unique way. Available from the usual outlets at approximately £10.00.

Quadrophenia – A Way of Life - by Simon Wells (Countdown Books 2014 – ISBN 9-780992-830441)

In June 2014, Quadrophenia finally got the book it deserved when this excellent publication became available. Simon has authored many other books, including ones on both The Beatles and Rolling Stones. This book concentrates on the making of the film and has been critically acclaimed, even including an introduction from Bill Curbishley no less! A great launch party was held in Soho, which saw stars from the film along with Franc Roddam, and Bill Curbishley, join a parade of scooters to welcome this much-awaited book onto the shelves. Available from the usual outlets at £9.99.

PROMOTIONAL MATERIAL.

Always harder to obtain these items, but can sometimes be picked up for a bargain, although perhaps not so much in recent years! Items to keep an eye out for are, Press Books and information packs (prices range from £30 to £250, Promotional LP's (which were made for radio DJ's and included various interviews – priced at around £15). Cinema information packs (expect to pay £15), Promotional fold out posters (expect to pay £15). Also, keep an eye out for competition flyers and even adverts from local and music press (prices vary!)

DVD's / VIDEOS ETC.

There are many different formats that the film is available on, with various different releases on both VHS, BETAMAX and DVD. Also, occasionally you will be able to hunt-down copies on Laser Disc and CD (made for computer!) Some of them available are viewed in the following photograph.

MISCLEANEOUS.

As mentioned earlier there are many other Quadrophenia items available out there such as the usual Mugs, T-Shirts and Badges. There are also some other not so usual items that have appeared over the years, such as light switch covers, Quadrophenia Ale, and even a back scratcher!

CHAPTER 6.
QUADS & SODS!

WE'LL FIGHT THEM ON THE BEACHES!

The over exaggeration of the events of May Bank Holiday in 1964 by the media are known to irritate many who were there! For the record, there was an estimated 1000+ Mods and Rockers present in Brighton, with just 75 being charged! Many events, like the infamous shot in the Newspapers of a Mod kicking a Rocker on the floor was a financially induced re-enactment! During the Bank Holiday in 1981 there was a 'copycat' riot, this time between Mods and Skinheads, One Skinhead told the Brighton Argus 'The only reason we came here is because of that film – Quadrophenia'.

DRESS LIKE JIMMY AND STEPH!

It was originally planned to launch a Mod related clothing range, this being a joint project between The Who and a fashion company! Phil Daniels and Leslie Ash were lined up to model the range, however the plan never got off the ground!

BRIGHTON – THE MOD MECCA!

Brighton at the time of Quadrophenia's release was something of an unwanted noose around its neck, with many blaming it for bringing unwanted visitors and trouble-makers to the town!

However, it soon came to be seen in a more positive light, with the film being credited as giving the area a much-needed boost to its tourism trade. Indeed, when the film was re-released in 1997 a special train the 'Quadrophenia Express' left London to celebrate in Brighton, and was met by none other than the Mayor of Brighton, before going on to a special screening which was followed by a civic reception at the Grand Hotel!

These days Brighton is something of a Mod Mecca, with a couple of Mod related shops, and countless retro outlets that will keep the most ardent Modernist happy! There are also of course, the many locations, none more so than Quadrophenia Alley that are still pretty much unchanged, but also the famous Mod-Weekender in August when Madeira Drive is festooned with hundreds of Mods and their scooters!

BRIGHTON – HOTELS AND RAY WINSTONE!

Of course, when you think of Brighton Hotels you instantly think of The Grand and the Ace Face, which is where Franc Roddam along with Phil Daniels and Lesley Ash stayed during filming! Gary Shail, Mark Wingett and other cast members stayed at the Salisbury (now the Brighton Hotel) just along the road opposite the new i360 vertical pier. Many of the extras were assigned to the Queens Hotel at the bottom of East Street, with various other Bed and Breakfast outlets nearby also being utilised! Indeed, one guest not involved in the filming was none other than, Ray Winstone, he made a visit to meet fellow cast members and get measured for costume!

WORLD GALA PREMIER.

WORLD GALA PREMIERE

QUADROPHENIA

Plaza 1, Lower Regent Street,
Thursday, 16th August 1979
7.15 pm for 8.00 pm

Black Tie

L 27

Amongst the backdrop of a throng of scooters Quadrophenia was given its World Premiere in the West End, on Thursday 16th August 1979. Phil Daniels, was ferried to the event with his Parents in a stretch limousine. Mark Wingett who would have been too young to watch it a few months prior, also travelled up with his Parents, stopping on-route to change into his tuxedo in a toilet. John Altman met the actress, Desiree Erasmus at the event, and the pair went on to date each other for eighteen months!

THIS IS YOUR LIFE!

Three Quadrophenia actors have been presented with the famous Red Book; they are Glenn Murphy in 1992, Toyah Wilcox in 1996 and Mark Wingett in 2000.

AUF WIEDERSEHEN PET!

Auf Wiedersehen Pet, was the brilliant comedy-drama show that originally aired in 1983 until 1986, returning in 2002 until 2004 and was created by Franc Roddam. The show came about when Roddam was talking to an old friend who was a bricklayer that was forced to seek employment in Germany. The main cast features Gary Holton as Wayne Norris, who sadly died during the second series, and Timothy Spall as Barry Taylor. Also, featured during Series 1 are Ray Winston who played a British Soldier, Colin Latham, and Michael Elphick who played Magowan in 3 episodes.

SCOOTER CLUB'S

It is impossible to imagine how Quadrophenia would have been made without the help and cooperation of many Scooter Clubs up and down the country! Modrapheniacs were, and still are, a Dorset based club who were formed in 1976, and supplied many extras and scooters, also represented were the Modern Coaster, 5.15 and the Barnsley Vikings.

The following pictures show a flyer that was given to Scooterist's at a rally in Southend, and a letter given to Scooter owners who used their own machines and were asked to inform their relevant insurance companies about the filming (apparently in most cases this was paid no more than lip service). Also pictured is a stick-on period number plate that was issued by the production company. My grateful thanks are extended to Michael McGarry for these photographs.

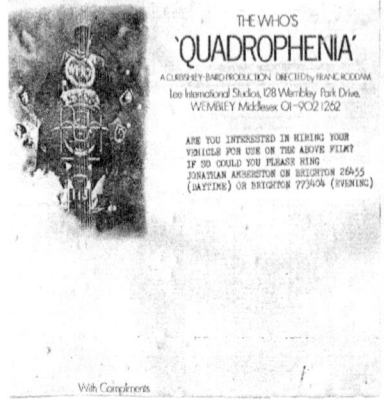

POLITICALLY CORRECT?

There are certain controversial subjects within the film that were very much of the time, none more so than the way the only black character, Ferdy is sometimes described and portrayed! Indeed, it must have been particularly hard for Phil Daniels to witness, as Trevor Laird was, and still is, one of his closest friends!

In his 2013 book, Mod – A Very British Style, Richard Weight elaborates; *'In the 1979 film Quadrophenia, for example the sole black character was a drug dealer on the fringes of the Mod gang; and although a controversial element of the film, it reflected the marginal role of the black youth in the movement during the sixties'*. Weight hits the nail very much on the head, and whilst some of the language and actions used may be a bit tough to take these days, it was correct that the film didn't ignore them, as many other films have gone on to do! Surely you can't just airbrush history keeping only those bits that suit, and it is to the films credit that they didn't try to hide it, however easy that may have been!

EXTRA'S / DELETED SCENES ETC!

Sadly, it would appear that any extras and deleted scenes have disappeared, it is rumoured that any unused footage was skipped during a clear-out at Elstree Studios which is where much of the editing stage was carried out! Also, when the film was finally transferred to digital, it was revealed that there were only two usable prints of the film still left!

ROCK IS DEAD – LONG LIVE ROCK!

Quadrophenia began life with the above name, and was originally going to be a film and album that looked at The Who's career and history, much like The Kids are Alright!

QUADROPHENIA – THE VEHICLES!

If you are curious about the make of the various cars, vans, motorbikes and scooters that are viewed in Quadrophenia, then you can visit the Internet Movie Cars Database at IMCDb.org. This incredible site has screen grabs of over 90 vehicles that are seen throughout the film, such as the 1960 Morris LD05 Royal Mail Van!

CHAPTER 7

QUADROPHENIA – THE SEQUEL?

Phil Daniels - 'Nobody ever suggested Quadrophenia 2 seriously; at least I hope they didn't'.
Phil Daniels – 'We were hoping that there was going to be Quadrophenia 2'
talking about the fact that Jimmy did not kill himself at the end of the film

Franc Roddam – 'He would have probably ended up supporting Margaret Thatcher'.
Talking about Jimmy's fate in the 2001 book, Your Face Here by Ali Catterall and Simon Wells.

Franc Roddam – It would be good to do a prequel. Or a Pre-Quad. You know it would be good to do a film in 1962 when the Mod movement was getting going.
Scootering Magazine August 2004

Phil Daniels – 'We are in talks about Quadrophenia 2, we will beat the Rockers up with our Zimmer frames, and go riding around on invalid scooters'
Quadrophenia cast re-union London, September 2nd 2007

Phil Daniels – Well I think it's a great idea!

Quadrophenia Convention – Brighton, April 2008

Toyah - Let's get a petition together and get it made!
Quadrophenia Convention – Brighton, April 2008

Could there really have been a sequel to this classic piece of cult British cinema? Well yes, no and possibly, is the complicated answer to that one (maybe one has already been made!).

Surely though, an all-out sequel - Quadrophenia 2 would be about as viable as say The Italian Job 2 or The Great Escape 2, some things are probably best left alone! For example, how often has the average person watched the disastrous Grease 2 compared to the original Grease film?

In an interview with Paolo Sedazzari, Phil Daniels revealed that the idea for a sequel had been mentioned jokingly. 'Jimmy would return to London and get into the advertising game, and end up as someone like Alan Parker (the director of Evita began his career directing adverts). But you know what sequels are like, they're never any good.' Franc Roddam has also said that it was mooted that Jimmy could go on a hippy trail to India, but adds that he fended off all serious attempts to put any of these into action.

Certainly, there was quite a lot of scope left in the original offering to make a sequel, with many unanswered questions;

1. Did Jimmy return to face the music in London, and make up with his parents and Dave?
2. Did the police arrest him for stealing the Ace Face's scooter?
3. What did he do for work, and what ever happened to his Lambretta?
4. Did Harry North's heavies find him and break a few of his bones?
5. Did Jimmy (as is suggested in the closing sequences) really reject his Mod ideals?
6. Did he get back with Steph?

However, isn't it best that we never actually found out the answers to these questions? The viewer is, therefore, able to decide what was to be Jimmy's fate, and the classic status of the film is able to be retained! The beauty of a film such as Quadrophenia, is surely that it leaves us with so many unanswered questions!

However, in 1985 we were (possibly) given an update on Jimmy's current situation in Pete Townshend's, White City. The forty-year-old, Townshend was now pursuing many solo-projects such as writing, and editing, for the publishing company Faber and Faber. In what was to prove a watershed period he decided to develop the White City idea into a musical film, with the sum of $350,000 of his own money being ploughed into the project. The project developed into a forty-minute production being shot on 35mm film, and accompanied by the obligatory soundtrack.

Townshend's idea had developed after a visit to the famous White City council estate (which is situated just off the Westway, and behind The BBC Television Centre), the area was very near to where he had grown up, and spent his formative years, and was also within spitting distance of Jimmy's old stomping area of Shepherds Bush.

Townshend said at the time that he was shocked at the deterioration of the area, which was dominated by the grand sounding, Commonwealth Avenue and other names relating to the old empire such as, India Way. The huge estate had been built after the second world war, and had a tough but clean reputation attached to it, what Townshend found were street corners full of pushers and pimps.

It had developed into a large immigrant community, dominated by Jamaicans, Africans, Irish and Gypsies all of whom lived in a fortress like estate bordered by walls, and with boarded up shops and disrepair everywhere. The impression was that the fortress had been long forgotten by the authorities, and that the estate could in effect administer its own rules and regulations.

Many of the very people who had come to Britain to help rebuild the country after the war now felt trapped in a monster-like creation that they had helped to create! And as they had now served their purpose, it suited the authorities to leave them where they were hoping that they would create as few problems as possible.

The production lasting forty minutes revolves in the main around a married couple, Jim and Alice. Jim who is unemployed is said to be an older update of Jimmy Cooper. Although this is somewhat vague, as we never learn his actual surname, his wife, Alice is the coach at the local swimming bath's. The bath's act as a real focal part in the film and as an escape from the mundane lives of the estate's inhabitants.

Jim's old pal, Pete Fountain is now a rock-star, and returns to his old manor to shoot a video, finding the area somewhat different to his last visit (as did Townshend, who plays the part superbly!) with Jim and Alice, like most others on the estate suffering acute economic problems.

The theme is that hope is there for all in the form of the White City swimming pool, the unifying element for the whole community.

Townshend said 'I felt the people to be good, in essence trying hard to live clean lives'. 'I found there was a sense of optimism and roots I was quite jealous of. Despite all my achievements and success, roots are one thing I don't feel I have'. The finished project received a mixed reception, with some very notable critical acclaim, however this failed to help sales of either the video or album.

Townshend's appraisal of the project was 'I wanted to make a metaphor and I got a bit confused, to be honest I wasn't sure of what I was trying to make a metaphor of'.

White City is (or probably is!), the closest that there is to a Quadrophenia 2, and is well worth a listen, and a view, for dedicated fans of the original film, however, do not expect too much, and don't expect to find the answer to unanswered questions from it, as the dates simply do not add up! Jimmy played by, Andrew Wilde bears absolutely no resemblance to Daniels incarnate at all in looks or personality.

What is known, is that in 1988 Roy Baird commissioned and co-wrote a script with Charles Preece, and Sam Hogue. Along with his son Marc Baird a meeting was held with Phil Daniels to discuss a proposed film, with a working title of ,Wont get Fooled Again! For whatever reason the film was never made and little is known of the contents of the script, apart from the fact that Jimmy ends up in Tunisia before returning to work in an Advertising Agency.
Following picture shows the cover of the script outline.

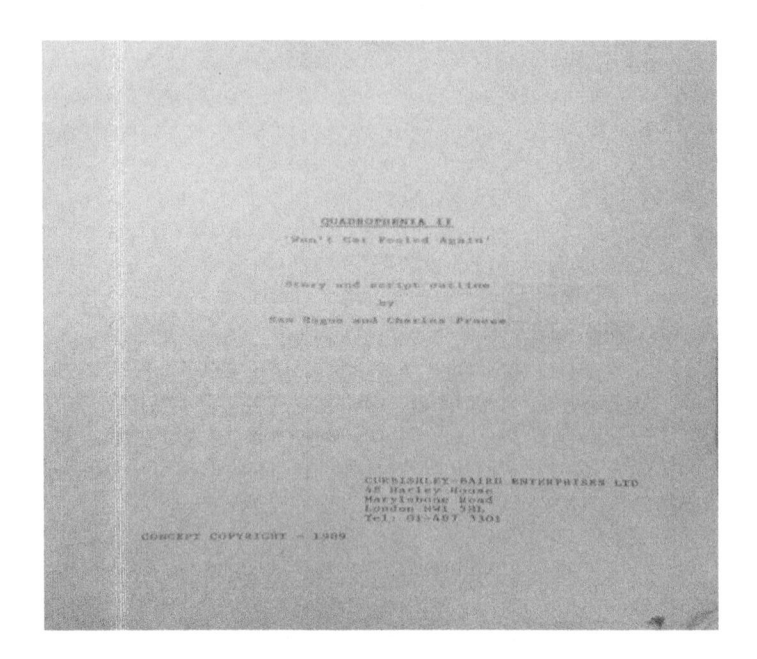

The Quadrophenia convention in Brighton, in April 2008, saw the subject debated in quite lengthy detail, with the actors present seemingly open to the idea, however the fans were probably less so!

In 2012 very strong rumours surfaced that Martin Stellman had written a script for a sequel, with ex-Skids front man, Richard Jobson being lined up to direct it! This was said to coincide with The Who's Quadrophenia live tour!

There have also been a couple of spin-off projects that hit the headlines in 2016; firstly, a crowd funded short film called Being.
Being is a thirty-minute production that has at its centre a young lad called Buddy caring for his Mother who is suffering from multiple sclerosis, and is very much into the film Quadrophenia, and sixties music. Buddy is subsequently befriended by Mark Wingett's character playing the part an out of work actor, and is also later joined by Trevor Laird. Buddy is given a chance to claim his childhood back again by his new-found friend in what promises to be a delightful little film made by Devin Crow, who grew up in Brighton where the film is set! Devlin is assisted in the film by his wife, who is currently fighting the debilitating disease herself in real-life! Although never billed, or claimed by the film-makers as a sequel, it will be interesting to see Wingett back in Brighton on a scooter! The support that this film has received from many parties will hopefully ensure that it

receives the success it surely deserves, in what is a very personal film by Devlin Crow, and is also his own personal nod to Quadrophenia and The Who!

In 2017, production is due to begin on a film called, To Be Someone, a film adaption of two books by Peter Meadows, they being, To Be Someone and To Be Someone 2. The first book was released in 2011, and followed up with its sequel in 2013. The original books saw the lead character, Jimmy now residing in Stevenage and involved in some shady dealings. Pete Townshend had given permission for Meadows to use the strapline, Jimmy's story continues, and inspired by Quadrophenia! However, contractually many names of the characters had to be changed, but a degree in Quadrophenia was not required to work out who they were based on! Both books were good gritty stories, and would have easily worked as well without the Jimmy connection, Meadows must be applauded for his work, and it's hard to believe that these were his first attempts at writing!

In May of 2016 it was announced that after a long journey a script was now available, and that virtually all the original cast of Quadrophenia had signed up for it, with Ray Burdis the man behind putting the project together. Predictably, sometimes due to 'lazy' journalism it was reported as being an out and out sequel – Quadrophenia 2, and things began to get messy for a while! The Who made it known it was not an official sequel, and the lawyers moved in! In late 2016 it seemed to have all been resolved, with the film being now talked about as a stand-alone project, however with all the lead roles being played by Quadrophenia stars, if, and when it happens the comparisons are bound to continue, whether anyone likes it or not!

So, it probably rightly looks as if unless Pete Townshend decides otherwise, we will never know what Jimmy is up to these days! The ambiguity of the Quadrophenia story is its true beauty, and surely its creator is the only one that has the right to decide what route his 'monster' ultimately took!

However, if you are still eager to find out the eventual fate of a certain Jimmy Cooper, 'Irish' Jack Lyons offers the following tongue in cheek answer on his website 'It's obvious what happens. He walks away from a miraculous brush with death, moves to Ireland and becomes a postman'.

CHAPTER 8.
MEMORIES and QUOTES!

One day I decided to adopt some method acting, had some Special Brew for breakfast and half a gram of speed. After a few hours of running up and down Brighton Beach I was as sick as a dog in the sea.

PAUL HARRISON – EXTRA

Despite what some people have said, the Alley scene was not played for real!

LESLEY ASH – STEPH.

Franc used to bollock me quite a lot in those days! I was a bit clumsy.

MARK WINGETT – DAVE.

People see the state of my eyes during the scene on the train and say you must have been on something; it was the only time I wasn't!

PHIL DANIELS – JIMMY

The movie was perfect timing for me!

PHIL DANIELS – JIMMY (talking at the 2007 Quadrophenia convention)

As I was a 'Rocker' it was our job to run down to the beach hollering! We were after the Mods and loving it! Stones (Ok potatoes!) were thrown fights ensued, even in the sea!

I remember there was a tea urn to keep us going. Unfortunately, I turned it on, but couldn't turn it off, and practically emptied the entire contents onto the esplanade!

I was up to my thighs in the water as someone convinced this would make it onto the screen, sadly it didn't but it was fun anyway! I lost count of the number of times we charged down the beach, but the adrenalin rush just kept us going. There were a mass of people watching the filming from the prom it was so exhilarating!

Franc Roddam the director was nice enough to buy some of us a drink. The filming on the beach alone took the best part of the day, and we were all exhausted but, had the best time. At the end of the day I even nearly forgot to pick up my £10 fee!

I would have gladly done it for nothing as it was, and remains, one of the best days of my life. If you watch the film very slowly frame by frame you may just spot me!

I am now approaching my 50th year mum to two teenagers, and living happily married in Leicestershire where I work as a teaching Assistant in a local High School. But, I can still be heard to say "Oh yes Toyah I met her when I was in a film" or "Sting? Didn't like him much when I met him!"

Happy days!

LOLLY DOBROJEVIC (NEE CLARKE) – EXTRA

There was a terrific camaraderie amongst everybody even the Mods and Rockers (until the cameras rolled that is).

LOLLY DOBROJEVIC (NEE CLARKE) – EXTRA

I saw Quadrophenia when it was released at the cinema in East Street. I came out of the cinema straight in to the middle of where it had all been filmed, can you imagine how that felt?

GLENDA CLARKE – BRIGHTON TOUR GUIDE/QUADROPHENIA FAN

I was in a motorcycle club at a pub called the Eagles Nest in Kent, and this guy turned up and said he needed some Rockers to be in a film. I said no problem and offered to help him get more people, which I did. I rode a 1956 Matchless with a sidecar as they needed a sidecar for the film. They built me a special one which was modeled on a picture from the sixties. The front came to a point at shin height and I believe was designed to ram scooters or Mods. I never did. Unfortunately, it never got used in the film.

We were in Brighton for over a week if I remember right. They put us up in local bed and breakfasts. One very big thing I remember was how well all the Mods & Rockers who were extras got on with each other. Everyone seemed to enjoy it. We were all trying to figure out who were real Mods and Rockers and who were actors, so that was always the question. Looking back on it now, that showed how well made the film was.

The police van scene was a lot of fun and I think it was 5 or 6 takes. I was just standing by the side of the road with everyone else and someone said, 'you, can you get in the van?' So I did. I think that took about half a day and I got to chat with Sting a lot. At that time, he was basically unknown. He was the opposite of his character. I found him very friendly and chatty. When it was time to leave, he came over to me to say goodbye which shows how well we got on. The cigarette case idea was Sting's I think. It cut the top of my finger.

My sister was also an extra in the film but you only saw her in the background. A few weeks later she was standing on Clapham Junction station and Toyah Wilcox was on the station and went up to my sister and said 'you were in Quadrophenia, weren't you'? She still remembers that day and how friendly Toyah was.

The whole Quadrophenia experience has stayed with me. A week has never gone by without someone mentioning it and the scene I was in. Even here in California people mention it. It has also opened many doors for me. I do some acting here and many agents and casting directors know that scene and are really pleased to meet me. I never realized at the time of filming that the film would have such an impact on my life and the lives of so many other people.

My biggest regret about Quadrophenia is having not stayed in touch with people from the film. As I stated, Sting and I got on very well and I often wonder if we met anywhere now what his reaction would be. The same goes for Phil Daniels. I know he is a big Chelsea fan and sits near a friend of mine who is a Chelsea season ticket holder, so maybe I will bump in to him the next time I go to the UK to see a match.

TOM INGRAM – ROCKER IN VAN AT BRIGHTON.

My only regrets are that I didn't take enough photos and didn't stay until the end of shooting. I was an apprentice at the time and had a supervisor that you didn't mess with, you just didn't do things like that at the time.

TOM PETCH – EXTRA.

Oh, how things changed when Quadrophenia was released in 1979 – everyone had to be a Mod!

WOLFY – LIFELONG MOD.

I don't think any of us had proper training. We just knew what we wanted to do!

MARK WINGETT – DAVE.

This was one of the biggest piss-ups of my life!

GUILIO PASTORELLI – EXTRA.

I took a stall on Portobello Road. It was a horrible, wet Saturday and this guy came up out of nowhere and said 'we're about to make a film set in the 60s. Could you supply us? It's about Mods.' Of course, it was totally my era, so I jumped at the chance.

ROGER BURTON – CLOTHING SUPPLIER.

The chemist scene was one that sticks in my mind, and was something we had improvised at Franc Roddam's house.

PHIL DAVIS – CHALKY.

I'm afraid I looked a complete prat in 1979, I had very long hair and a moustache. But it's interesting that the Mods still look cool today, while the flared trousers we were wearing during the shoot are a bit of an embarrassment.

FRANC RODDAM – DIRECTOR.

I remember constantly trying to stay on my scooter; it had all those mirrors, and was very awkward. They had to have three of them!

PHIL DAVIS – CHALKY.

After the re-release party in Brighton a guy came up to me and said that Quadrophenia had saved his life! Another time I was in a New York taxi and the driver told me he had watched it over 200 times!

FRANC RODDAM – DIRECTOR.

Gary (Shail) was very good, I was very young when I did that movie, I just remember being really scared when they were filming the fights on the beach because all the Hells Angels were really fighting!

CLAIRE TOEMAN – UNCREDITED ACTRESS.

Mobs coming up from London to fight on the beeches (I used to do that twenty years before, only at Bognor Regis, not Brighton.
When I think how stupid I was in the late 50s early 60s to travel all that way to get into a punch up I might as well have stayed at home and had a row with the geezer next door. (Saves time!)
This time it was different as I was dressed as a copper (you do stand out a bit!)
After two days filming we all had a few bruises but were well paid for our trouble and headed back to London.

HARRY 'AITCH' FIELDER – UNCREDITED ACTOR.

It's never gone so far as me wishing I'd never done Quadrophenia, but there was a time when I wouldn't talk about it when I was doing interviews, because I wanted people to be interested in me for other things as well.

PHIL DANIELS – JIMMY.

Looking back, it's amazing how much of a turning point that film was for me. Everything else seems to revolve around it.

PHIL DANIELS – JIMMY.

My daughter has never seen Quadrophenia – I don't mind though!

PHIL DANIELS – JIMMY.

I remember meeting Liam Gallagher in a toilet once and he told me how much he liked Quadrophenia, but said what are you doing hanging around with that lot from Blur though!

PHIL DANIELS – JIMMY.

They wanted me to cut my hair short for the role, but I refused and went for the Jane Asher look; make-up would be done in doorways and cars etc.

LESLEY ASH – STEPH.

I was very self-conscious but the cast and crew gave me loads of confidence. We all became very good friends. The party scenes were done at about 3.00am, and it wasn't unusual to work from 8.00 am until midnight. My fee was about £500.

LESLEY ASH – STEPH.

I think the film celebrates energy, but is also a condemnation of violence! There was a lot of improvising; actors were actively encouraged to change lines. The language used in the film means that it has never been played on an aircraft.

FRANC RODDAM – DIRECTOR.

I was originally up for the part of Jimmy, and auditioned 3 or 4 scenes but although I didn't get that role I was really chuffed to be in it. Everybody wanted to be in it, it was the film to be in.

PHIL DAVIS – CHALKY.

Franc offered me the scooter when we finished filming, but I was sick of it by then, I didn't want to be a Mod anymore!

PHIL DANIELS – JIMMY.

Steph would have ended up having a few kids and become a hairdresser, not ageing very well in a dead-end job!

LESLEY ASH – STEPH.

I know Kids today can enjoy watching the film as much as we did making it!

FRANC RODDAM – DIRECTOR.

The biggest danger is that it could come out looking like That'll be the Day or Stardust, because low production British pictures have that look about them. I suppose I'm banking on the fact that Franc Roddam is, I think, the only British TV director who's going to make that transition to Film. If he does pull it off I don't think, there's going to be any stopping him.

PETE TOWNSHEND (talking at the time of filming)

I have six children, and one by one they've all fallen in love with it.

FRANC RODDAM – DIRECTOR.

I was obviously only in the filming of it for just a few seconds as filler, but I will remember it all as if it were yesterday, for the rest of my life!

NEIL COLLINS – ROCKER EXTRA.

I had to wear different wigs in different scenes, and think it was 3 or 4 parts. It was great fun but a long time ago!

MARY THERESA WALSH-PAMMEN – Mod Girl Special Extra.

(Talking about Sting in his 2010 book, it's Only a Movie). Oh, and for the record, I thought he was crap in Quadrophenia too. Ace Face my arse!

MARK KERMODE – FILM CRITIC.

(Talking to The Brighton Argus in 1997). Quadrophenia was one of the best things I have been involved with because it was such fun to film.

JOHN ALTMAN – JOHN THE MOD

I was an extra on Quadrophenia back in 1978 and my claim to fame is having a chat with Sting, unaware that he was one of the lead actors! And a very sharp tonic mohair suit he was wearing at the time too! (source My favourite film website 2005)

LOUISE SHORT – Uncredited Extra in Night Club scene.

Ah the party scene! was it for real? Let's just say we were very young and there was a lot of Champagne flowing during the filming!

KATHERINE ROGERS – Played Dave's girlfriend at the house party.

By 1979 a film came out called 'Quadrophenia'. In this film, I saw everything I needed to know and I was hooked!

DAVE WYBURN – Quadrophenia fan and finder/restorer of Ace's scooter.

Looking back there's not much that I would change in the film. We got lucky in many ways. Finding such a great actor as Phil Daniels who became Jimmy and the terrific supporting cast is something that a producer hopes for but can never guarantee.

BILL CURBISHLEY – Producer (talking about the film in Quadrophenia a Way of Life – Countdown Books 2014)

When I met Pete, he wanted to do it like Tommy. He bought me some orchestration tapes with strings and violins. I said, 'No, that is Tommy – this is Quadrophenia. This is about street kids, this is going to be about Rock and Roll; this is going to be very raw and that suits my style as a film-maker'. And he immediately kind of folded in the nicest possible way and said: 'Make the film you want to make, I'm with you'. And I felt that was an incredible freedom to be given to me'.

FRANC RODDAM – Director (talking to Cast and Crew – BBC 2004)

Tom Ingram told me of the upcoming filming whilst we were having a drink at 'The Railway' in West Wickham. All he said was 'want to be in a film?' and I was sold. The filmmakers apparently took a shine to Tom. They paid for the engine on his A.J.S to be rebuilt and had a wedge-shaped sidecar made and fitted, for him to mow down Mods on Brighton seafront. We got to The Queens hotel in Brighton at the allotted time, where we were all given a fiver (enough for a good drink at the time) and the addresses of a B&B that had already been paid for, and a pub where they were having a 'Rock'n'Roll' night. We turned up (bleary-eyed) the next morning, where all our bikes had blankets tied on the back, and the guy on the 70's Bonneville had his yellow number plate and indicators taped over. Then, one by one, we were called into the 'wardrobe' department, where everyone had either a white scarf wrapped round their necks, their hair re-styled or their jeans turned up, or all three! They took one look at me and just waved me through - much to the chagrin of my fellow 'Rockers'. They wanted us in the car park on Beachey Head, so we set off along the coast road with a noise that would wake the dead. They had arranged for the road at Beachey Head to be closed off so we could ride around without crash helmets, and after one or two 'passes' with the sound man to record our engines, it was time for the filming. Tom Ingram's A.J.S just would not start having made it that far, so nearly in tears; they promised him a piece of the 'action' later in the filming. Judging where they had placed the camera, and how they wanted us to ride by in a group, I decided to risk being chucked out by being the first to venture wildly onto the wrong side of the road. Several people behind me had a similar idea, but I am the first to do it in that scene, which starts at 59 minutes, 59 seconds into the film, (if anyone's interested) anyway, after this excitement, we were assembled out of shot in the car park, watching the Mods all doing the same thing with some amusement. It was a blustery day, so when the Mods disappeared, we all took shelter in the furniture van full of props the film people had parked there, and to pass the time. Tigger, did a very good job of simulating several different kinds of sex acts with the mannequin he found, right in front of his girlfriend Bonnie, causing much hilarity. A lone scooter was heard approaching so we all went out to investigate. It was Phil Daniels on his mirror-festooned monstrosity. Quite brave, I thought, as there had been some tensions between the Mods and Rockers, even though it had been over ten years since hostilities proper. He pulled up right in front of us and with his unmistakable cockney accent said 'How you doin' boys? You all right then?' I immediately said (also with an unmistakable cockney accent) 'cor lets 'ave a go then' looking (as if in awe) at his Scooter. Surprisingly, he let me, saying 'don't smash it up or they'll kill me'. I rode it round the car park (causing a stir) a couple of times as if on a Sunday outing, and returned it intact. He went off and a coach turned up. The Director informed us that we were going to Brighton for the 'court scene' and would anyone like to volunteer to look after all the bikes, they would arrange a Mod to be there as well for company. I just was not prepared to leave my bike unattended so I stuck my arm up. Then all the Mods returned and everyone got on the coach except me. There was a pub and a cafe within walking distance, so when the pub landlord refused to serve me because of what I looked like, I was forced into the cafe for the couple of cups of tea I could afford. Upon returning to the Bikes and Scooters, found the wind had really picked up and I was actually able to lay back into the wind at a 45-degree angle (I've never known wind like it before or since) then a dozen or so Scooters fell over in the wind like a pack of cards. I felt duty-bound to rescue them, and just as I was doing this, a huge group of Mods on Scooters turned up. I was rather relieved when, instead of kicking the shit out of me, politely enquired about being in the film, as they had just travelled down from Yorkshire! Apart from this interruption, I was on my tod for nearly 12 hours. Tom Ingram inadvertently fell into the sea during the Brighton Beach fight sequence, so they paid him quite a lot of money in compensation for a new leather jacket, belt and boots. They even paid him £35 for a cut he got when Sting snapped a cigarette tin shut on his finger in the 'police van' scene. He had to join Equity too because he exclaimed the 'F' word. He is now a highly paid and respected Rock'n'Roll DJ somewhere in America. Why couldn't my bloody bike have broken down instead?

NEIL COLLINS – Uncredited Rocker at Beachey Head and Brighton.

I did Quadrophenia for other reasons. It was at a time when Mods hadn't re-occurred and I loved the fashion and I loved the music…and then it re-occurred and I fucking hated it. I still like the music, I just hated the hype.

TOYAH – Monkey (talking in 1980).

Franc Roddam was a very good master of a very big ship!

TOYAH - Monkey

Quadrophenia is The Who album I am most proud of!
PETE TOWNSHEND.

I was in Manhattan talking about the film when one of the audience said that they had noticed there were two yellow lines painted on the side of the road – out of the blue I said 'What are you some kind of fucking Traffic Warden?'
FRANC RODDAM – Director.

'I recognised a lot of myself in Jimmy!'

ROGER DALTREY.

When it came to the film, you were confronted with Sting. What's he got to do with Quadrophenia?

BRETT 'BUDDY' ASCOTT – ex Drummer with The Chords.

The film was a disappointment to me because it didn't match the complexities of the issues of the album.

BRETT 'BUDDY' ASCOTT – ex Drummer with The Chords.

Punk influenced Quadrophenia in that it chose to eschew the article of the rock opera of a few years previously, like the other film based on a Who album, Tommy (1975). It shied away from being a musical and was essentially a drama with songs, representing the Mods as an earlier form of youth rebellion along the lines that could be understood by a late 1970's punk influenced audience.

K.J. DONNELLY – (Popular Music in British Cinema a Study – BFI

I remember preparing for a second take in Brighton, when a little old lady scuttled by and muttered 'oh dear it's happening all over again'.

JOHN ALTMAN – John.

'Just about everything I dislike is to be found in Quadrophenia. The music is so loud and raucous that there should be ear-plugs with every ticket.
The film reeks with mindless violence. Without any meaning in their lives, the characters constantly take refuge in noisy vulgarity.
The first word spoken consists of four letters staring with F and if all the times the word is used were expurgated, the film would be half its length!
Sex is treated as cattle market traffic with an explicit scene of a pair of teenagers coupling standing up in a Brighton alley.
In the face of all this, why do I consider Quadrophenia one of the best films to have been made in Britain for a very long time?
Quite simply because it is utterly realistic – an uncompromising honest picture of a way of life that existed in the early 1960's'.

FELIX BARKER – Film Reviewer in 1979.

My scooter had been hired for the filming and as Terry Adcock couldn't get any time off, he kindly lent me his to ride down for the Brighton filming. He was also a Modrapheniac. I ended up sneaking his GP in to several scenes that subsequently never appeared, including a major one which is in posters where Sting was supposed to lead us down on to the beach. I've often wondered if that was because I sneaked a GP in! One day we visited the garage where the hired scooters where being stored, I asked about mine and they said they wanted to use it but it wouldn't start. I went over and it started first kick! They ended up hiring a few that didn't make it in to the film.

ROB 'YOB' WILLIAMS –Club. Extra and member of Modrapheniacs Scooter

The film crew provided girls with clothing. And they weren't all dressed the same each day. One day I wore a wig for one of the shots. A blonde dodgy one, wearing a green long coat. Other times I had my hair down and another in a ponytail with white top. Quite a few of the extras stayed at the same B&B as us including Ray Winstone!

ANGIE MULVIE - Extra and member of Modrapheniacs Scooter Club.

At the start of the summer of 1973 I began to read in the weekly music papers, (I used to get the Melody Maker, NME, Sounds and Disc) of an upcoming Who album that Pete Townshend was writing songs for, but there was very little detail just a few lines. As the summer progressed. a little more info came out, with wrong titles etc., but one day a photo and a better more detailed article appeared with Keith Moon outdoors at their apparent new recording studio, Ramport, which was still under construction. It was also my last year in High School, and I was more intrigued than ever, so along with a couple mates of mine set off one day, in search of Ramport in Battersea, but after a bit of looking around and asking people where it was we still could not find it so we gave up! Anyway, we got a job cleaning factory floors at a Record manufacturing plant along the North Circular Road in Walthamstow, a place called Phonodisc, and to my great surprise and delight while we were sweeping up one day, on the factory floor were stacks of Quadrophenia, the new Who album! I was in Heaven! There were also in another heap not far away, loads of scrapped album covers as something had gone wrong and they were not usable!

A bit later came the announcement of the release of the album and the subsequent Tour. I have read and heard of the Oil embargo at the same time as the release of the album, but I really cannot remember at all that it affecting the production of the album, but some people say it did which resulted in delays in its production, but from my viewpoint this was not the case at all! I was seeing it in the shops where I lived, so maybe other parts of the country perhaps? Anyway, I was walking down Walthamstow Market one day and a bloke had a copy on his stall and I got my copy for a Fiver which was a little cheaper than the shops!

I was due to leave school, had already taken my exams and had saved money all summer long to buy tickets for the forthcoming concerts which I hoped to go to. An announcement that tickets were going to go on sale came, I can't remember the exact date but it was on a Monday morning, and you had to queue up in person to buy them, the only place in London where The Who were going to play was the Lyceum in the Strand, and tickets were £2.20, and were limited to two per person due to an inevitable high demand. So, I went down there on the Sunday night on the last tube, and must have got there just before Midnight. The flipping Line was already half a mile long! Crikey! I wondered if I would get any tickets at all!

Anyway, I got to the Strand and joined the end of the queue, several people were playing Who music on cassette recorders so although I was at the end of the line it helped make up for it. Then I recognised a pal from Brighton, a bloke called Bill, I had seen him several times at different Who concerts and we would have talked about The Who a bit! Bill and maybe 5 or 6 Who fans were the only people I knew, as most seemed to keep to themselves back then and not interact much at all. So Bill and I kept each other company for a little while, until there was a bit of a commotion and shouting going on, up ahead apparently a gap had developed in the queue (this was to happen two or three times during the night) so I stood up and began running behind everybody else who were now moving up the queue, I looked around but did not see Bill right away, it was only then to my amusement and everybody else's that we saw that poor old Bill was running in his sleeping bag , and being hopelessly left behind ! But I kept a spot for him and most people were okay with that! By the time the morning arrived the crowd had swelled to huge numbers and the atmosphere began to turn a bit ugly as there was no apparent crowd control at all, a nice little line had become gigantic with loads of people gate-crashing, pushing in and almost riot like scenes began in the area. Tickets were due to go on sale at the Lyceum Box Office at 10am, and I began to seriously wonder if I would get any at all. Police had been called now and began to take a bit of control by erecting crash-barriers, and a few were on horseback trying to keep people in line, this was more like a football crowd, and as more gaps opened total chaos set in as the Police had clearly not expected anything like it. Some of the police began insisting we follow them around a corner and led a lot of people away, including me, but when they were not looking I left that line of people and snuck back in the line I was originally in! And there I met London's first ever black policeman! he was cool and he chatted with some of the fans and said that he liked The Who.

Finally, the queue started moving as it was now after 10am indicating sales had begun, and within half an hour I was now outside the box office! My turn came and I bought two tickets, one for the opening night and one for the last night, I intended to see all three if I could. By the time, I got home it was all over the radio, 'mobs run riot outside the Lyceum as fans queue for Who tickets'. Police estimated that over 20,000 people turned up for a total of about 9,000 tickets! an amazing experience, as I had queued for tickets before, but never like this!

By now I had played the album almost non-stop and already knew every word of it, I went down to Walthamstow Market and even had a T-shirt made saying Quadrophenia: The Who, which I started wearing everywhere, having bought it for the princely sum of £1.26! A girl I knew from High School, Kathy worked in the shop, and made it for me. I also went to a record shop in Leyton High Road called Ziggy's, as they had quite a spectacular Quadrophenia display in their window which was good to see! I knew the shop owner a guy called Phil, and he was a great bloke, always happy to chat about music with people and we would talk about Quadrophenia and what a great album it was, I remember he gave me a Quadrophenia sticker which I have now lost!

At the first Lyceum Gig, you had to go through a fair bit of security. I remember there were loads of blokes at the entrance, dressed up in suits with black bow ties who demanded to search people's bags and frisking them as they went in, they tore the tickets in half which kind of ruined them as there was no actual ticket stub. I got quite upset about it at time as where it said The Who had now been destroyed, so you could barely make it out! I quietly swore at them for doing that! In the foyer, there were a few Who T-shirts for sale, but I could only afford one so I got the Who Quadrophenia tour, like the design in the fallout shelter tour!

So, I'm at the back of the gig, and with an old mate from school Tony Boakes, a real Hippy, but didn't have a great view as everybody was taller than me and the floor was flat, no seats, and no slope! The place had a very expensive decor and lush carpeting which was very posh! Smoking was allowed in those days and the place was full of it, and you could also smell a lot of weed being smoked. I had a couple of drinks as there was a bar at the back and soon the concert started, but after a couple of songs they stopped the show as there was some severe crushing at the front, with Roger Daltrey appealing to fans to take steps backwards to help ease the pressure on those at the front, this seemed to take quite a long time , but was probably just a few minutes, that done they began to carry on. It was quite loud, I don't really know if it was because the Lyceum itself is a small place or what, but I think the speaker bank was the biggest I had ever seen, and as I said was quite loud! They began to play the opening notes of Quadrophenia, and when it came to the ' is it me' part a lot of people shouted out ' is it me for a moment, for a moment 'which went on for a while until some people told them to shut up! Which was amusing! So clearly people already knew the album which to my mind dispels the story about the Oil embargo and how it affected the production of the album and that nobody could get hold of a copy! Anyway, they delivered a blistering set, and I remember John blowing the trumpet for his parts and Roger seemingly going crazy with the twirling of his microphone, with Pete seemingly flying, I could hardly see Keith because his drum kit was so massive, but I loved every second of that show. They seemed to be in a trance really, with nothing getting in their way and committed to delivering a great set, the one low point, for me, was the insistence of Pete and Roger to explain Quadrophenia to everybody, which kind of killed the continuity of the show, they seemed to forget that most of the audience had indeed lived out Quadrophenia in their teenage years and now were a little older so could identify with the songs! I know I could! The lines in the Real Me, say,' The girl I used to love, lives in this yellow house, yesterday she passed me by she doesn't want to know me now?' How many young lads has that happened to? answer Millions! So, the talk between the songs was not needed, but sadly continued into The American Fallout Shelter Tour. At the end of the gig I stuck around and noticed that the carpet on the floor had been ruined as many people had stubbed their cigarettes out!

DERRICK BHUPSINGH - Who Fan and previous convention coordinator, now based in Trinidad & Tobago.

At the age of 13 I was at Plymouth Argyle's match against Luton Town on Saturday 19th October 1968, and it was where I first witnessed a youth subculture gang, Skinheads. Luton fans infiltrated the Devonport End of Home Park. They looked fearsome, shaved heads, grandad vests, braces, boots. Fights were breaking out throughout the match. With the Police struggling to control the mayhem.

A few weeks later, I was a mini Skinhead, riding my little bike around on my paper round.

A couple of years later, after buying the Richard Allen paperback, a natural progression was made to Suedehead.

I changed to Mod in 1972 when at 17 years old I bought a Vespa GS 160 from a mate. I had the Vespa for about a year before moving on to the Disco scene, with suits, shirts and ties the look!

None of my close friends at the time of these fashion phases were so image conscious, I was doing my own thing dress-wise.

Then in 1977 a group of us became Punks, not the safety-pin spikey hair bondage type, but a sort of Oxfam 'Are they? Aren't they?' look.

Bored with this when it became mainstream, I gradually morphed into Mod again after buying a new Lambretta Jet 200 in 1978 (£400 on Hire Purchase if I remember correctly!) Within a few months there were six of us on Lambretta's (three bought new), turning heads as we scooted around Plymouth.

I can't remember where it happened, but on one excursion in the summer of 1978, maybe at Torquay, we met the Modrapheniacs, a big gang of Mods of more than a dozen scooters. We exchanged addresses and, back in Plymouth, decided to call ourselves The Modern Coasters.

In August, the Modrapheniacs invited us to join them on a week-long tour of England including a 'Lambretta Club GB' Rally at Southend, then on to Manchester, Blackpool and Preston. A couple of us made it to Southend, but due to work commitments perhaps, I was the only Modern Coaster that completed the whole trip.

At the Southend Rally, some guy was giving out flyers calling for anyone interested in being in a film that The Who were making of their Quadrophenia album. To be honest we thought it was a wind-up, some geezer doing it for a laugh. One other memory of this England tour was when we went to an Army Surplus store in Stockport that sold the original US Army Parkas, several Modrapheniacs already had one and I was waiting to buy mine here, including the detachable wool lining, I now looked the part!

 Back home in Plymouth, we were all concluding that this Quadrophenia film was nothing more than a tease. However, there was a telephone number to call on the Quadrophenia flyer, we followed this up and registered our interest, but weeks passed with no news. Then one day someone telephoned and confirmed it was real. We were told to ride up to Brighton and we were booked into a certain B&B in the town for the evening of 27th September and following five nights. We were to report to the sea front by the pier at 9.30am the following morning to "begin filming".

I must have a cynical aspect to my character, because up to the point that we arrived at this B&B in Brighton and were in fact greeted by the landlady, I was still doubting that I was going to be in a film version of Quadrophenia!

The following morning in a sea front Cafe we signed disclaimer forms, we were given lunch vouchers for the cafe, some stick-on 1960s number plates, and reported to wardrobe in the centre of Brighton ...... The Modern Coasters were told "You guys look the part already, carry on down to Marine Parade." This acknowledgement encouraged us to joke, even more, about some of the appalling sights that called themselves Mods, we were elitist!

The next five days involved filming the riot scenes, the big meet along by the arcades (Sting stalling his Vespa countless times), charging up from the beach (ten takes, I was told off for looking directly at the camera, I thought it was a Documentary style film!), running through the back streets (those Police dogs were a bit too close for comfort! Leslie Ash crying, Sting had bought a bag of sweets and offered them around, trying to gain favour after his riding embarrassments). There was a lot of standing around in-between takes, we needed a rest from all the running, and we did become bored sometimes.

I was singled out for a scooter scene at dusk in which Sting and five of us rode slowly around a children's playground. Thirty-five years later I was pleased to read in Simon Wells book 'Inside the Making of Britain's Greatest Youth Film' that reference to this particular scene echoed Townshend's vision for Quadrophenia more than any other factor, it replayed an August night in 1964 when he finished a Who concert in Brighton and took a walk to wind-down. As if on cue a few hardy Mods stepped onto their scooters and drove around in a circular formation before moving off into the darkness. To him it was "the most perfect moment of my life".

After each day's filming, we returned to our B&B for dinner. In the evening we would go in to The Hungry Years pub by the pier, I remember chatting to Mark Wingett in there simply because he had a red V Neck jumper exactly like mine, I always thought of this when he later became famous in The Bill. Same with Sting and the sweets, he was Gordon Sumner and unknown at the time!

On the final morning, we reported to the Cafe on the beach for our wages - £15 per day with scooter, £10 per day without + petrol expenses for the travel to Brighton.

I remember the journey back to Plymouth being melancholic, what a week, fantastic, but it was over, the fleeting friendships with other cast members, the experiences shared never to be repeated, all confined to memory now!

It was about a year before the film was released. Waiting for it, we were concerned it would turn out naff, like a Mod version of Grease, or just as bad, a rock opera like Tommy. We were pleasantly surprised. We unanimously declared we would now be proud to boast that we were in it, the only disappointment being a couple of us did not spot themselves in the finished version and missed their chance to be famous for fifteen minutes.

MIKE McGARRY – Uncredited Mod in Brighton Scenes.

To a great extent as a young man I was Jimmy!

BILL CURBISHLEY – Producer (talking about his time with The Who on BBC Radio London 2017)

CHAPTER 9.

QUADROPHENIA - APPENDIX

QUADROPHENIA FILM - THE CAST

JIMMY (James Michael Cooper)	PHIL DANIELS
DAVE	MARK WINGETT
CHALKY	PHILIP DAVIS
STEPH	LESLIE ASH
PETE (Peter Fenton)	GARRY COOPER
MONKEY	TOYAH WILCOX
THE ACE FACE	STING
FERDY	TREVOR LAIRD
JIMMY'S MOTHER	KATE WILLIAMS
JIMMY'S FATHER (George Cooper)	MICHAEL ELPHICK
YVONNE (Cooper)	KIM NEVE
KEVIN (Herriot)	RAYMOND WINSTONE
SPIDER	GARY SHAIL
DANNY	DANIEL PEACOCK
MR (Simon) FULFORD	BENJAMIN WHITROW
MICHAEL (Agency Man)	JEREMY CHILD
MAGISTRATE	JOHN PHILLIPS
HARRY (Projectionist)	TIMOTHY SPALL
TAILOR	OLIVER PIERRE
ALFREDO'S CAFÉ PROPRIETOR	GEORGE INNES

MR CALE	HUGH LLOYD
HARRY NORTH	JOHN BINDON
BARMAN (at Villains Pub)	P.H. MORIARTY
HARRY NORTH'S ASSOCIATE	DON HANN*
HARRY NORTH'S ASSOCIATE	JIMMY MUIR*
RINGSIDE TRAINER	BOBBY RAMSEY*
BAND (at The Goldhawk Club)	CROSS SECTION
ROCKER #1 Wesley'Wez'Brooks	GARY HOLTON
ROCKER #2 (Lenny)	JESSE BIRDSALL*
ROCKER IN POLICE VAN	TOM INGRAM*
ROCKER AT SEA WALL/STUNTMAN	COLIN SKEAPING*
ROCKER IN BRIGHTON	JOHN BLUNDELL*
ROCKER IN BRIGHTON#2	WILF HARVEY*
ROCKER IN BRIGHTON#3	PAUL HARRISON*
ROCKER IN BRIGHTON#4	RAY (COLINDALE)*
ROCKER IN BRIGHTON#5	GLEN MURPHY*
ROCKER GIRL IN BRIGHTON #1	LOLLY CLARKE*
ROCKER GIRL IN BRIGHTON #2	CHRISSIE HANCOCK*
ROCKER GIRL IN BRIGHTON #3	CATHY INGRAM*
POLICEMAN IN BRIGHTON	HARRY FIELDER*
ROCKER ON ROAD TO BRIGHTON #1	JENNY CAMPBELL*
ROCKER ON ROAD TO BRIGHTON #2	MICK BONNER (TWIZZEL)*
ROCKER ON ROAD TO BRIGHTON #3	NEIL COLLINS*
ROCKER ON ROAD TO BRIGHTON #4	TIGGER? *
LEAD ROCKER GIRL	LINDA REGAN*
ROCKER GIRL ON ROAD TO BRIGHTON #1	BONNIE? *
FERDY'S MOTHER	LUCITA LIJERTWOOD*
SPIDER'S GIRLFRIEND	TAMMY JACOBS*
DES	PATRICK MURRAY*
BOUNCER AT NIGHTCLUB	CHRIS PARSONS*

JOHNNY FAGIN	JOHN ALTMAN*
MICHAEL	JULIAN FIRTH*
ERIC	PERRY BENSON*
GEORGE (Dave's Boss)	ERIC KENT*
KEN 'JONESY' JONES	MICKEY ROYCE*
KENNY	ANDY SAYCE*
NICKY	JAMES LOMBARD*
LOU	JOHN GAY*
ADVERTISING AGENCY CLIENT	BARRIE HOLLAND*
UN-NAMED MOD#1	DEREK LYONS*
UN-NAMED MOD#2	RUPERT FARLEY*
UN-NAMED MOD#3	ROBERT GLENISTER*
SHIRL (Steph's friend)	LOREN DAY*
MOD GIRL (Dave's Girlfriend)	KATHERINE ROGERS*
MOD GIRL#1	LESLEY DODD*
MOD GIRL#2	CLAIRE TOEMAN*
MOD GIRL#3	NICOLE MURPHY*
MOD GIRL#4	LOUISE SHORT*
MOD GIRL#5	BARBARA FRANKLAND*
MOD GIRL#6	ANGIE MULVEY*
MOD GIRL#7	LAVERNE JANES*
VOICE OVER ARTIST	RAY BROOKS*
RADIO LONDON ANNOUNCER	DAVE CASH*
SANDRA'S BOYFRIEND AT PARTY	SIMON GIPPS-KENT*
PARTYGOER #1	BEN ELTON*
PARTYGOER #2	PETER McNAMARA*
PARTYGOER #3	LINDA?*
PARTYGOER #4/MOD GIRL AT CLUB	MARY THERESA, WALSH-PAMMEN*
RECORD STORE ASSISTANT	CAROL HARRISON*

SCHOOLGIRL ON TRAIN	CAROLINE EMBLING*
RIOTING MOD	PETE McCARTHY*
MOD EXTRA #1	PHIL TERRY*
MOD EXTRA #2	STUART TURTON*
MOD EXTRA #3	GARY SANDERS*
MOD EXTRA #4	ROYSTON EDWARDS*
MOD EXTRA #5	TOM PETCH*
MOD EXTRA #6	MARTYN SCULLY*
MOD EXTRA #7/ROCKER IN POLICE VAN	KEVIN LAWTON (GINGER)*
MOD EXTRA #8	STEVE ORRIDGE*
MOD EXTRA #9	DOUGIE MACDONALD*
MOD EXTRA #10	PAUL CURBISHLEY*
MOD EXTRA #11	ROBIN (YOB) WILLIAMS*
MOD EXTRA #12	JOHN LOVING*
MOD EXTRA #13	MARK ELLIS*
MOD EXTRA #14	CHRIS PEARCEY*
MOD EXTRA #15	MICK?*
MOD EXTRA #16	PETE WALKER*
MOD EXTRA #17	MIDGE?*
MOD EXTRA #18	PHIL.B?*
MOD EXTRA #19	MICHAEL DICKINS*
MOD EXTRA #20	GUILIO PASTORELLI*
MOD EXTRA #21	GUIDO PASTORELLI*
MOD EXTRA #22	DAVID GRIGGLESTONE*
MOD EXTRA #23	TONY STANHOPE*
MOD EXTRA #24	SCOTT WILLIS*
MOD EXTRA #25	FRANK MAIDMENT*
MOD EXTRA #26	JOHN WARDZINSKI*
MOD EXTRA #27	HAPPY? *
MOD EXTRA #28	STIG? *

MOD EXTRA #29	JOHN HENRY ODDY*
MOD EXTRA #30	SIMON SCULLY*
MOD EXTRA #31	ROBERT GLOVER*
MOD EXTRA #32	DAVID KAY*
MOD EXTRA #33	DAVID WADDINGTON*
MOD EXTRA #34	ELLY BONGO*
MOD EXTRA #35	KEVIN LAWN*
MOD EXTRA #36	BINGO? *
MOD EXTRA #37	FLEAGAL? *
MOD EXTRA #38	GARY ROBERTSON*
MOD EXTRA #39	MARK HAZELGROVE*
MOD EXTRA #40	BRENDAN?*
MOD EXTRA #41	COLIN HAWKER*
MOD EXTRA #42	ADEY COBB*
MOD EXTRA #43	DAVE CLAYTON*
MOD EXTRA #44	PHIL BIRCH*
MOD EXTRA #45	MIKE McGARRY*
STUNTMAN/ROCKER	GARETH MILNE*
YOUTH ON BICYCLE	MICHAEL BARRY*
VOICE OVER ARTIST	ANGELA MARSHALL*
WAITRESS AT BRIGHTON CAFÉ	MAUREEN WELLS*
AIR CADET IN BRIGHTON	NEIL SYKES*
TV SHOW APPEARANCE	WILLOUGHBY GODDARD*
TV SHOW APPEARANCE	PHILIP LOCKE*

*uncredited performance

QUADROPHENIA FILM - THE CREW

Producers

ROY BAIRD, BILL CURBISHLY

Executive Producers
THE WHO
Director
FRANC RODDAM
Musical Directors
JOHN ENTWISTLE, PETE TOWNSHEND
Associate Producer
JOHN PEVERALL
Unit Manager
DAVID ANDERSON
Location Managers
BRYAN COATES / REDMOND MORRIS
Production Assistant
CAROLINE HAGEN
Assistant Director
RAY CORBETT
2nd Assistant Directors
MIKE FLYNN, KIERON PHIPPS

Director of Photography
BRIAN TUFANO B.Sc.

Camera Operator
DEWI HUMPHRIES

Camera Focus
JEFF PAYNTER

Continuity

MELINDA REES

Sound Mixer

CHRISTIAN WRANGLER

Sound Editor

JOHN IRELAND

Dubbing Mixer
BILL ROWE

Music Re-Mix Engineer

CY LANGSTON

Music Co-ordinator

MIKE SHAW

Boom Operator

ALBERT BAILEY

Production Designer
SIMON HOLLAND

Chief Make-Up Artist
GILLI WAKEFORD

Chief Hairdresser
SIMON THOMPSON

Wardrobe Supervisor

JOYCE STONEMAN

Stunt Arranger
PETER BRAYHAM

Stuntman

COLIN SKEAPING

GARETH MILNE

Choreographer

GILLIAN GREGORY

Property Master
TERRY WELLS

Construction Manager
JACK CARTER

Construction Supervisor

LEON APSEY

Casting Director

PATSY POLLOCK

Casting Assistant

ESTA CHARKHAM

Editors

MIKE TAYLOR / SEAN BARTON

Assistant Art Director

ANDREW SANDERS
Production Accountant
KEVIN O'DRISCOLL

Set Dresser

KEN WHEATLEY

Producers Assistant
KEN TUOHY

Production Buyer

TED HIGH

Electrical Supervisor for POLYTEL Films / Lee Electric's

MARTIN EVANS

Stills Photographer

FRANK CONNOR

Public Relations
DENNIS DAVIDSON, ASSOCIATES LTD

Unit Publicist

GEOFF FREEMAN
Screenplay

DAVE HUMPHRIES, MARTIN STELLMAN

Story Consultants
ALAN FLETCHER, PETE TOWNSHEND, CHRIS STAMP

Executive Producer for Polytel Films

DAVID GIDEON THOMPSON

Assistant Choreographer

JEFF DEXTER

Best Boy

RONNIE RAMPTON (uncredited)

Camera Operator – Second Unit
GEOFF MULLIGAN (uncredited)

Second Boom Operator / Sound Maintenance

MALCOLM HIRST (uncredited)

Producer of Cigarette Advertisement

RICHARD BRYAN (uncredited)

Music Editor

PAUL B. CLAY (uncredited)

Tailor for Phil Daniels

MITCH WAX (Dave Wax Outfitters) – (uncredited)

Clothing Suppliers

JOHNSON'S MODERN OUTFITTERS – (uncredited)

ROGER K. BURTON (Contemporary Wardrobes)– (uncredited)

Advisor

ALAN MORRIS aka DJ KING JERRY – (uncredited)

Scooter Advisor

BILL DRAKE – (uncredited)

Scooter Consultant

WILLIAM WOODHOUSE – (uncredited)

Scooter Supplier

STERLING SCOOTERS

Script Consultant

'IRISH' JACK LYONS – (uncredited)

Security Consultant

BOBBY RAMSEY – (uncredited)

Painter

ADRIAN START – (uncredited)

Clapper Loader

DEREK SUTER – (uncredited)

Advisor

TOMMY SHELLEY – (uncredited)

Title Designer

RICHARD MORRISON (uncredited)

Special Effects Technician

STEVE HAMILTON – (uncredited)

Misc. production role

JOHNATHAN AMBERSTON

Driver and Stand in for Phil Daniels

JOHNNY NOYCE

Without Who and Thanks

FREDDIE HAAVEN

Sound Recording – Dolby Digital 5.1 and DVD Version

MICHAEL JORDAN (uncredited)

Promotional Material Coordinator

BERTIE NICHOLAS

MISC

A POLYTEL FILM
The Producers Wish to Thank
FREDDIE HAAYEN and JAMES SWANN without whom…
Made by
THE WHO FILMS LIMITED

at

LEE INTERNATIONAL STUDIOS, WEMBLEY, ENGLAND

and on Location.

Processed by

RANK LABORATORIES

Recorded in

DOLBY STEREO

Re-recorded at

EMI STUDIOS, ELSTREE, ENGLAND

Jeans by

LEVI

Police Vehicles by

JOHN NICHOLSON CAR SALES

MUSIC

Hi Heel Sneakers........................CROSS SECTION..........The Who Group Limited
Dimples...................................CROSS SECTION......... The Who Group Limited

    Zoot Suit......................... THE HIGH NUMBERS. ....Phonogram

    Wishin & Hopin................ THE MERSEYBEATS........... Phonogram

    Blazing Fire................ DERRICK MORGAN.... Island Records

    Night Train........................ JAMES BROWN................... Polydor

    Be My Baby........................ THE RONNETTES...... Phil Spector Records

    Da Doo Ron Ron................... THE CRYSTALS...................... Polydor

    Wah Wahtusi........................THE ORLONS............ Abbeco Records

    Rhythm of the Rain................ THE CASCADES............ United Artists

    Baby Love......................... THE SUPREMES......... Motown Records

    Baby Don't You Do It............. MARVIN GAYE........... Motown Records

    He's So Fine.......................THE CHIFFONS................ Phonogram

Louie, Louie............................ THE KINGSMEN........... Springboard Records

    5-4-3-2-1........................... MANFRED MANN..................... EMI

Anyway, Anyhow, Anywhere.................. THE WHO................... The Who Group/EMCA

My Generation................................ THE WHO................... The Who Group/EMCA

    Green Onions...................... BOOKER.T & THE M. G's.................. WEA

MISC MUSICAL CONTRIBUTIONS

THE KINKS

JOHN LEE HOOKER

Music from the Soundtrack available on
POLYDOR RECORDS

VHS / DVD SPECIAL FEATURETTE

Photography
FRANK CONNOR

Editor

JOHN PIEDOT

Assistant Editor

DANNY PERKINS

Music

THE WHO

Video and Film Services

POLYGRAM VIDEO

FEATURE FILM COMPANY

HOLLOWAY FILM &TV

QUADROPHENIA– PERSONNEL A-Z.

A
AFFEJEE, Rafick	*Sound for Cast & Crew Documentary.*
ALLAN, Gregory	*Graphic Design – A Way of Life DVD Documentary.*
ALLEN, Patrick	*Voice-Over for UK Trailer.*
ALTMAN, John	*Johnny (John the Mod) Fagin.*
AMBERSTON, Jonathan	*Undesignated role in production.*
AMOS, Dallas	*Hair Stylist for 1973 album cover and booklet.*
ANDERSON, David	*Unit Manager.*

ANT, Adam	Potential actor in film.
APSEY, Leon	Construction Supervisor.
ARORA, Krishan	Executive Producer (BBC) for Cast & Crew Documentary.
ARTHAN, Louise	Researcher for Cast & Crew Documentary.
ASH, Leslie	Steph.
ASTLEY, John	Sound Engineer. / 1973 album re-issue Producer.
AUCOIN, Bill	Co-Producer of LA stage version.

B

BAILEY, Albert	Boom Operator.
BAIRD, Roy	Producer.
BARNES, Richard	Special Thanks (1973 album).
BARRIE, Amanda	Actress recruited to cast and subsequently sacked.
BARRY, Michael	Uncredited extra.
BARTON, Sean	Film Editor.
BENSON, Perry	Played the part of Eric.
BINDON, John	Played the part of Harry North.
BINGO?	Uncredited extra.
BIRCH, Michael	Played John Entwistle in LA stage show.
BIRCH, Phil	Uncredited extra.
BIRDSALL, Jesse	Played the part of Lenny the hostile rocker.
BJORKLAND, Johan	Camera Assistant for Cast & Crew Documentary.
BLAKE, Amanda	Production Manager for Cast & Crew Documentary.
BLUNDELL, John	Rocker on road to and in Brighton (uncredited).
BONGO, Elly	Uncredited extra.
BOOKER T& The M.G.'s	Musical Contribution.
BONNER, Mick (Twizzel)	Rocker on road to and in Brighton (uncredited).

BONNIE?	Uncredited Female Rocker.
BOURNE, John	Special Thanks – A Way of Life DVD Documentary.
BRANCH, Danielle	Played Guardian Angel in RWCMD adaptation – 2007.
BRAYHAM, Peter	Stunt Arranger.
BRENDAN?	Uncredited extra.
BRINTON, Tim	Newscaster (scene cut!)
BROOKS, Ray	Voice over for the cigarette advertisement.
BROWN, James	Musical Contribution.
BRYAN, Richard	Produced cigarette advertisement.
BRYDEN, Alan	Music for Cast & Crew Documentary.
BURDIS, Ray	Potential Actor.
BURTON, Roger K	Clothing supplier to film.

C

CAMPBELL, Jenny	Rocker on road to Brighton (uncredited).
CARTER, Jack	Construction Manager.
The CASCADES	Musical Contribution.
CASH, Dave	Radio London Announcer.
CASH, Nicky	Special Thanks – A Way of Life DVD Documentary.
CAVANAGH, Darren	Director – A Way of Life DVD Documentary.
CHAUHAN, Natasha	VT Editor – A Way of Life DVD Documentary.
CHARKHAM, Esta	Casting Crew.
CHARLESWORTH, Chris	Re-issue Executive Producer (1973 album).
CHENG, David	Editor – A Way of Life DVD Documentary.
The CHIFFONS	Musical Contribution.
CHILD, Jeremy	Played the part of Michael (Jimmy's work).
CLARKE, Lolly	Uncredited extra.
CLAY, Paul.B	Music Editor on film.
CLAYTON, Dave	Uncredited extra.

CLEMENTS, Alan	Executive Producer for Cast & Crew Documentary.
CLOUGH, Russell	Played Jimmy#1 in RWCMD adaptation – 2007.
COATES, Bryan	Location Manager.
COBB, Adey	Uncredited extra.
COLLINS, Neil	Uncredited extra.
CONNOR, Frank	Unit Photographer.
COOK, Lewis	Played Preacher in RWCMD adaptation – 2007.
COOPER, Garry	Peter Fenton.
CORBET, Ray	First Assistant Director.
COUTTS, Don	Series Director for Cast & Crew Documentary.
CRITCHLEY, Tom	Director, 2007 stage adaption.
CROSS SECTION	Band at the Goldhawk Club.
The CRYSTALS	Musical Contribution.
CULL, Simon	Editor for Cast & Crew Documentary.
CURBISHLEY, Paul	Uncredited extra.
CURBISHLEY, Bill	Producer. Re-issue Executive producer (1973 album).
	The Who Management with Trinifold Management.
CURL, John	Newsreader (1973 – original album- Cut My Hair).
CURTIS, Daniel	Played Jimmy#2 in RWCMD adaptation – 2007.

D

DALTREY, Roger	Executive Producer and Musical Director.
DANIELS, Phil	Jimmy Cooper.
DAVIS, Philip	Chalky.
DAY, Loren	Played the part of Steph's friend, Shirl.
DENNIS DAVIDSON ASSC.	Public Relations.
DEXTER, Jeff	Assistant Choreographer.

DiCARALO, Franco	Played Keith Moon in LA stage show.
DICKINS, Michael	Uncredited extra.
DODD, Lesley	Uncredited extra.
DRAKE, Bill	Scooter advisor (uncredited).
DWYFOR, Dyfan	Played Jimmy#3 in RWCMD adaptation – 2007.

E

EDENSOR, Joanne	Special Thanks – A Way of Life DVD Documentary.
EDMONSON, Adrian	Ace Face at Hyde Park show 1996.
EDWARDS, Neil	Camera Assistant/Sound Recordist- A Way of Life DVD Documentary.
EDWARDS, Royston	Uncredited extra.
ELLIS, Mark	Uncredited extra.
ELMS, Robert	Narrator of - A Way of Life DVD Documentary.
ELPHICK, Michael	George Cooper.
ELTON, Ben	Played the part of a youth at the house party.
EMBLING, Caroline	Played the part of schoolgirl on train.
EMSON, Julie	Mod girl in 1973 album booklet.
ENTWISTLE, John	Executive Producer, Music Director and Music Producer.
EVANS, Martin	Electrical Supervisor for Polytel.
EVANS, Richard	Designer and Art Director for reissued album.

F

FARLEY, Rupert	Uncredited Mod in London and Brighton.
FAWCUS, Ron	Mixing Continuity and Engineering Assistant (1973 album).
FIELDER, Harry	Played the part of a Brighton policeman.
FIELDS, Tommy	Played Roger Daltrey in LA stage version.
FIRTH, Julian	Played the part of Michael a Mod.
FLEAGAL?	Uncredited extra.
FLETCHER, Alan	Consultant and author of Novel.

FLYNN, Michael	Second Assistant Director.
FRANKLAND, Barbara	Played the part of Mod Girl in Club.
FREEMAN, Geoff	Unit Publicist.
FRIEND, Tim	Special Thanks – A Way of Life DVD Documentary.
FRY, Stephen	Played the part of Hotel Manager at Hyde Park show 1996.

G

GAY, John	Lou the Mod uncredited extra.
GAYE, Marvin	Musical contribution.
GILMOUR, David	Musician at Hyde Park show 1996.
GIPPS-KENT, Simon	Uncredited role as Sandra's boyfriend.
GLENISTER, Robert	Uncredited role of un-named Mod.
GLITTER, Gary	Rocker and Godfather on 1996 tour.
GLOVER, Robert	Uncredited extra.
GODDARD, Willoughby	Appears in TV show watched by the Coopers.
GREGORY, Gillian	Choreographer.
GRIGGLESTONE, David	Uncredited extra.
GRILLO, Joseph	Played Roger Daltrey in LA stage show.
GWYNNE, Lowri	Played Mum in RWCMD adaptation – 2007.

H

HAAYEN, Freddie	'without whom' credit for supporting project.
HAGEN, Caroline	Production Assistant.
HAMILTON, Steve	Special Effects Technician (uncredited).
HANCOCK, Chrissie	Uncredited extra.
HANN, Don	Played the part of associate of Harry North.
HAPPY?	Uncredited extra.
HARRISON, Carol	Played the part of the record shop assistant.
HARRISON, Paul	Uncredited extra.

HENDERSON, Kahl	Sound Dubbing for Cast & Crew Documentary.
HERDEN, Darren	Camera for Cast & Crew Documentary.
HARVEY, Wilf	Uncredited Rocker in Brighton.
HAWKER, Colin	Uncredited extra.
HAZELGROVE, Mark	Uncredited extra.
HIGH, Ted	Production Buyer.
The HIGH NUMBERS	Musical Contribution.
HIRST, Malcolm	Sound Boom Operator/Sound Maintenance.
HO, Michael	Graphic Design – A Way of Life DVD Documentary.
HOGUE, Sam	Script and Story for Quadrophenia 2.
HOLLAND, Barrie	Advertising Agency Client.
HOLLAND, Simon	Production Designer.
HOLTON, Gary	Aggressive Rocker (Wesley 'Wez' Brooks).
HOOKER, John Lee	Musical Contribution.
HOUISON, Ron	Special Effects (1973 album).
HUGHES, Graham	Photography and design (1973 album).
HUMPHRIES, Dave	Screenplay.
HUMPHRIES, Dewi	Camera Operator.

I
IDOL, Billy	Played the part of the Ace Face in stage version/Classic Quadrophenia.
INGRAM, Cathy	Uncredited extra.
INGRAM, Tom	Played the part of Rocker in Police Van – uncredited.
INNES, George	Café Proprietor (Alfredo's).
IRELAND, John	Sound Engineer.
ISENMAN, Maxine	Mod girl in 1973 album booklet.
I.S.O.	Titles for Cast & Crew Documentary.

J
JACOBS, Tammy	Spiders Girlfriend.

JAMES, Tony	Potential Actor.
JANES, Laverne	Uncredited extra.
JOBSON, Richard	Potential Director of Quadrophenia sequel.
JOHNS, Glyn	Associate Producer on Love Reign O'er Me and Is It In My Head.
JOHNSON, Lloyd	(from Johnson's Modern Outfitters) clothing supplier.
JONES, Taylor, Rees	Played Godfather in RWCMD adaptation – 2007.
JORDAN, Michael	Sound Recording (Dolby Digital and DVD versions).

K

KAY, David	Uncredited extra.
KAMERON, Pete	Executive Producer (1973 album).
KELLY, Jerry	Lighting Director for Cast & Crew Documentary.
KENDRICK, Rob	Played Jimmy#4 in RWCMD adaptation – 2007.
KENNETT, Ray 'Chad'	Jimmy in photographs (1973 album).
KENT, Eric	Played the part of Dave's boss George.
The KINGSMEN	Musical Contribution.
The KINKS	Musical Contribution.
KIRBY, Lydon	Advisor for 1973 album booklet.
KOLB, Jim	Choreographer of LA stage version.

L

LAMBERT, Kit	Pre-Production and Executive Producer (1973 album).
LANGDON, Alex	Jimmy 1996/7 Quadrophenia Tour.
LANGTON, Cy	Re-mixing Engineer.
LAIRD, Trevor	Ferdy.
LAWN, Kevin	Uncredited extra.
LAWTON, Kevin (Ginger)	Uncredited extra.
LEFFMAN, Jonathan	Sound Recordist – A Way of Life DVD Documentary.

LINDA?	Uncredited extra.
LIJERTWOOD, Lucita	Played the part of Ferdy's Mother.
LlOYD, Benedict	Sound Editor – A Way of Life DVD Documentary.
LlOYD, Hugh	Played the part of Mr Cale.
LOCKE, Philip	Appears in TV show watched by the Coopers.
LOLK, Darren	Played Pete Townshend in LA stage show.
LOMBARD, James	Played the part of Nicky.
LONDON ORIANA CHOIR.	Choir for Classic Quadrophenia.
LOVING, John	Uncredited extra.
LUCAS, James	Played Ace-Face in RWCMD adaptation – 2007.
LUDWIG, Bob	Re-issue (1973 album) Remastering.
LYONS, Derek	Uncredited Mod extra.
LYONS, 'Irish' Jack	Special Thanks (1973 album), Script Consultant (uncredited).

M

McCARTHY, Pete	Played the part of a rioting Mod.
McDONALD, Trevor, Sir	Played the part of newscaster at Hyde Park 1996.
McGARRY, Mike	Uncredited extra.
McKAIE, Andy	Special Thanks (1973 album).
McLOORE, Briad	Researcher for Cast & Crew Documentary.
McMANUS, George	Special Thanks (1973 album).
McMICHAEL, Joe	Special Thanks (1973 album).
McNAMARA, Peter	Played the part of a youth at the house party.
McMULLAN, Sophie	Production Manager – A Way of Life DVD Documentary.
MACDONALD, Dougie	Uncredited extra.
MACPHERSON, Andy	Mixer on re-issued album.

MAIDMENT, Frank	Uncredited extra.
MARSHALL, Angela	Uncredited extra voice-over.
The MERSEYBEATS	Musical Contribution.
MEYER, Guy	Executive producer – A Way of Life DVD Documentary.
MICK?	Uncredited extra.
MIDGE?	Uncredited extra.
MILNE, Gareth	Stuntman and Rocker in film.
MILLER, Randy	Special Thanks (1973 album).
MOCHRIE, Steven	Camera for Cast & Crew Documentary.
MOON, Keith	Executive Producer.
MORGAN, Derrick	Musical Contribution.
MORIARTY, P.H.	Barman.
MORRIS, Alan aka DJ King Jerry	Advisor to Film.
MORRIS, Redmond	Location Manager.
MORRISON, Niamih	Make-Up for Cast & Crew Documentary.
MORRISON, Richard	Title Designer (uncredited).
MUIR, Jimmy	Played the part of associate of Harry North.
MULLHOLLAND, Mathew	Editor – A Way of Life DVD Documentary.
MULLIGAN, Geoff	Camera Operator – Second Unit.
MUNRO, Scott	Cameraman - A Way of Life DVD Documentary.
MURPHY, Glen	Rocker extra in Brighton.
MURPHY, Nicole	Mod girl extra in Brighton.
MANFRED MANN	Musical Contribution.
MURRAY, Patrick	Played the part of Des.

N

NELL, Dirk	Lighting Director for Cast & Crew Documentary.
NEVE, Kim	Yvonne Cooper.

NEWCOMBE, Bodie	*Director of LA stage version.*
NEWMAN, Frances	*Choreographer, 2007 stage adaption.*
NEVISON, Ron	*Engineer and Special Effects (1973 album).*
NICHOLAS, Bertie	*Coordinator of Promotional Material.*
NICHOLLS, Rob	*Equipment Supervisor – A Way of Life DVD Documentary.*
NICHOLSON, John	*Supplied Police Vans for the film.*
NIXON, Kimberley	*Played Mod Girl in RWCMD adaptation – 2007.*
NOYCE, Jonny	*Driver and stand-in for Phil Daniels.*

O

ODDY, John Henry	*Uncredited extra.*
O'DRISCOLL, Kevin	*Production Manager and Accountant.*
O'HARA, John	*Musical Director, 2007 stage adaption.*
O'HARE, Elspeth	*Series Producer for Cast & Crew Documentary.*
OLLEY, Michelle	*Writer of, A Way of Life DVD Documentary.*
ORRIDGE, Steve	*Uncredited extra.*
The ORLONS	*Musical Contribution.*
OXLEY, Ray	*Designer for Cast & Crew Documentary.*

P

PARKER, Charlie	*Musical Inspiration.*
PARSONS, Chris	*Bouncer at Nightclub.*
PASTORELLI, GUIDO	*Uncredited extra.*
PASTORELLI, GUILIO	*Uncredited extra.*
PAYNTER, Jeff	*Camera Focus.*
PEACOCK, Daniel	*played the part of Dan.*
PEARCE, Scott	*Camera Assistant for Cast & Crew Documentary.*
PEARCEY, Chris	*Uncredited extra.*
PERKINS, Danny	*Assistant Editor of Featurette – video/DVD.*

PETCH, Tom	Uncredited extra.
PEVERALL, John	Assistant Producer.
PHIL.B	Uncredited extra.
PHILLIPS, John	Played the part of the Magistrate.
PHIPPS, Kieron	Second Assistant Director.
PIERRE, Oliver	Played the part of the Tailor.
PIEDOT, John	Editor of Featurette.
PLANET X	Music – A Way of Life DVD Documentary.
POLLOCK, Patsy	Casting Director.
PREECE, Charles	Script and Story for Quadrophenia 2.
PRIDDEN, Bobby	Studio Earphone Mix (1973 album).
PROBY, P.J.	Played the part of The Godfather on UK tour.
PROKOFIEV, Sergei	Musical Contribution.

R

RAMPTON, Ronnie	Best Boy.
RAMSEY, Bobby	Played the part of ring-side referee/ security co-ordinator.
RAY (Colindale)	Played the part of uncredited Rocker.
REES, Melinda	Continuity.
REGAN, Linda	Rocker Girl.
ROBERTSON, Gary	Uncredited extra.
RODDAM, Franc	Director and Screenplay.
ROGERS, Katherine	Played the part of Dave's Girlfriend at Party/Mod Girl.
The RONETTES	Musical Contribution.
ROSENBERG, Robert	Re-issue Executive Producer (1973 album).
ROTTEN, Johnny	Screen tested for the part of Jimmy.
ROWE, Bill	Sound re-recording.
ROYAL PHILHARMONIC	

ORCHESTRA	Orchestra for PT Classic Quadrophenia.
ROYAL WELSH COLLEGE OF MUSIC AND ARTS	
	Production and Stage for 2007 adaption.
ROYCE, Mickey	Played the part of Ken 'Jonesy' Jones.
RUSSELL, Ethan, A.	Original Art Direction (1973 album).

S

SANDALL, Robert	Contributor - A Way of Life DVD Documentary.
SANDERS, Andrew	Assistant Art Director.
SANDERS, Gary	Uncredited extra.
SAYCE, Andy	Played the part of Kenny.
SCHULTZ, Bill	Producer of LA stage version.
SCHUMACHER, John	Played Dad in RWCMD adaptation – 2007.
SCULLY, Martyn	Uncredited extra.
SCULLY, Simon	Uncredited extra.
SHAIL, Gary	Spider.
SHAREAUX, Stephen	Played the part of Jimmy in LA stage version.
SHAW, Mike	Music co-ordinator.
SHELLEY, Tommy	Uncredited advisor.
SHORT, Louise	Uncredited extra.
SKEAPING, Colin	Played the part of a Rocker also stuntman.
SKITTLES, Sophie	Producer – A Way of Life DVD Documentary.
The SKUNKS	Potential Band in film.
SMART, James	1964 Mod.
SPALL, Timothy	Played the part of Harry the projectionist.
STAMP, Chris	Story Consultant. Executive Producer (1973 album).
STAINTON, Chris	Pianist on Dirty Jobs, 5.15 and Drowned.
STANHOPE, Tony	Uncredited extra.
START, Adrian	Uncredited painter.

STEELE-WALKER, Georgiana	Ramport Studios Secretary.
STELLMAN, Martin	Screenplay.
STERLING SCOOTERS	Scooter suppliers to film.
STEVENS, Phil	Lighting for Cast & Crew Documentary.
STIG	Uncredited extra.
STING	Ace Face.
STONEMAN, Joyce	Wardrobe Supervisor.
STRAIGHT 8	Potential band in film.
SUTER, Derek	Clapper Loader.
The SUPREMES	Musical Contribution.
SWANN, James	'without whom' credit for supporting project.
SYKES, Neil	Air Cadet in Brighton scene.

T

TAIT, Samantha	Production Manager – A Way of Life DVD Documentary.
TAMMARA, Angela	Special Thanks – A Way of Life DVD Documentary.
TAYLOR, Mike	Film Editor.
TEGLAS, Zoltan	Played Ace Face in LA stage show.
TERRY, Phil	Uncredited extra.
THOMPSON, David Gideon	Executive Producer (Polytel).
THOMPSON, Simon	Hairdresser.
TIGGER?	Uncredited Rocker.
TOEMAN, Claire	Uncredited extra.
TOWNSHEND, Pete	Executive Producer, Story Consultant, Music Director, and Screenplay (Uncredited). Various Production credits (1973) album.
TOY, Adam	Sound for Cast & Crew Documentary.
TUFANO, Brian	Director of Photography.
TURTON, Stuart	Uncredited extra.
TUOHY, Ken	Production Assistant.

TYDESLEY, Heath	Special Thanks – A Way of Life DVD Documentary.

U

URIBE, Peter	Director of LA stage version.

W

WADDINGTON, David	Uncredited extra.
WAKEFORD, Gilli	Make-up Artist.
WALKER, Pete	Uncredited extra.
WALSH-PAMMEN, Mary, Theresa	Special Extra (Mod Girl).
WARDZINSKI, John	Uncredited extra.
WARK, Kirsty	Presenter, Cast & Crew Documentary.
WAX, Mitch	Tailor (from Dave Wax Outfitters) for Phil Daniels.
WELLS, Maureen	Waitress at Brighton Café.
WELLS, Terry	Property Master.
WHEATLEY, Ken	Set Director.
WHITROW, Benjamin	Played the part of Simon Fulford.
THE WHO	Various musical and production roles.
WILCOX, Toyah	played the part of Monkey.
WILDE, Andrew	Played Jimmy in White City.
WILKIN, Amanda	Played Guardian Angel in RWCMD adaptation – 2007.
WILLIAMS, Kate	Mrs Cooper.
WILLIAMS, Robin(Yob)	Uncredited extra.
WILLIS, Scott	Uncredited extra.
WINGETT, Mark	Dave.
WINEHOUSE, Amy	Possible Female Lead in Stage Version.
WINSTONE, Ray	Played the part of Kevin Herriot.
WOODHOUSE, William	Scooter consultant.
WRANGLER, Christian	Sound Mixer.

X/Y/Z

YOUNG, Jeff	Writer, 2007 stage adaption.

ZIEGLER, Robert   *Conductor Royal Philharmonic Orchestra PT-Classic Quadrophenia.*

QUADROPHENIA – TIMELINE.

1891

April 27th   **Sergei Prokofiev** – born in Russia.

1914

July 16th   **John Phillips** – born in Birmingham.

1917

August 22nd   **John Lee Hooker** – born.

1920

?   **Bobby Ramsey** – born.

February 8th   **Lucita Lijertwood** – born in Trinidad.

1923

April 22nd   **Hugh Lloyd** – born in Chester.

1927

March 17th   **Patrick Allen** – is born.

1928

January 30th   **Geoff Mulligan** – born in Camberwell, London.

1929

December 24th   **Tim Brinton** – born in Hampstead.

1931

February 2nd   **Bill Rowe** – born in Durham.

1933

?   **Roy Baird** – born in Elstree.

1935

May 11th   **Kit Lambert** - is born.

September 14th   **Amanda Barrie** – is born.

1936

July 12th	**Peter Brayham** - is born.

1937

February 17th	**Benjamin Whitrow** - born in Oxford.

1938

?	**David Gideon Thompson** - is born.
March 8th	**George Innes** - born in London.
November 6th	**P.J. Proby** – born in Houston, Texas.

1939

?	**Brian Tufano** – born in London.
February 27th	**P.H. Moriarty** - born in London.
April 2nd	**Marvin Gaye** – born in Washington DC.
April 20th	**Ray Brooks** – born in Brighton.
August 16th	**Sir Trevor McDonald** – born in Trinidad & Tobago.

1940

?	**Manfred Mann** – born in South Africa.
April 26th	**Harry Fielder** – born in Islington.

1941

?	**Kate Williams** – born.
February 11th	**Freddie Haayen** – born.
April 29th	**Franc Roddam** – born in Stockton-On-Tees.

1942

?	**Alan Morris** aka **DJ King Jerry** – born.
February 15th	**Glyn Johns** – born in Epsom, Surrey.
July 7th	**Chris Stamp** – born in London.
July 18th	**Dave Cash** – born in Bushey, Hertfordshire.

1943

October 4th	**John Bindon** – born in London.

1944

March 1st	**Roger Daltrey** – born in Shepherds Bush, West London.
March 29th	**Sean Barton** – born in Hampton Court, Surrey.

May 8th	**Gary Glitter** – born in Oxfordshire.
September 20th	**Jeremy Child** – born in Woking, Surrey.
October 9th	**John Entwistle** – born in Chiswick, West London.
1945	
February 6th	**Michael Jordan** - born in Alaska.
May 19th	**Pete Townshend** – born in Chiswick, West London.
1946	
March 6th	**David Gilmour** – born in Cambridge.
August 23rd	**Keith Moon** – born in Willesden, Middlesex.
September 19th	**Michael Elphick** – born in Chichester, Hampshire.
1948	
?	**Martin Stellman** – born in London.
June?	**Alan Fletcher** – born in Newark.
1950	
?	**Terry(Chad)Kennett**- born.
1951	
October 2nd	**Gordon Sumner (aka Sting)** – born in Newcastle.
November 9th	**Pete McCarthy** – born in Warrington, Cheshire.
1952	
February 9th	**James Lombard** - born in Battersea.
March 2nd	**John Altman** – born in Reading, Berkshire.
September 22nd	**Gary Holton** – born in London.
1953	
March 5th	**Sergei Prokofiev** – dies.
July 30th	**Phillip Davis** – born in Grays, Essex.
October 19th	**Oliver Pierre** – born in France.
1955	
June 2nd	**Garry Cooper** – born in Hull.
November 30th	**Billy Idol** – born in Middlesex.
1956	

January 31st	**Johnny Lydon aka Rotten** – born in London.
December 17th	**Patrick Murray** – born in London.

1957

January 24th	**Adrian Edmonson** – born in Bradford.
February 19th	**Ray Winstone** – born in Plaistow, London.
February 27th	**Timothy Spall** – born in Battersea, London.
August 24th	**Stephen Fry** – born in London.
August 30th	**Trevor Laird** – born in Islington, London.

1958

February 8th	**Carol Harrison** – born in West Ham, London.
May 18th	**Toyah Wilcox** – born in Birmingham.
September 25th	**Derek Lyons** – born.
October 25th	**Philip William Daniels** – born in Kings Cross, London.
October 25th	**Simon Gipps-Kent** – born.
November 14th	**Claire Toeman** – born.

1959

?	**John Entwistle** - invites his school pal, **Pete Townshend** to join Trad-Jazz band – **The Confederates**.
May 3rd	**Ben Elton** – born in Catford, London.
November 10th	**Gary Shail** – born in Hendon, Middlesex.

1960

February 19th	**Leslie Ash** – born in Mitcham, Surrey.
March 11th	**Robert Glenister** – born in Watford.
March 12th	**Julian Firth** – born in London.
December?	**Loren Day** - born.
December 21st	**Katherine Rogers** – born in London.

1961

January 1st	**Mark Wingett** – born in Melton Mowbray, Leicestershire.

January 25th	**Tom Ingram** – born in Hampshire.
1962	
?	**John Entwistle** joins **Roger Daltrey'** group, **The Detours** and is soon followed by **Pete Townshend**.
1963	
February 13th	**Jesse Birdsall** – born in Highbury, London.
1964	
	The Detours are renamed as **The Who**. **Pete Townshend** smashes his guitar into the ceiling of The Railway Tavern, Wealdstone, Middlesex thus starting a trend that would continue for many years.
	Pete Meaden takes over as the bands new manager, their name is changed yet again, this time to **The High Numbers**.
	In April **Keith Moon** joins the group, as its new drummer.
	In July **Meaden** resigns and is replaced by **Chris Stamp** and **Kit Lambert**.
May 16th – 18th	The infamous bank-holiday weekend when thousands descended on Brighton to cause mayhem.
May 18th	**Barry Prior** a Mod thought to have influenced **Pete Townshend** in the writing of **Quadrophenia** is found dead just along the coast from Brighton.
July	**The High Numbers** release **I'm The Face/Zoot Suit** in the UK on **Fontana Records**.
1965	
January 26th	**The Who** make their first appearance on **Ready Steady Go**.
May 21st	**The Who** appear on **Ready Steady Go** singing **Anyway, Anyhow, Anywhere** (probably this clip is the one used in the film). The single is released the same month on **Brunswick** in the UK.
November	**My Generation** is released as a single in the UK on **Brunswick**.

November 20th	**Melody Maker** reports that **The Who** are splitting after the other members of the group sack **Roger Daltrey**. However, **Daltrey** returns within the week.
December	**My Generation** is released as an album in the UK on **Brunswick**.
1971	
July 12th	A version of **Love Reign O'er Me** is recorded at Olympic Studios.
1972	
?	The Road Traffic Act of 1972 makes it illegal to ride a Scooter or Motorbike without a crash helmet.
?	**Pete Townshend** releases his first solo album, **Who Came First** on **Track Records**.
1973	In the spring **The Who** commence the recording of their most ambitious project to date, **Quadrophenia**. **5.15**, climbs to number 20 in the charts during September. In October, a ten show British tour is undertaken to promote **Quadrophenia** and **5.15** is debuted on **Top of the Pops**.
October	**Love Reign O'er Me** is released in the USA on **Track**.
October 29th	**The Who** receive a gold disc for **Quadrophenia**.
November	**Quadrophenia** has its world-wide release.
1974	
January	**The Real Me/ I'm One** is released in the USA on **Track**.
1975	
December 9th	**Tommy** the movie is released in the UK.
1978	
May 25th	**Keith Moon** plays his final gig with **The Who** at Shepperton Studios.
June 13th	**Franc Roddam** commences work on **Quadrophenia**.
July	**Who Are You? /Had Enough** released on **Polydor** in UK.

	Phil Daniels answers an advert in **The Sun** for the part of **Jimmy Cooper**.
August	**Who Are You? /Had enough** released on **MCA** in USA.
August 15th	**Pete Meaden** - the bands ex- manager dies.
September 7th	**Keith Moon** - dies of an accidental overdose of a prescription medicine, Heminevrin that he was taking to overcome his alcoholism.
	Bill Curbishley finalises funding from **Polygram** for **Quadrophenia**.
September 26th	Location filming begins in Brighton.
1979	
April 26th	**Quadrophenia** is reviewed at the British Film and Television Arts screening room in London.
May 12th	**The Kids are Alright** is released in British cinemas.
August 16th	**Quadrophenia** is released in British cinemas with the world Gala premier being held at the (now closed) Plaza Cinema, in Lower Regent Street, London.
September 7th	**Quadrophenia** is featured on the BBC programme, **Talking Pictures** with a special location report.
September 14th	**Quadrophenia** is released at the Toronto Film Festival in Canada.
October	**Quadrophenia** soundtrack released in UK and USA.
October 2nd	**Quadrophenia** is released in America.
October 9th	**Quadrophenia** is released in West Germany.
December	**Quadrophenia** is voted as 'the most distasteful film of 1979' in an annual pole. **Green Onions** reaches number 7 in the charts on the back of a post **Quadrophenia** re-release.
1980	
January 9th	**Quadrophenia** is released in Sweden.
January 25th	**Quadrophenia** is released in Finland.
March	**I'm Free / Zoot Suit** re-released in USA.
April	**I'm Free / Zoot Suit** re-released in the UK.
1981	

April 4th	**Kit Lambert** falls down the stairs at his mother's home and is killed.
?	The film is made available to buy on VHS at the princely sum of £89.99.
1983	
November	**The Style Council,** release **Solid Bond in Your Heart** which has a promotional video that is said to be their own personal mini-**Quadrophenia**.
December 16th	**Pete Townshend** officially leaves **The Who.**
1984	
March?	**Bobby Ramsey** – dies.
April 1st	**Marvin Gaye** – killed by his father in Los Angeles.
1985	
March 19th	**Bryan Coates** – dies in a plane crash in Morocco.
September 24th	**Kimberley Nixon** – born.
October 25th	**Gary Holton** – dies of a drug overdose in Wembley, Middx.
November 1st	**Pete Townshend's** solo project **White City** is released in November as both an album and as a long-form video,
1987	
September 16th	**Simon Gipps-Kent** – dies of drug overdose.
1988	
?	**Roy Baird** sets the wheels in motion for a Potential sequel called **Won't Get Fooled Again!**
November 26th	**Quadrophenia** is given its TV premier on ITV in a heavily edited version that was not warmly received!
1992	
?	**Bill Rowe** – dies in Northwood, Middlesex.
August?	**Lucita Lijertwood** – dies in Southwark, London.
1993	
October 10th	**John Bindon** – dies of an Aids related illness in London.

1995

February?	**Phil Daniels** and **Blur** are at The BRITS to collect the award for best single and best video.
May 11th	**John Phillips** who played the part of the Brighton magistrate dies in Oswestry.
October 31st	**Phish** cover **Quadrophenia** in its entirety as part of their 'Halloween Musical Costume Extravaganza' which is later released on cd.

1997

January 29th	**Quadrophenia** is premiered at The Odeon Cinema, West Street in Brighton prior to its re-release.
January 31st	**Quadrophenia** is re-released up and down the country.

1999

December 31st	**Timothy Spall** is awarded the OBE in the new-year honours list.

2000

May 21st	**The Simpsons** parody the 1973 album in an episode entitled Behind the Laughter. The album is renamed **Krustophenia** after **Krusty the Clown** and sees him astride a scooter!

2001

?	**John Altman** has the dubious honour of being voted rear of the year.
March	Comedian **Phil Jupitus** releases a live video and audio cassette of a recent tour which sees him pose as a slightly larger than life Jimmy on the back of a scooter. The name of this offering being, **Quadrophobia**.
April	**Pete Townshend** attempts to get a **Quadrophenia** workshop up and running at The Bush Hall in Shepherds Bush.
June 21st	**John Lee Hooker** – dies.
July 28th	**Pete Townshend** announces that he hopes to follow the success of the **Quadrophenia** workshop with a production at The National Theatre. **Trevor Nunn** is said to be very interested in the project.

2002

	Chasing the Wind: A Quadrophenia Anthology is released by **Gary Wharton**.
June 27th	**John Entwistle** - dies at the age of 57 in a Las Vegas Hotel bedroom.
September 7th	**Michael Elphick** - dies at the age of 55 after being rushed to hospital from his home in Willesden, North West London. He suffers a heart attack thought to have been caused by his alcoholism.
2003	
January	**Leslie Ash** creates many newspaper headlines following her recent cosmetic surgery to her lips.
	Friends rush to the support of **Pete Townshend** after he is released on police bail following investigations into child pornography.
February 14th	Sting is reported to have earned a massive £25million in the Last eight months alone!
March 15th	An exact replica of Jimmy's Lambretta is offered on the auction website **e-bay** for the sum of $12,500.
March 28th	The famous Brighton, West Pier featured in the film is virtually destroyed in a fire, just weeks after securing a grant to have it restored to its former glory. The pier had remained closed for almost 30 years.
April 28th	**Toyah Willcox** is installed as bookies favourite to win the ITV reality show, **I'm a Celebrity Get Me Out of Here.**
May 7th	**Pete Townshend** learns that he will not face charges following on from police investigations into child pornography. It is later reported that he had no case to answer to in the first place!
August 24th	**Quadrophenia** is shown as part of 'The Cool World' a special season of Mod related films put on by the **BFI** at **The National Film Theatre.** It shares a double bill with the rare 1979, **Talking Pictures,** which was originally shown on **BBC** and shows an in-depth location report of the film – lasting 23 minutes.
October 10th	**Sting** receives his CBE from the Queen at Buckingham Palace in recognition of his services to the British music industry.
December 30th	**David Gilmour** is awarded the CBE.
?	**Quadrophenia** is voted the 86th greatest album of all time by **VH1** viewers.

2004

February 4th — I'm a Celebrity Get Me Out of Here sees **Quadrophenia** hopeful, **John Lydon** aka **Johnny Rotten** walk out of the show. Rumours are abounding that **Carol Harrison,** who had a small role in the film is to replace him. The **Quadrophenia** connection is furthered when **Toyah Wilcox** appears on the show to talk about their experience when auditioning for the film.

March 15th — **Franc Roddam** makes the national news after discovering a novice author in a supermarket who has gone on to write an award-winning children's book.

June/July — **Leslie Ash** appears almost daily in the press after she is hospitalised following an incident at home. Whilst in hospital for treatment she picks up a virus, and there are initial fears that she may never walk again, however she proves experts wrong, although she faces a long and painful road to full recovery.

July 21st — **Phil Daniels** stars in the BBC drama **The Long Firm**. The drama is set in the sixties with **Daniels** taking the role of, Jimmy. He reveals in interviews to publicise the show that he still has some of the costumes at his home from **Quadrophenia**.

July 26th — A special 25th Anniversary showing of **Quadrophenia** takes place on a huge outdoor screen on Brighton Beach.

September 21st — **Green Day** release their successful rock-opera, **American Idiot** which is said to be partly influenced by **Quadrophenia**.

October 6th — **Pete McCarthy** the well-known travel writer and extra in **Quadrophenia** dies of cancer at the age of 51.

November 21st — **Quadrophenia** is screened as part of the Brighton Film Festival to celebrate its 25th anniversary. The film is dedicated to the memory of the late **Pete McCarthy**.

December 31st — **Roger Daltrey** receives a C.B.E in the Queens new year's honours list.

Hugh Lloyd receives an M.B.E.

2005

? — **Luna C Productions** stage a theatrical version in Los Angeles of **Quadrophenia** which stars **Stephen Shareaux**. The play is revived in March and November the following year.

January — **Phil Daniels** receives critical acclaim for his role as a Lawyer in the new BBC series **Outlaws**.

February — **Mark Wingett** leaves ITV's **The Bill** after 21 years.

March?	**Oliver Pierre** - dies in France.
March 8th	**Leslie Ash** speaks out publicly about the cleanliness in Hospitals, which was said to be a contributory factor in the virus that she picked up whilst hospitalised the previous year.
March 15th	**Toyah Wilcox** goes on a nation-wide tour to promote her book about her recent facelift.
March 22nd	**Phil Daniels** and **Franc Roddam** appear in BBC4's **Cast & Crew** to discuss the making of **Quadrophenia**.
April	Readers of **MOJO** magazine vote **Quadrophenia** as the eighth greatest music movie ever, the winner being **This Is Spinal Tap**.
May 29th	**Quadrophenia** is included in the inaugural **MOJO** Film Festival.
August 24th	**Quadrophenia** wannabe's **Jimmy Pursey** and **John Lydon** are involved in a punch up at the USA embassy whilst renewing their visa's, the pair have been feuding on and off for over 25 years.
September 6th	**Franc Roddam** talks about his work on **Quadrophenia** during a BBC show called, **Drama Connections** that was dedicated to **Auf Weidershen Pet**. **Timothy Spall** and **Gary Holton** also appear.
September 26th	**Mark Wingett** joins the cast of **EastEnders**.
September 28th.	**Phil Daniels** is to join **EastEnders** in January 2006 playing the part of **Kevin Wicks**.
October 30th	A new film, **We Are the Mods** is announced. The story revolves around 2 girls in a Californian high school who are retro-mods being heavily influenced by **Quadrophenia**.
November 2nd	The European premier of **Tommy/Quadrophenia Live** on DVD is held at the Curzon Cinema in Mayfair. **Daltrey** and **Townshend** are joined by a packed cinema, including **Leslie Ash** looking great following her recent and ongoing illness. The reviews that follow are extremely favourable with **The Sun** giving it a 5/5 review.
November 7th	**Tommy/Quadrophenia Live** is released in the UK.

2006

February	Pete **Townshend** reveals that he has written a song about **Leslie Ash** called, **Cinderella** for **The Who's** long-awaited new album due out later in the year.
March 7th	**Phil Daniels** and **Mark Wingett** share their first scene together in **EastEnders**.
April 7th	**Tommy/Quadrophenia** wins an award in the second annual Music DVD awards in California, in the best special features/bonus materials section.
April 29th	**Alan Curbishley** announces that he is to leave his role as Manager of Charlton Athletic after fifteen years.
May 23rd	**Leslie Ash** presents an award at **The British Soap Awards**, **Phil Daniels** and **Mark Wingett** are also in attendance.
July 1st	Radio Two's, **The Day the Music Dies** features probably the first and only **Quadrophenia** based comedy sketch which sees a quasi-**Paul Weller** take the lead role. The lead character travels to Brighton in search of **Leslie Ash** and some Rocker's!
July 28th	**Patrick Allen** – dies at the age of 79.
August 7th	at last the digitally remastered DVD is available in region 2 retailing at £17.99.
August 27th	**Geoff Freeman** - dies of Pulmonary Fibrosis.
September	**Shane Meadows** releases **This Is England**, which includes **Perry Benson** in its cast. The film's poster is said to be a homage to **Quadrophenia**.
September 4th.	It is announced that **Trevor Laird** will appear in the forthcoming series of **Doctor Who** as the father of the Doctors new assistant, Martha.
September 12th	**Kate Williams** and **Phil Daniels** share a brief scene in **EastEnders** the former joins the show as the mother-in-law of his girlfriend.
November	**Quad** returns for a short run in Los Angeles.
December 7th	**Peter Brayham** - dies outside his home in London.
December 25th	**James Brown** dies of pneumonia at the age of 73.

2007

February 10th	The BBC2 programme **The Culture Show** announces that it would like to erect a plaque at Beachey Head to mark the exact spot where Jimmy sends the GS scooter over the cliff.
February 9th	**The Royal Welsh College of Music** stage a stage show of **Quadrophenia** at the Sherman Theatre in Cardiff.
June 19th	**Lambretta** announce the launch of a new clothing range in conjunction with **The Who** with one of its highlights being an exact replica of the parka used on the cover of the 1973 album.
July 14th	**Leslie Ash** makes a rare television appearance on the BBC show, **Would I Lie to You?**
July 22nd	**Freddie Haayen** dies.
July 28th	**Quadrophenia** is voted third in the 'Social Realism' category of the **Radio Times/BBC2** poll in their **British Film Forever** competition.
August 18th	**Phil Daniels** reveals he is to leave **EastEnders** when his current contract expires.
September 1st	**Phil Daniels**, **Phil Davis**, **Trevor H. Laird**, **Mark Wingett**, **Gary Shail**, **Garry Cooper**, **Toyah Wilcox**, and **John Altman** are re-united at Earls Court for **The London Film and Comic Convention**.
September 2nd	**Franc Roddam** joins the above for the second day of the re-union, and all take part in a Q and A session that goes down extremely well with a packed audience.
September 6th	**Garry Cooper** wins The Stage actor of the year award for his portrayal at the Edinburgh Festival of **Grizzly** in **Long Time Dead**.
October	**Ray Winstone** receives the **Richard Harris** award for Outstanding Achievement by an actor, at the British Independent Film awards.
November 24th/25th	**Phil Daniels, Mark Wingett** and **Trevor Laird** appear at a mini-Quadrophenia re-union at the NEC in Birmingham.

2008

January 1st	**Phil Daniels** is seen for the last time as Kevin Wickes in **EastEnders,** his character is killed in a car accident.

January 10th	The Camden New Journal carries a story that **Phil Daniels** Parka as worn in Quadrophenia was stolen from a friend's car some three days previous. A cash reward is offered but to date it remains unfound.
January 16th	**Leslie Ash** is awarded the sum of £5M as compensation for her injury and loss of earnings relating to the MSSA virus that she contracted whilst in hospital in 2005.
April 5th/6th	Brighton stages the first ever **Quadrophenia** Convention culminating with a special showing of the film at The Duke of York Cinema.
April 13th	**Phil Daniels** and **John Altman** are amongst 30,000 runners at the Flora London Marathon. **Phil Daniels** finishes in 4:49:11 with **John Altman** coming in at 5:18:36.
July 14th	**Hugh Lloyd** – dies aged 85.
September 20th	**Phil Daniels** makes his debut on the BBC TV show **Strictly Come Dancing**, his dance partner is **Flavia Cacace**. **Bruce Forsyth** welcomes him with a **Quadrophenia** related joke, however it turns out to be a brief stay as he is voted off in a Dance-off the following night.
September 23rd	**Leslie Ash** starts her TV comeback with a brutally honest Documentary, **Face to Face** which looks at cosmetic surgery **Toyah** is also featured in a programme which is well received by the critics.
October 4th	**John Altman** reveals he is returning to EastEnders to reprise his role of **Nick Cotton**.
October 7th	**Roger Daltrey** states that he is looking to turn **Quadrophenia** into a West End Musical with his two leads of choice being **Carl Barat** and **Amy Winehouse**.
November 15th	**Phil Daniels** appears on **Soccer AM** on Sky TV in which he reminisces about his time on **Quadrophenia**. A spoof sketch of the film is shown entitled, **Codrophenia**.
November 25th	**Bonham's** Auction House in London sell the original Lambretta used by **Phil Daniels** in the film for a staggering £36,000, which is £9,000 above their top estimated guide price.

2009

March 24th	**Tim Brinton** - dies in Folkestone aged 79.
August 15th	**Modrophenia'79** a Mod/**Quadrophenia** inspired event is held in Brighton to celebrate the films 30th birthday, **Gary Shail** is the star guest.
October 13th	**Leslie Ash** makes her long awaited return to acting when she takes on a role in the BBC show, Holby.

2010

April	'Dreamland in Margate hosts a special screening of **Quadrophenia** to promote the iconic amusement parks preservation. A £12 ticket includes an introduction by well-known Mod author, **Paolo Hewitt**.
May?	**Roy Baird** - passes away at the age of 77.
July 17th	**Quadrophenia Night** is held at The Artrix Centre in Bromsgrove which includes the film being shown to a packed house followed by a band called **The Coopers** who play all the hits from the film and a Who tribute band called **The Whoo**!

2011

January 28th	**Leslie Ash** is named as one of the many famous people who may have been subject to phone hacking in the infamous News of the World scandal.
February 2nd	**P.J. Proby** appears in court in a £47,000 benefits fraud case.
March 12th	**Toyah** is part of an 80's super-group that appear in the 2011 final of **Let's Dance for Comic Relief** she shares the stage with amongst others, **Claire Grogan**.

July 23rd	**Amy Winehouse** once mooted as a potential female lead in a West End production of **Quadrophenia** dies at the tragically young age of 27 due to alcohol poisoning.
October?	**The Independent** curiously credits **Alan Parker** as the Director of **Quadrophenia**.
October 25th	**The Who's** official website launch a competition to make a new promo-video for the re-released **5.15**.
October 27th	**Liam Gallagher** owned clothes shop, **Pretty Green** in Carnaby Street hosts a **Quadrophenia** exhibition to celebrate the new Directors-cut of the original album.
November 1st	**Mojo** magazine is released and celebrates the imminent release of **Quadrophenia** the Directors-cut with a special edition that includes a CD entitled **the route to Quadrophenia**.
November 9th	An evening with **Pete Townshend** is held at the Bush Hall in Shepherds Bush to celebrate the launch of the new directors cut of **Quadrophenia**. Later the same night he and **Roger Daltrey** attend **The Classic Rock Awards** to receive the award for classic Album of the year.
. November 14th	**Quadrophenia** is released on the Blu-ray format for the first time.
	The new Directors Cut and Deluxe edition of the original 1973 album is released.

2012

?	Rumours are again rife about an Official sequel with **Martin Stellman** allegedly working on the script.
June 29th	**BBC 4** has a dedicated **Quadrophenia** night, which includes **Quadrophenia… Can You See the Real Me?** Followed by the film and **The Who – Live at the Electric Proms**.
October?	**Phil Daniels** partner **Jan Stevens** sadly dies from Pancreatic Cancer.
November 24th	**Chris Stamp** dies of Cancer in New York.
December 5th	**Eric Kent** who played the part of Dave's boss George dies.

2013

April 14th — A cavalcade of scooters lead the runners of the Brighton Marathon to mark the 40th Anniversary of the original album.

July 14th — **NK Theatre Arts** present a stage adaptation of **Quadrophenia** at The Palace Theatre in Manchester.

2015

May 16th — **Phil Daniels** and **Leslie Ash** are reunited in a special edition of **Pointless Celebrities,** in a superb effort that sees them reach the final!

May 22nd — an unexploded World War2 bomb is discovered at Fountain Studios in Wembley.

June 10th — **Leslie Ash** reveals that she no longer requires her medication and walking stick after her long illness, and is planning to make a full return to acting.

2016

May 28th — **Toyah Willcox** announces that she is to appear in the **Quadrophenia** sequel with other members of the original cast also being lined up. After a lot of confusion, it is confirmed that the film, **To Be Someone** is not a sequel but a stand-alone movie that has no connection with the original or indeed **The Who** at all!

2017

April — **Being** the **Quadrophenia** inspired film is premiered in London.

Roger Daltrey slams the possible **Quadrophenia** reboot as 'fucking irrelevant' and a few days later **Phil Daniels** rules himself out!

June/July Beccles, Suffolk. — **Quadrophenia** the stage play opens in

ABOUT THE AUTHOR: -

Layne Patterson is based in Norfolk, having relocated from Harrow in Middlesex sixteen years ago, married to Liz, with three grown-up sons he also has four grandchildren. Layne is a massive fan of The Who, and all things Quadrophenia, and supports Wealdstone and Manchester United. This is Layne's first solo book, but he has, in the past contributed to three books about his beloved Wealdstone FC.

CAN YOU HELP?

THE ONES THAT GOT AWAY! – IF YOU ARE ABE TO HELP WITH THE IDENTITY OF THE FOLLOWING ACTORS, PLEASE CONTACT THE AUTHOR.

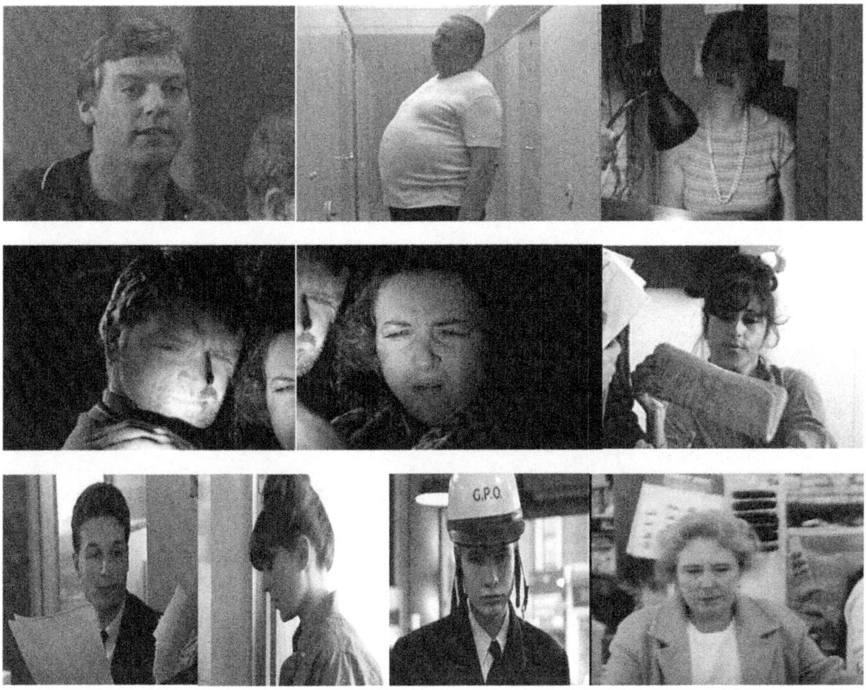
G.P.O.

Printed in Great Britain
by Amazon